ns and outcomes in turbulent environments

(2014)

Edited by Paul Trowler

Preface to this edition

This book originated in the Society for Research into Higher Education annual conference at Leicester University in 2000. Papers were selected for publication around the theme of the implementation of policy at different levels of higher education. The book as a whole is structured around the notion of the 'implementation staircase', as the first chapter explains. It was originally published 2002 by Open University Press/SRHE. Because the book went out of print copyright reverted to me, at my request. I wanted to make it available to researchers, managers and others for whom the content remains important and relevant.

I did little to the text of the original book other than give it a new cover, update or remove web links and optimize it for the Kindle and the Kindle Reader operating on PC and Mac.

After publication for the Kindle format in 2012 I used CreateSpace (an Amazon company) to make it available in physical form again, this time in the 2014 edition.

All Rights Reserved © 2014 Paul Trowler

Contents

Preface to this edition 2
The Contributors 7
   Abbreviations and Glossary (2001) 10
1 Introduction: Higher Education Policy, Institutional Change **13**
   Higher Education Policy 13
      The Rational-Purposive Model of Policy 13
   Institutional Change 15
      Loose Coupling 16
      Policy Reception in Higher Education Institutions 17
   The Book's Structure 19
      The Rationale 19
      The Chapters' Content 19
   A selective theoretical commentary 22
   References 35
2 Explaining Change in Higher Education Policy **38**
   Introduction 38
   Policy Design, Reform and Change 39
      Changes in policy design 40
   Policy Regimes 46
      Dimensions of policy regimes 47
      Regime dynamics 49
   Regime Changes 51
      Actors and influence 51
      Actor networks and cohesion 55
   Conclusion 57
   References 60
3 The Role of Different Groups in Policy-Making and Implementation. **64**
   Different Groups in Policy-Making and Implementation 64
      Contextual factors 65
      Prime actors 65
      Elites 65
      Interest Representation and Interest Politics 69
      What happened in the UK 71

> Role and behaviour of civil servants. 73
>
> Parliament 74

Conclusions..**74**

> The impact of policy changes on institutional government 74
>
> Factors making for change 76

References..**80**

4 Access and Recruitment: Institutional policy in widening participation. 85

Introduction: The creation of an access imperative. **85**

What is To Be Done? Asking questions about access **86**

Mapping Access in Action **87**

The Access Agenda **89**

Institutional Survival and Recruitment **91**

Widening Participation and Institutional Competition **93**

Conclusion **97**

References..**99**

5 Resources in the Management of Change in Higher Education 101

Introduction..**101**

The significance of resources in public sector policy..**102**

The significance of resources to organizations **104**

Sustaining the organization: definitions of 'survival' **108**

> Survival strategies:...109
>
> Surviving dependencies:..111
>
> The HoD role as survival strategy:..112
>
> Survival skills:...112
>
> Survival of the fittest: 114
>
> Survival of the maverick. Back door dealing: 116
>
> Agents of change. Survival and autonomy:..118

A balancing act: managing and surviving change **119**

> Slicing the cake. Cordiality and budgets: 120
>
> The geese that lay the golden eggs: 121
>
> A fair wage. Balancing income and activity:..122

Changed responsibilities: accounting for the accounts **123**

Conclusion **127**

References..**128**

6 The Unintended Consequences of Deregulation. 131

Introduction **131**
Sources of data **132**
    Decreased funding 132
    Fee-paying students 133
    Student:staff ratios 133
    Teaching technologies 133
    Entrepreneurialism 134
Intended Outcomes: From unity to competition **135**
    Government intentions 135
    Institutional strategies 136
Unintended Consequences **139**
    'Brain drain' 139
    Curriculum and cultural imperialism 140
    Intellectual property issues 141
    Workload and work quality 141
    Transparency versus commercial-in-confidence 142
    Reputation 144
    The competencies of managers 145
The 'Learning Organisation' and its Future **146**
    Maintaining the essential attributes of a university education 148
References **150**

7 A Comedy of Manners: Quality and power in higher education **152**

Setting the Stage **152**
What a Performance! **156**
The Aliens are Coming! **157**
Suspending Disbelief **157**
The Comfort of Commodities **159**
At Your Service: Changing social relations in the academy **161**
Challenging Students: Is the customer always right? **162**
Quality, Equity and Change **165**
References **167**

8 Exploring the Implementation Gap **172**

Introduction **172**
Conceptualizing Institutional Change **173**
An Alternative Perspective **176**

An Illustration: The 'new route' to the PhD 181
    Policy Formulation at National Level 181
    At Hilltop…. 183
    An Analytical Pause in the Narrative 183
    Narrative and Analysis at the Workgroup Level 185
    Social Practice Theory: the significance of this vignette 186
    The enacted organization 187
Implications for Practices 188
References 195

The Contributors

Di Adams
Di has spent most of her working life as a teacher in pre-schools, public and private schools, TAFE (Technical and Further Education) colleges, community classes, distance education for health care workers, and universities. For many years she worked in universities as an educational developer, instructional designer, and as a lecturer in higher education, latterly at the University of Canberra, Australia. Her research interests cover the nature of academic work, particularly the enculturation of new academic staff, the process of change, and policy implementation in universities.

Ivar Bleiklie
Ivar Bleiklie is a Professor in Administration and Organization Theory and the director of the Norwegian Research Centre in Organization and Management at the University of Bergen and the Norwegian School of Economics and Business Administration. He has published several books and articles on higher education and public welfare administration in Norway and the Nordic countries.

Peter T Knight
Peter was a friend and colleague of the editor and many of the contributors. He was widely known and respected by academics, university managers and educational developers around the world. His many publications on the enhancement of teaching, learning and assessment in higher education are a valuable and permanent legacy for the higher education community and to students everywhere. He is sadly missed by his many friends.

Rachel Johnson
Dr Rachel Johnson worked at Lancaster University as Research Associate to an ESRC study of 'New Managerialism and the Management of UK Universities from Oct 1998 - Sept 2000. In 2000 she obtained her PhD from Sheffield Hallam University/University of Sheffield; this was a qualitative study of student feedback/student course evaluation. From October 2000 worked as a Lecturer in Educational Evaluation and Research, and as a member of the Centre for Developing and Evaluating Lifelong Learning, School of Education, University of Nottingham.

Maurice Kogan

Maurice was Professor of Government and Social Administration (Emeritus) and Joint Director of the Centre for the Evaluation of Public Policy and Practice at Brunel University where he had also been head of the Department of Government, Dean, Faculty of Social Sciences and Acting Vice-Chancellor. He authored several books and articles on higher education, local government, education, health, social services and science policy. He was the editor of the OECD's journal Higher Education Management and an examiner in five of the OECD's reviews of national education policies. He was a founding Academician of the Academy of Learned Societies for the Social Sciences. Very sadly Maurice died in 2007. This was a great loss to the higher education research community.

Brenda Morgan-Klein
Brenda is Senior Lecturer in Adult Education at the Institute of Education, University of Stirling. Her previous research and publications span higher education policy and the student experience in higher education. Specific interests include: student access and equity but she has a wider interest in hierarchies and inequalities in further and higher education. This includes a range of issues such as institutional difference and epistemological aspects of educational change and related to this, the relationship between further and higher education and between further education and schools.

Louise Morley
Louise Morley AcSS is a Professor of Education and Director of the Centre for Higher Education and Equity Research (CHEER) (**www.sussex.ac.uk/cheer**) at the University of Sussex, UK. Her previous posts were at the Institute of Education, University of London, the University of Reading and the Inner London Education Authority. She is an Academician of the Academy of Social Sciences and a Fellow of the Society for Research into Higher Education. Louise has an international profile in the field of sociology of higher education studies. Her research and publication interests focus on international higher education policy, gender, equity, micropolitics, quality, and power.

Mark Murphy
Dr. Mark Murphy is Senior Lecturer in Education and Programme Leader for Education Studies in the Faculty of Education and Children's Services, University of Chester. Previously he worked as a Lecturer in Education and Programme Director of a Teacher Training Programme at the University of Stirling (2000-2006). During the period 1992-1999, he was employed at different times by University College Dublin, The National University of Ireland Maynooth and Northern Illinois University, USA.

Paul Trowler
Paul is Professor in Higher Education, Lancaster University and Research Director of here@Lancaster (the higher education research and evaluation centre there). He has research interests which include: enhancing student engagement; academic 'tribes' and their disciplinary territories; planning and managing change in universities; the implementation of planned change particularly related to the enhancement of the curriculum, teaching, learning and assessment; higher education policy-making and environmental change; cultures in universities; and approaches to evaluation.

Abbreviations and Glossary (2001)

ABRC: Advisory Board for the Research Councils (UK)
ABS: Australian Bureau of Statistics
ANU: Australian National University
Australia Institute: an independent think tank based in Canberra
   http://www.tai.org.au
AUT: Association of University Teachers - Professional body representing the interests of pre-1992 university lecturers in the UK
AV-CC: Australian Vice-Chancellors' Committee
CDP: Committee of Directors of Polytechnics
CIHE: Council for Industry and Higher Education
CVCP: Committee of Vice Chancellors and Principals (UK) now called *Universities UK*
DES: Department of Education and Science (subsequently renamed several times), (UK)
DETYA: Department of Education, Training and Youth Affairs (Australia)
EFTSU: Equivalent full time student unit (Australia)
EHE: Enterprise in Higher Education, (UK)
FBA: Fellow(s) of the British Academy, (UK)
FEC: Further Education College (UK)
FRS: Fellow(s) of the Royal Society ; (UK)
FTE: Full time equivalent
GATS: General Agreement on Trades and Services (Australia)
HECS: Higher Education Contribution Scheme (Australia)
HEFC: Higher Education Funding Council
HEFCE: Higher Education Funding Council for England
Higher Still: Introduced in August 1999 by the Scottish Qualifications Authority, Higher Still is a Curriculum and assessment development programme for the 16+ stage of education (Schools, Further Education Colleges, Adult Education). The aim is to gradually replace the existing Scottish Higher courses (see below) n order to provide students with the opportunity to progress through their studies at a level appropriate to them.
Högskoleutredningen 89: Swedish reform commission
IDP: IDP Education Australia Limited (an independent organization contracted to promote Australian education services abroad)
Jarratt Report, 1985: Charged with reviewing and making recommendations about university management, it recommended a raft of measures designed to make universities more effective and efficient through clearer management structures and styles. (UK)

Melbourne IT Ltd: began as a subsidiary of the University of Melbourne. It is now a publicly listed global company supplying software products and services.

MSC: Manpower Services Commission (UK). Now defunct.

NAB: National Advisory Board. Responsible for advice on funding of polytechnics in the UK for a short period.

NTEU: National Tertiary Education Union (Australia)

NUS: National Union of Students (UK)

OECD: Organization for Economic Co-operation and Development

OST: Office of Science and Technology

Oxbridge: used to jointly refer to the elite English universities of Oxford and Cambridge

PAC: Public Accounts Committee

PCFC: Polytechnics and Colleges Funding Council, (UK). Now defunct.

Quality Assurance Agency (QAA): Established in 1997 to provide an integrated quality assurance service for UK higher education institutions. Its mission is to promote public confidence that quality of provision and standards of awards in higher education are being safeguarded and enhanced. (UK)

RAE: Research Assessment Exercise, (UK). Now the Research Excellence Framework.

RMIT: Royal Melbourne Institute of Technology University

Robbins Report (1963): Government-appointed committee of enquiry tasked to review the provision of full time higher education and make proposals for its development, (UK).

RTX: Research, teaching and mixed types of university

Russell Group: an organization of research-led universities in the UK.

Scottish Highers: are advanced level qualifications that act as entrance routes into university. They are taken by students in their 5th Year of School. A number of these are normally accepted for entry into Scottish HE institutions.

SPT: social practice theory. An approach which combines activity theory and approaches which emphasize the significance of communities of practice. It is employed in Chapter 8.

Subject Review: the QAA's process for reviewing the quality of teaching, learning and assessment provision in UK HE academic departments. Now defunct.

TQA: Teaching Quality Assessment, (UK), later renamed Subject Review (see above)

U68: Swedish reform commission

UCAS: Universities and Colleges Admissions Service

UNE: University of New England (Australia)

Universitas 21: A company incorporated in the UK with a network of 23 leading research-intensive universities in fifteen countries. http://www.universitas21.com/

University Compacts: agreements between universities and school pupils, that if the pupils meet agreed goals (enhancement of personal and social qualities, key information and communication skills), they can be guaranteed a university place.

University Grants Commission: body charged with the allocation of funding to UK universities. An intermediary between higher education and the state, now replaced by other bodies.

1 Introduction: Higher Education Policy, Institutional Change

Paul Trowler

As its title suggests, the subject matter of this edited collection is higher education policy, institutional change and the ways in which they inter-relate. It does not, however, see policy and policy-making as distinct from or 'above' processes of implementation and change, located only in formal settings of policy design or strategy formulation. Instead it draws on a model of policy-making and implementation which acknowledges that policy is made in ways other than in formal settings of government or Vice-Chancellors' offices and which sees 'implementation' processes as essentially creative – and therefore also part of the policy-making process. Implementation of formal policy initiatives is also seen as contextually contingent in this model, taking different forms in different institutional and departmental contexts.

This chapter begins by briefly setting out that model as it relates to, first, higher education policy and then institutional change. The chapter goes on to discuss the rationale for the structuring of the collection and to review the contents of the chapters which follow. The final section draws attention to the links between chapters by highlighting some of the key theoretical and conceptual issues that they raise, either individually or considered together. Foregrounding them here is also intended to help the reader 'read' each chapter more fully. These issues include: the tensions between agency and structure in the policy process; the often-incoherent nature of policy-making; the situated character of policy reception; and the problems with policy 'problems' and 'solutions'.

Higher Education Policy

The Rational-Purposive Model of Policy

There is a common-sense and usually tacit conception of the educational policy process, often found among students, as progressing along a clearly defined path which starts from the carefully considered intentions of those in formal positions of power, often in response to a problem which has become apparent to them. These intentions – the 'vision' - are encapsulated in careful, formal, policy statements. Explicit decisions are made about policy implementation, including the choice of appropriate levers to use to ensure compliance. These are engaged and changes on the ground in accordance with original intentions are achieved relatively unproblematically. Such changes are usually behavioural and sometimes attitudinal as well. To take some examples from the chapters which follow they might include changes in recruitment patters of universities and colleges, changes in the ways PhDs are conceptualized, planned and delivered, or new, marketized patterns of interaction between institutions and their students. We can recognize this in the view of policy articulated by Harman (1984: 13):

> [Policy is] the implicit or explicit specification of courses of purposive action being followed or to be followed in dealing with a recognised [educational] problem or matter of concern, and directed towards the accomplishment of some intended or desired set of goals. Policy also can be thought of as a position or stance developed in response to a problem or issue of conflict, and directed towards a particular [educational] objective.

In this rational-purposive account of policy-making and implementation, 'policy' is defined is seen as the explicit articulation of current actions or preferred actions undertaken in pursuit of a stated objective. It is conceived as formulated only or mainly at the highest level of a country or an institution and is portrayed as generally being coherent and rational. The issues and goals it addresses capable of being unproblematically identified and articulated from this perspective. Finally, successful realization of policy goals is viewed as being achieved through the use of rewards, sanctions or simply by the fact that the values and goals of implementers are congruent with those of policy-makers (Browbrow and Dryzek, 1987).

From an academic perspective this conception almost self-evidently fails to capture adequately the messiness of policy-making and its implementation. It is, nonetheless, one that frequently informs the thinking of institutional managers and others charged with bringing about change. Moreover the rational-purposive model is an attractive one to governments and managers alike: the notion that there are levers to pull to effect change in desired directions in order to fix clearly identified problems is undeniably appealing: if only things were that simple.

I would like to counterpose this with an alternative model that sees the policy process as more organic and complex. In this alternative there is only a limited distinction between policy-making and policy implementation: policy is also made as it is put into practice because important social processes necessarily occur as this happens and because unforeseen circumstances on the ground mean that actors need to exercise discretion. Here policy is not just manifested in policy documents: white and green papers, acts of parliament, institutional strategies and the rest. Nor does it just reside in the announcements of politicians or the pronouncements of Vice Chancellors, important though these clearly are. Policy in this sense is understood in a very broad way as 'any course of action (or inaction) related to the selection of goals, the definition of values or the allocation of resources' (Codd, 1988: 235). The locale of policy-making and articulation thus becomes diffuse. From this perspective:

> ...policy is expressed in a number of practices, e.g. the production of texts and rhetoric and the expression of project and national policy management, in school [and university], in classrooms, and in staffrooms. Policy is also expressed by different participants who exist in a matrix of differential, although not simply, hierarchic power. Finally, participants are both receivers and agents of policy and, as such, their 'production' of policy reflect priorities, pressures and interests characterising their location on an implementation staircase. (Reynolds and Saunders, 1987: 44).

In this view, then, policy is also 'made' as it is received in different locales (sometimes with loss or fuzziness in parts of the message), interpreted and implemented. It is made too as practitioners go about their daily business, whether they are aware of it or not, as recurrent practices, sets of attitudes and assumptions are realized in specific contexts of practice.

Reynolds and Saunders' notion of the implementation staircase emphasizes how the location of individuals and groups in the hierarchy of the policy process can shape their interests and perceptions about the nature and relevance of particular policies. The situationally contingent nature of the processes they are engaged in also places boundaries upon how they conceive of their task. The staircase model helps to explain the reasons for the development of an 'implementation gap' (the distance between original purposes and actual outcomes) as policy is refracted during its trajectory down, and up, the staircase (Lingard and Garrick, 1997; Gale, 1999). The character of policy trajectories in HE thus represents an important issue for both researchers and those concerned with the future of higher education.

Institutional Change

Loose Coupling

It has long been recognized by academic theorists that there is a loosely coupled relationship between policy initiatives at the upper level of the implementation staircase and outcomes on the ground (March and Olsen, 1976). As Cohen and March's (1974: 206) say:

> [in universities] anything that requires the co-ordinated effort of the organization in order to start is unlikely to be started. Anything that requires a co-ordinated effort of the organization in order to be stopped is unlikely to be stopped.

Likening universities to 'organized anarchies' Cohen and March say they have the following characteristics:

- problematic goals - 'it [the university] discovers preferences through actions more often than it acts on the basis of preferences' (p. 3)
- unclear technology - it operates on the basis of a set of trial-and-error procedures, the residue of learning from the accidents of past experiences, imitation, and the inventions born of necessity
- fluid participation - the boundaries of the organization appear to be uncertain and changing.

Decisions associated with change in a situation of organized anarchy closely approximate to a 'garbage can model' in which various problems and solutions are dumped by participants:

> The mix of garbage in a single can depends partly on the labels attached to the alternative cans; but it also depends on what garbage is being produced at the moment, on the mix of cans available and on the speed with which garbage is collected and removed from the scene. (Cohen and March, 1974: 81).

At the institutional level, as at the national, policy making and policy implementation are more likely to be the result of negotiation, compromise and conflict than of rational decisions and technical solutions, of complex social and political processes than careful planning and the incremental realization of coherent strategy. This was recognized by early institutional theorists such as Selznick (1949): drawing on Merton (1936 and1968) he recognized the importance of the unanticipated consequences of purposive action and the importance of context to those outcomes. He showed too how the explicit, front-of-stage, goals of organizations differ from the 'real', and organically developing, objectives which have a tendency to become increasingly divergent in different locales. Empirical research in a number of educational contexts has confirmed that outcomes are contextually contingent, as the model of loose coupling would predict (Gewirtz et al., 1995; Arnot et al., 1996; Woods et al., 1996).

Brown and Duguid (1996) show how this divergence is inevitable because of the complexity of reality on the ground. They draw attention to the disparities between canonical and non-canonical practices in organizations. Canonical practices refers to statements of prescribed practices as set down in official documents, mission statements and elsewhere. They are the road maps which organizational members are intended to follow. In higher education descriptions of espoused, canonical, practice are requested by and presented to quality monitoring organizations such as the QAA. Non-canonical practices are those conditioned by the complex and diverse practice on the ground. These are necessarily different from canonical practice because of, at one level, the complexity and variability of events on the ground: the 'rough terrain' that is missed by the large-scale maps. It is necessarily different too because of the dynamic character of knowledge, knowing and expertise: new ideas, developed understandings, work-arounds, re-interpretations and re-constructions of tasks, projects and roles mean that the relatively static nature of canonical practice can never keep up with the realities faced by 'street-level bureaucrats' (Lipsky, 1980). Both canonical and non-canonical practice represent policy, but of different sorts:

> Policy is both text and action, words and deeds, it is what is enacted as well as what is intended. Policies are always incomplete insofar as they relate to or map on to the 'wild profusion' of local practice. (Ball, 1994: 10).

Policy Reception in Higher Education Institutions

In discussing the nature of hearing, the neurological specialist Professor Susan Greenfield (1997: 66) points out that that our perceptions involve more than simply physical auditory sensations:

> There is much more to hearing, for example, than mere vibrations. We do not hear a symphony as vibrations any more than we see a face as lines and contrasts. Rather, our perceptions are unified wholes, shot through with memories, hopes, prejudices, and other internalized cognitive idiosyncrasies.

This is a useful analogy for our purposes. First let us consider formal policy texts: the acoustic signals. They originate from a source which is not itself simple: certainly not an symphony orchestra following a score, more like a group of untrained musicians competing to be heard and following different scores, often markedly different and some with pages missing. Meanwhile the transmission of the audio signal is both 'lossy' - some parts never making it to the ear - and it meets interference from environmental 'noise'.

Important processes occur when the audio signal enters the ear and is processed by the brain, when the policy is received and interpreted locally by those charged with implementing it. As Tierney's (1989) discussion of changes in leadership and management policy at a small American Catholic liberal arts college indicates, even something so simple as the new director's literal open door, meant to indicate an 'open door policy' was received and interpreted quite differently by staff at that college. Their interpretation was conditioned by both tacit and explicit remembrance of the previous leader's behaviour and their response to it. Also significant to this interpretive work were the new leader's other behaviours, demeanour and actions in both formal and informal contexts. Together such factors generated a series of connotative codes, dispositions in the attribution of meaning and affect, which were attached to the new leader's actions and pronouncements, invisible to the leader herself but immensely significant in conditioning staff responses and so the outcomes of initiatives.

These interpretative responses are founded on 'internalized cognitive idiosyncrasies' which equate to Greenfield's 'memories, hopes, prejudices'. They are not randomly generated, nor (in the case of policy reception) are they the products of individual responses only: such responses are in part socially constituted in activity systems and communities of practice as well in larger social structural groupings.

Stephen Ball is right to say, then, that:

> A response to policy must...be put together, constructed in context, offset against other expectations. All this involves creative social action, not robotic activity. (Ball, 1994: 19)

This constructive work is, however, tacit as well as explicit, unconscious as well as conscious, sometimes unrecognized even by those involved in doing it.

The Book's Structure

The Rationale

The structure of the book follows that of the implementation staircase: each chapter represents a move down the staircase as the level of analysis shifts from the national contexts right down to the domain of the 'street level bureaucrats' (Lipsky, 1980) in specific institutional locations. Progressively shifting the level of analysis in this way helps address the analytical limitation that Graham Allison (1971: 4) identified some years ago:

> Bundles of…assumptions constitute basic frames of reference or conceptual models in terms of which analysts and ordinary laymen ask and answer the questions: What happened? Why did it happen? What will happen? Assumptions [about the character of puzzles, the categories in which problems should be considered, the types of evidence that are relevant, and the determinants of occurrences] are central to the activities of explanation and prediction. In attempting to explain a particular event, the analyst cannot simply describe the full state of the world leading up to that event. …Conceptual models not only fix the mesh of the nets that the analyst drags through the material in order to explain a particular action; they also direct him [or her] to cast his [or her] nets in select ponds, at certain depths, in order to catch the fish he [or she] is after.

Switching for a moment from the staircase to the fishing metaphor, this book includes chapters in which some authors cast their nets cast near the surface, others at the sea bed and still others at various points in between. They ask different sorts of questions and use evidence drawn from different locations in the policy process. Bleiklie's focus is on the policy environment: the nature of the waters themselves in different geographical areas, while Kogan is interested in the nature of and relations between the fish swimming near the surface. Kirby and Morgan-Klein take us a little deeper, to the institutional level. They explore how leaders in higher education institutions (HEIs) and Further Education Colleges (FECs) both respond to a particular policy initiative from higher up and effectively re-make it in adapting it to local circumstances. Johnson takes us deeper still, focussing on the Heads of Department (HoDs) within HEIs and exploring their responses to often-competing and conflicting demands. We travel to the lower levels in the final three chapters, by Morley, Adams and Trowler and Knight, exploring how policy is received and re-made (albeit in unintended and often unconscious ways) in universities in England and Australia.

The Chapters' Content

Chapters 2 and 3 by Bleiklie and Kogan respectively focus on the policy process in national higher education policy systems. Their work are based on the three-country study of higher education policies funded by the Swedish Council for Higher Education Studies (Henkel, 2000; Kogan and Hanney, 2000; Kogan et al., 2000). Bleiklie explores the ways in which the different policy regimes in Norway, Sweden and England are influential in the processes that bring about HE policy in those countries. Kogan picks up the theme raised by Bleiklie of the differences between policy communities and issue networks as distinctive policy regimes. Conducting what Maguire and Ball (1994) would categorize as an 'elite study' of the UK. He examines the groups involved at the upper levels of the higher education policy process and his aim is to explore the forces at work there in creating policy and putting it into effect. His chapter uncovers for us the workings of what has increasingly become an 'issue network regime' as the elite involved in higher education policy-making has fragmented in the UK.

Chapter 4, by Murphy and Holden-Smith, draws on data from a five-country study of widening participation policy funded by the Scottish Executive. The authors look at the institutional responses elicited in Scotland by the central initiative to widen participation in higher education in that country. They use data from those in key positions in different institutions to demonstrate the differentiated character of institutional responses. They explore the interaction between the marketization of the further and higher education system on the one hand, and the governmental push to widen participation on the other. Particularly significant here is the context declining demand for post-compulsory education generally. This, then, is an 'implementation study' (Maguire and Ball, 1994: 280) focussing as it does on 'interpretation of and engagement in policy texts and the translation of these texts into practice'.

Johnson's Chapter 5 comes out of research conducted for a large ESRC funded project entitled 'New Managerialism and the Management of UK Universities'. She examines how HoDs respond to policy developments in an increasingly managerialist environment and to what extent their behaviour is in line with that predicted by competing theoretical models. These HoDs had to cope with tensions between mangerialist understandings and discourse from the university and its environment on the one hand, and ground level understandings, practices and pressures on the other. In particular Johnson is interested in the power of what Bleiklie calls 'incentive tools': the giving or withholding of resources to ensure compliance with policy intentions by those on the ground: HoDs in this case. The incentive tools have become much more significant in a climate of resource constraint and progressive withdrawal of the state from underwriting the cost of HE world-wide. Thus, for example, in the UK universities suffer financial penalties for recruiting too many or too few students, but benefit financially if they recruit students from particular socio-economic groups, defined by postcode. At the same time, however, other levers – what Bleiklie calls 'learning tools' - are used to amplify and extend feedback to managers and policy-makers through evaluative, reporting and accounting procedures so that proximity to intended policy outcomes can be assessed and corrective measures taken when appropriate. Their use is linked to new managerialist approaches to establishing compliance, particularly the 'new public management' variety (Clarke, Gewirtz and McLaughlin, eds., 2000).

While Chapters 6, 7 and 8 take us to the ground level of institutional life, each makes links back to the upper levels of developments in the national and international policy environments. Chapter 6, from Adams, explores in detail the latent dysfunctionality of the unintended outcomes of progressive 'liberalization' of HE under Labor and then Liberal Australian governments. As Meek and Wood (1997) predicted, these measures have disturbed relationships within and between institutions in quite fundamental and often deleterious ways. Adams draws on evidence from her interviews with academic and general staff within a number of Australian universities, from interviews with research officers and industrial officers of the National Tertiary Education Union, from newspaper reports, government documents, and from participant observation within two universities in that country.

Morley's Chapter 7 examines the ways in which processes associated with quality audit resulted in affective responses on the ground in one UK university and so to consequences which were unanticipated and unintended by national policy-makers in government and the Quality Assurance Agency. While the data used here are specific to one site, the issues are virtually universal. The 'evaluative' or 'regulatory' state (Neave, 1997; Sporn, 1999) is today found everywhere across the globe as higher education expands and costs rise. Morley's important argument that local responses to this will be affective as well as cognitive is therefore of broad significance, as are the consequences of this fact.

The final chapter, from Trowler and Knight, continues this theme, again using an example from one English university to illustrate processes at different levels on the implementation staircase. Their chapter has the components which distinguish a 'policy trajectory study' (Maguire and Ball, 1994) in that it follows a specific policy through the stages of its cycle, though the focus of attention is primarily at the ground level. The case study here involves an initiative to alter the shape the nature of doctoral study in the face of competition in an increasingly global market. Trowler and Knight use the analytical lens of social practice theory (SPT) to view this initiative, showing how the aspirations of innovators can be undermined when they base their ideas on technical-rational principles. Again, the responses of those on the ground, together with the apparent invisibility of these to national and institutional innovators, constitute an important dimension of this analysis. The chapter also engages, though, with the question of why policy makers tend to unreflectively adopt rational-purposive understandings of the policy process when they are quite clearly flawed.

A selective theoretical commentary

In this section I want to introduce some theoretical tools and perspectives which are important to have at hand for a fuller appreciation of the chapters in the book. They tend to surface and resurface across the different authors' work, though none of them individually has the space to explore them. They are also intended to help the reader apprehend the book as whole, rather than as a collection of discrete chapters.

Agency and structure, discourse and text

I want first to highlight the issue of agency and structure, which Bleiklie frames in terms of the actor's perspective and the structural perspective. Agentic understandings of the policy process prioritize actors' perceptions, perspectives, preferences, actions and interactions. By contrast structuralist perspectives emphasize the ways in which these are conditioned by forces beyond the individual and which, consequently, give rise to a certain degree of regularity and predictability in social behaviour which would not be present if behaviour were wholly agentic.

Ball highlights the significance of this contrast for policy-making and implementation in his discussion of policy as text and policy as discourse. Viewing policy as discourse draws attention to the ways in which discursive repertoires delimit what can and cannot be thought about as well as what is on, and off, the policy agenda. Discourses do not simply describe reality, they help create it by offering or denying the communicative resources available to frame it. Here the emphasis is on the way behaviour and ideas are constrained by factors external to the individual and the group. The perspective is a structural one: the constraining effect of the discursive context comes to the fore, a context which can affect formal policy-makers as well as those at the ground level (Bacchi, 2000). Pring's excellent book provides an illustration in relation to the language of business applied to higher education, including the mechanistic language of educational outcomes much used by the British Quality Assurance Agency in its subject reviews – the focus of Morley's chapter:

> …the language of education through which we are asked to 'think in business terms' constitutes a new way of thinking about the relation of teacher and learner. It employs different metaphors, different ways of describing and evaluating educational activities. In so doing it changes those activities into something else. It transforms the moral context in which education takes place and is judged successful or otherwise…So mezmerized have we become with the importance of 'cost efficiency' and 'effectiveness' that we have failed to see that the very nature of the enterprise has been redefined…Once the teacher 'delivers' someone else's curriculum with its precisely defined 'product', there is little room for that *transaction* in which the teacher, rooted in a particular cultural tradition, responds to the needs of the learner. When the learner becomes a 'client' or 'customer', there is no room for the traditional apprenticeship into the community of learners. When the 'product' is the measureable 'targets' on which 'performance' is 'audited', then little significance is attached to the 'struggle to make sense' or the deviant and creative response. (Pring, 2000: 25-26. Emphasis in original).

While we can see several examples of the unreflective use of managerialist discourse by F/HE managers quoted in Murphy and Morgan-Klein's chapter, for example, Pring is over-generalizing when he claims that we - educationalists, researchers, educational managers - have all become mezmerized by the language of outcomes and of business and finance. A more agentic perspective which views policy as *text* stresses the role of actors in the policy process, including their ability to contest, negotiate and reconstruct both policy *and* the discourse in which it is encoded (Trowler, 2001). Policy decoding is an active (re)interpretive process from this perspective: one involving creative reinvention by those who 'receive' policy texts.

The ESRC-funded project on managerialism from which Johnson's chapter in this volume derives concludes that the extent of new managerialist discursive capture that occurs is probably limited by managers' ability to be 'bilingual' (Gewirtz *et al.*, 1995). The concept of bilingualism refers to the situation in which two or more sets of values and cultures exist side by side are invoked in appropriate contexts (Deem, 1998: 50).

Two other studies support this position. Prichard's (2000: 90) interview-based study of managerialism in further and higher education suggests that:

> The manager is not a coherent distinct human being, but a multiple of subject positions within various discursive practices, which in this case sit uncomfortably together.

Managers move between the 'managerial station' and other subject positions, particularly localized knowledges which address professional and academic expertise. The manager, then, suggests that the manager's professional identity, and the discourses drawn on, is dynamic and protean. He or she will move between the managerial station, drawing on managerialist discourse - constituting students as 'funding units' and colleagues as 'their staff', for example - and more authentic 'locales', situated in specific contexts of professional practice. These are 'localized cultures of practices which produce other relations to the self - that is individualized identities, which variably resist and subvert managerially individuated identities (stationings[i])' (Prichard, 2000: 41). They are the grounds from which agentic resistance to structural stations are mounted.

So, for example, while senior post-holders devote considerable time and attention to developing and implementing performance review processes, staff members engage in counter moves to resist the intrusion of such reporting and surveillance: they ignore requests and advice, fail to attend meetings or 'lose' important documents. These sorts of struggles between what Prichard calls 'power blocs' and 'the people' occur not only within groups but, most importantly, 'within' people as they struggle with alternative identity positionings and discourses: 'In other words, we all move in and out of relations which maintain and extend the power bloc into and across our lives and the lives of others' (p. 41). Bleiklie agrees that both agency and structure operate in real social situations and this is one reason why we should see the pattern of influence in the implementation staircase as being both down *and* up: if structural forces predominated then influence would only be in a downward direction.

These issues, of structure and agency, discourse and text, surface in each of the chapters which follow but are particularly evident in Johnson's discussion of Heads of Departments' (HoDs') responses to the managerialist environment and its associated discursive repertoires. They are applied too in Trowler and Knight's discussion of the reception at ground level of a curricular innovation wrapped up in managerialist discourse and assumptions.

Incoherence in policy-making

Both Bleiklie and Kogan take issue with the rational-purposive policy model, particularly its depiction of the policy-making process as coherent, incremental and cumulative. They note that policy design is frequently quite different from this picture. Only too frequently policy is far from simply 'the mechanical application of means [by the policy architect or engineer] in order to realise given ends' (Bleiklie, 2000: 54-55). Instead the process of 'encoding' policy is a complex one in which policy texts are developed as a process of negotiation, compromise and the exercise of power. As a result these policy texts are usually laden with multiple agendas, attitudes, values and sets of meaning. Policy encoding thus involves complex practices of interpreting, negotiating and refining proposals. The consequence is that 'processes of change at the level of national policy, within academic institutions and disciplinary groups, are only partially co-ordinated' (Kogan *et al.*, 2000: 30).

Ball sums up this view of the policy formulation process as follows:

> [Education] policies themselves...are not necessarily clear or closed or complete. [They] are the product of compromises at various stages (at points of initial influence, in the micropolitics of legislative formulation, in the parliamentary process and in the politics and micropolitics of interest group articulation.) They are typically the cannibalized products of multiple (but circumscribed) influences and agendas. There is ad hocery,

> negotiation and serendipity within...the policy formulation process. (Ball, 1994: 16).

The contested character of policy-making is part of the explanation for the often paradoxical nature of higher education policy. It means that any government will find it extremely difficult to properly 'join up' its policy innovations. Many forces act at different points in the policy process and render coherence extremely difficult if not impossible to realize (Rothblatt, 2000: 9). Even discounting outside influence and turbulence, governments themselves often behave like `a tribe of hyper–active children' (King 1996). Watson and Bowden (1999) show, for example, how the personalities of Education Secretaries led to swings in policy even during a period of administration by one party. They trace the paradoxes in British HE policy which resulted from the clash of ideologically driven neo-liberal marketizing preferences of individuals in government at the time and a reluctance to follow these ideas to their logical conclusion:

> the politicians, perhaps unduly inhibited by their officials in this respect, never displayed the nerve really to make this happen. Not only did it conflict with the`technological steer' [towards 'economically relevant' courses]...but it also ran the risk of institutional instability. Instead of a consumer-driven market for public services, the Conservative government invented the `quango' - of which the HEFCE became, in spending terms, the prime example. Intermediate and formally `arm-length' bodies would do the government's bidding, sustained by formal `direction. (Watson and Bowden, 1999: 249).

At the level of the political party too there are strains which jeopardize coherent policy formulation. Gamble and Wright (1999: 2-3) identify the tensions inherent in the new social democracy as being the need to assemble a majority electoral coalition and retaining the focus on the kind of society social democrats want to bring about. Party leaders no longer represent a unified and disciplined labour movement. Rather they act as brokers in an extremely diverse, dynamic and pluralist political environment, a helmsman rather than the rower (Coote, 1999).

There are strains too between the different departments in government. Ball offers an illustration, described the policy-making environment during the Thatcher period in this way:

> Old conservative...interests are at odds with new, manufacturing capital with finance capital, the Treasury with the DTI [Department of Trade and Industry], the neo-liberals with the neo-conservatives, wets with drys, Elizabeth House with Number 10, the DES with itself, Conservative Central Office with the Shires. (Ball, 1990: 19).

This array of difficulties has led New Labour to restrict its conceptualization of 'joining up' to one which addresses only the superficial avoidance of administrative duplication and costs rather than a more fundamental and holistic effort to establish coherence in its policy drive (McCormick and Leicester, 1999).

Examples of mutually contradictory policy initiatives which result from competing pressures on policy-making are legion. In the UK there is a central policy drive to widen participation but, simultaneously, concerns that the higher education system should not grow in an unrestricted way and a push for students themselves to be responsible for part of the cost of their own learning. The resultant incongruities in policy - what Gleeson (1989) has called 'policy paradoxes' - have been both puzzling and difficult to cope with for those on the ground. Similarly Newby (1999) has highlighted the concurrent yet incompatible policies which, on the one side, encourage the marketization of higher education yet on the other act to preserve a more dirigiste model:

> Despite the rhetoric of fees, competition and market forces, regulation of the UK higher education sector is strong in terms of student numbers distribution, public accountability, quality assurance and selectivity in research funding. It follows that there is unlikely to be a real higher education market on the American model in the UK in the near future. (Newby, 1999: 13, quoted in Benmore, 2000: 144)

Again, Maggie Woodrow (1999), reflecting on policy contradictions surrounding the push to lifelong learning, notes that:

> Lifelong learning can only be for all if those who are currently benefiting least are given priority in the allocation of opportunities and resources. The current trend in Europe for an increased proportion of the costs of post-school education to be met by the students themselves means that lifelong learning will certainly not be within everyone's reach).

In considering such paradoxes Bleiklie notes in an earlier volume arising from his study of HE in Norway, Sweden and England (2000: 55) that policy design

> …is not the outcome of any master plan, but reflects the decisions of many different people and organizational units, often acting in different contexts and places. They are not necessarily logical or even coherent.

He argues that variations in policy design can be explained in terms of policy regimes. These are networks of actors and patterns of influence that are dynamic in that actors and relationships change over time. It is its dynamism that distinguishes a policy regime a policy network as discussed, for example, by Rhodes and Marsh (1992) and Richardson (1997). The regime may be specific to an area of policy (for example higher education policy) or to a whole country. The actors and their actions need not be directly or exclusively engaged in the policy process, but to be relevant to a policy regime what they do must bear on public policy in some way. Moreover, as indicated above, the motivations for and goals of their actions need not be explicitly oriented to public policy goals: they may involve actions and motives which, from the actor's perspective, derive from and are oriented to, for example, recurrent practices in institutional contexts.

Knowing about the character of different policy regimes tells us quite a lot about the process of policy making in any particular context. Thus when Kogan and Hanney (2000) note that civil servants and vice chancellors in the UK not only once shared a common background and university education but frequently also membership of the same London club, the Athenaeum, they are commenting on the higher education policy regime in the UK and on the policy community there at that time. By the latter term is meant a group with

> ...limited membership; frequent interaction with shared basic values; all participants having a resource base and the ability to deliver their members' support; and a relatively equal power distribution among the network members. (Bleiklie, 2000: 67).

In some cases the policy regime is such that the rational-purposive depiction of policy design is closer to being the case, though it is rarely if ever fully realised. In such a circumstance we perhaps expect fewer policy paradoxes. Where such a regime exists there is a fairly tight constellation of actors combined with a hegemonic set of norms and values. Contrasted with this situation is the 'issue network' environment, in which there is a wide range of affected interests; fluctuations in contacts, access and congruence of viewpoint; unequal resource distribution; varying abilities to deliver members' support and unequal power levels among the actors involved. This is likely to result in numerous policy paradoxes of considerable significance.

In England there has been a drift since the 1960s from a policy community regime to one characterized as an issue network. As had happened in the compulsory education sector there was a progressive exclusion of some groups from the policy-making process and a simultaneous decline in trust as new managerialist ideology placed greater emphasis on market forces, accountability and performance assessment. Meanwhile an increase in the number of range of 'co-opted elites', such as academics appointed to RAE panels, created an even more mixed picture. Yet at the same time the ideological drive of Thatcherism did retain some consistency and coherence in central policy:

> There are continuities throughout the long period of Conservative stewardship: on the economic imperative (variously interpreted); on the desire for control; on the reluctance to intervene in the fate of individual institutions, or sub-sectoral groups, rather than that of the sector as a whole. (Watson and Bowden, 1999: 253).

In Norway the policy community retained its coherence for longer. There the relatively small size of the country and the HE system meant that there was an intimate and close community: top civil servants and university professors knew each other personally and shared a common background. The state did not become significantly involved in HE until the late 1980s. Meanwhile the picture in Sweden mirrored that in England: a switch from a policy community model to one closer to an issue network occurred, though this happened as late as the 1990s in Sweden. This change led to the break up there of a tradition of consensus-seeking among the multiple groups involved in the policy process and there was a new tendency to skip the traditional consultation process. Summarising the differences between the three countries, Bleiklie (2000: 86) says:

> English reforms were comparatively centralised, radical and relied more on tougher measures in order to discipline non-compliant institutions. Once introduced, the policy was pursued rather consistently. This pattern illustrates the confrontational style...: what we may call a *heroic style* of policy making....The Norwegian reforms, however, were less radical....They evolved gradually in a value-structure driven process with considerable local variation as to how the reforms were implemented...[We may call this] the *incremental style*. Swedish reforms were characterised by a more confrontational style than those of Norway, but also by less political stability. Government changes led to policy changes and varying central government control in terms of authority tools and use of incentives vis-à-vis educational institutions. The Swedish experience thus illustrates what we may call an *adversarial style* of policy making in the sense of an uneasy tug-of-war between two major political blocks with two very different versions of higher education.

The extent to which HE policy represents contested terrain, then, will differ from place to place, and from time to time. Maurice Kogan's Chapter explores some of the dynamics of these processes of policy-making.

The situated character of policy reception

I noted above that a situated understanding of policy implementation stresses how the 'same' policy is received and interpreted differently in different contexts according to institutional context, history and environment. Murphy and Morgan-Klein's chapter on the implementation of widening participation policy in Scotland and its mutation into recruitment practices there exemplifies this, substantiating Ball's point that:

> Policy is...an 'economy of power', a set of technologies and practices which are realized and struggled over in local settings. Policy is both text and action, words and deeds, it is what is enacted as well as what is intended. Policies are always incomplete in so far as they relate to or map on to the 'wild profusion' of local practice. Policies are crude and simple. Practice is sophisticated, contingent, complex and unstable. (Ball, 1994: 10.)

Different locations on the implementation staircase will be influenced by different sets of forces:

> ...it is thus an open question how and to what extent academic institutions and practices are affected by major policy changes. This depends on the extent to which changes are welcomed by, relevant to, and moulded and absorbed by academic institutions and practices. Conversely, academic disciplines and their development may, for instance, be formed by processes such as academic drift that may go unheeded by national policy actors. (Kogan *et al.*, 2000: 30)

Multiple factors, then, affect policy outcomes, not just the intentions of policy makers. Kogan *et al.* (2000: 28-9) point out that national socio-political peculiarities affect both the nature and pace of change in higher education systems at the national level too. Changes in student preferences for particular disciplines or for different types of degree - combined as against single honours, for example, can have a greater effect on HE systems than any government policy:

> Much of the rhetoric about higher education policy is based on the notion that higher education systems are shaped by political decisions and preferences....A number of events and processes, such as educational choices made by young people, the dynamics of the academic labour markets and academic prestige hierarchies, have exerted equally important influences on higher education. (Kogan *et al.*, 2000: 29).

Even the seismic shift to mass higher education was itself driven by forces other than just purposive policy. Fulton (1991b: 589), borrowing from the poet W. B. Yeats, describes the process in the UK as one of 'slouching towards mass higher education' and Scott describes it as being the result of a 'fit of absent-midedness' (Scott, 1995: 22). As for the formal abolition of the binary divide and policies associated with it, there was, as Pratt says: 'hard to discern in this history any sense of grand strategy. Much of the policy-making [in the 1980s] would be comfortably, possibly generously, described by Lindblom's (1959) term `muddling through' (Pratt, 1999: 265).

This multi-causality has the unfortunate consequence (from a central policy maker's perspective) that national (and indeed local) policies will have different outcomes in different locales - because each locale is likely to have a different set of forces and contextually contingent factors driving the reception and response to policy.

Many authors identify the strange fact that policy makers tend to be blind to the complexity of bringing about change, particularly to the processes that go on when policy is (re-)shaped at the ground level. Lingard and Garrick say (1997: 9) say that policy-makers tended to treat teachers as '"empty vessels", waiting to be filled with ideas and approaches emanating from Central Office'. Kogan *et al.* (2000: 29) point out that policies are usually formulated as though 'target groups can be counted on to act as if they are subject to no other influences than the policy itself'. Policy makers rarely take into account the need to support policy implementation, thinking that once the hard job of policy-making is done they can send out the finished documents and wait for results. As Lingard and Garrick put it (1997: 16): '...more energy is expended in the internal state micropolitics necessary to the production of a policy text than to its institutionalization'. Policy formulators tend not to appreciate either that the constant accumulation of educational policy leads to system overload. Finally, policy-makers usually develop an 'innovation bundle' and think of it as a single policy. In a bundle of loosely defined and loosely-coupled innovations each strand is subject to competing interpretations and alternative viewpoints. 'Implementation' in these circumstances becomes extremely complex and variable according to context. Trowler and Knight attempt to go some way in explaining this strange selective blindness of formal policy makers

The chapters in the later part of the book explore the local processes of policy-making and implementation, providing examples of the situated character of policy reception. The show how these processes can result in unintended, unpredicted behaviours and outcomes: to what Lingard and Garrick (1997) have called 'policy refraction'. This is evident in Johnson's account of HoD's responses to managerialist initiatives and in Adams' investigation of the unanticipated consequences of the 'liberalization' and marketization of HE in Australia. Morley's attention to the affective responses to policy initiatives illuminates their significance in the refractive process. She notes, with Adams, that marketization brings affective responses too, ones associated with loss of confidence, self-esteem and changes to personal and professional identities. So, a system designed to ensure the quality of British higher education not only involves considerable financial costs (£250m per year according to a HEFCE report: Baty, 2000) but personal costs too. More importantly for our purposes, however, these personal costs have important consequences for social practices and hence for the nature of and linkages between higher education policy and institutional change.

Problems with 'problems' and 'solutions'

Morley's chapter also highlights the politically contentious nature of problem-constitution, as does Murphy and Morgan-Klein's. The rational-purposive model of policy-making discussed above assumes that educational 'problems' are unproblematically recognizable (Bacchi, 2000). This is a simplistic understanding of the socially-constructed contested character of educational (and other) policy issues. Problems do not exist in isolation from the social and historical context: like the policies that are designed to address them they are created, given shape, in a social and discursive process of problem-constitution. Thus the 'problem' of how to widen participation in higher education is usually formulated as such on the basis of taken-for-granted assumptions about the nature of higher education, the forms of propositional knowledge that need to be acquired and notions of 'quality' and 'standards'. These in turn derive from ideological positions and usually-unsurfaced sets of values and attitudes. Such preconceptions give rise to the idea of the 'under-prepared' student and so constitute the site of the problem in individual deficiencies. They 'write out' alternative ways of looking at the issues in a fundamentally different way.

Murphy and Morgan-Klein demonstrate the ways in which the 'problem' of increasing access, as constituted by government, becomes entangled with concerns at institutional level, particularly the *institution's* problem of recruitment. This has potentially deleterious consequences for the widening participation agenda. Moreover, through their quotes from senior people in further and higher education they illustrate the ways in which managerialist discourse frames the problem, constituting it in particular ways and excluding other perspectives on it.

Morley too highlights the ways in which the 'quality problem', as constituted by the QAA, is politically driven and framed in a number of senses. Articulated and then addressed in a particular way, resolving the 'problem' leads to a clear shift in the HE agenda and in the locus of power. A power struggle is going on as academic labour is subjected to intensification and scrutiny in a context where knowledge is increasingly commodified so that HE bears ever-closer resemblance to a production facility. As Barnett (1997, 2000) has noted in his discussion of the shift to performativity, there is more than meets the eye. What appears to be 'just' a shift from propositional to operational knowledge (Ryle, 1949) in the HE curriculum actually represents a more fundamental displacement of the way we see the world, our way of knowing, and this is associated with a shift in who defines what counts as 'useful' knowledge,

Other chapters, too, raise the issue of the relational character of 'problems'. Trowler and Knight note the way in which the 'problems' connected with education at doctoral level are constituted from a managerialist perspective, personified in 'Professor Proselytizer'. Likewise Adams notes the ways in which Australia's higher education system was constituted as problematic by successive governments. Their solution was a switch to a marketized model, with the changes in power relations that brought.

These chapters too illustrate some of the complexities involved when a highly technical-rational approach to solving 'problems' hits the ground in an organization like a university. The technical-rational approach to change emphasizes efficient, goal- or vision- directed processes in the management of change. In that model roles and responsibilities in implementation locally are seen as ideally clearly delineated, hierarchical and assigned according to precisely defined and expressed tasks. The stages of accomplishment are regularly monitored. Objectives are assumed to be unproblematic and commonly understood and agreed. Properly-managed change processes are incremental and predictable in this view.

Technical-rational and top-down models of change have prompted searches for the pre-requisites of successful change processes and have led to lists of them such as this:

- creating and sustaining the commitment of those involved
- having clear and stable policy objectives
- ensuring that the policy innovation has priority over competing demands
- ensuring that there is a real expectation of solid outcomes inherent in policy, not just a symbolic one

- ensuring that the causal theory which underlies the policy reform is correct and adequate
- allocating sufficient financial resources
- creating, as far as possible, a stable environment within which policy is being implemented.

(adapted from Cerych and Sabatier, 1986)

Morley's chapter demonstrates some of the weaknesses in technical-rational approaches by exemplifying the ways in which managerialist versions of this thinking is necessarily some distance from teaching, learning and assessment practices on the ground. Her chapter thus reflects concerns of an earlier period about the technical-rational approach to policy and the management of change:

> ...much of the existing literature tends to take a 'managerial' perspective: the problems of implementation are defined in terms of co-ordination, control or obtaining 'compliance' with policy. Such a policy-centred...view of the process...tends to play down issues such as power relations, conflicting interests and value systems between individuals and agencies responsible for making policy and those responsible for taking action. (Barrett and Fudge (eds), 1981.)

Reprised throughout the book, then, is the theme of the complex, paradoxical and essentially 'messy' nature of the policy process, in contrast with the clean and logical model of it portrayed in the technical-rational approach. From the upper reaches of the policy implementation staircase, discussed in the early chapters, to the level of practices on the ground, addressed in the later ones, it is evident that improving higher education provision through policy initiatives is a complex and socially mediated affair.

References

Allison, G. T. (1971) *Essence of Decision: Explaining the Cuban missile crisis*. Boston: Little Brown.

Arnot, M., David, M. and Weiner, G. (1996) *Educational Reforms and Gender Equality in Schools*. Manchester: Equal Opportunities Commission.

Bacchi, C. (2000) Policy as Discourse: what does it mean? Where does it get us? *Discourse: studies in the cultural politics of education*, 21(1): 45-57.

Ball, S. (1990) *Politics and Policy Making in Education*. London: Routledge.

Ball, S. J. (1994) *Education Reform: a critical and post-structural approach*. Buckingham: Open University Press.

Barnett, R. (1997) *Higher Education: a critical business*. Milton Keynes, Open University Press.

Barnett, R. (2000) *Realizing the University in an Age of Supercomplexity*. Buckingham: Open University Press/SRHE.

Barrett, S. and Fudge, C. (eds) (1981) *Policy and Action*. London: Methuen.

Baty, P. (2000) Millions Go Down the Drain in Audit Fiasco. *Times Higher Education Supplement*, 4 August.

Benmore, G. J. (2000) Perceptions of the Contemporary Academic Employment Relationship. Unpublished thesis submitted for EdD, Sheffield University.

Bleiklie, I. (2000) Policy Regimes and Policy Making, in M. Kogan, M. Bauer, I. Bleiklie, and M. Henkel (eds) *Transforming Higher Education*. London: Jessica Kingsley, 53-87.

Blunkett, D. (2000) Modernising Higher Education: facing the global challenge. Speech on Higher Education, 15 February 2000 at Maritime Greenwich University.

Browbrow, D. B. and Dryzek, J. S. (1987) *Policy Analysis By Design*. Pittsburgh: University of Pittsburgh Press.

Brown, J. S. and Duguid, P. (1996) Universities in the Digital Age. *Change*, 28, 4, 11-19.

Cerych, L. and Sabatier, P. (1986) *Great Expectations and Mixed Performance*. London: Trentham.

Clarke, J., Gewirtz, S. and McLaughlin, E. (eds) *New Managerialism, New Welfare?* London: Sage.

Codd, J. (1988) The Construction and Deconstruction of Education Policy Documents. *Journal of Education Policy*, 3, 3, 235-247.

Cohen, M. D. and March, J. G. (1974) *Leadership and Ambiguity: the American College President*. New York: McGraw Hill.

Coote, A. (1999) The Helmsman and the Cattle Prod, in A. Gamble and T. Wright (eds) *The New Social Democracy*. London: Blackwell, 117-130.

Deem, R. (1998) New managerialism" and higher education: the management of performances and cultures in universities in the United Kingdom. *International Studies in Sociology of Education*, 8, 1: 47-70.

DfEE (2000) *The Excellence Challenge The Government's proposals for widening the participation of young people in Higher Education*. London: DfEE.

Fiske, J. (ed) (1993) *Power Plays, Power Works*. London: Verso.

Fulton, O. (1991) Slouching Towards a Mass System: society, government and institutions in the United Kingdom, *Higher Education*, 21, 589-605.

Gale, T. (1999) Policy Trajectories: treading the discursive path of policy analysis. *Discourse: studies in the cultural politics of education*, 20, 3, 393-407.

Gamble, A. and Wright T. (eds) (1999) *The New Social Democracy*. London: Blackwell.

Gewirtz, S., Ball, S. and Bowe, R. (eds) (1995) *Markets, Choice and Equity in Education*. Buckingham: Open University Press.

Gleeson, D (1989) *The Paradox of Training*. Buckingham: Open University Press

Greenfield, S. (ed) (1997) *The Human Brain: a guided tour*. London: Phoenix.

Harman, G. (1984) Conceptual and theoretical issues. In J.R. Hough, (Ed.), *Educational Policy: An International Survey* (pp. 13-29). London: Croom Helm.

Henkel, M. (2000) *Academic Identities and Policy Change in Higher Education*. London: Jessica Kingsley.

King, A. (ed) (1996) *Is Britain a Well-governedCountry?* London: Lloyds/TSB Forum.

Kogan, M. and Hanney, S. (2000) *Reforming Higher Education*. London: Jessica Kingsley.

Kogan, M., Bauer, M., Bleiklie, I., and Henkel, M. (2000) *Transforming Higher Education: A comparative study*. London: Jessica Kingsley.

Lindblom, C. E. (1959) The Science of 'Muddling Through', *Public Administration*, 19: 79-99.

Lingard, B. and Garrick, B. (1997) Producing and Practising Social Justice Policy in Education: A Policy Trajectory Study from Queensland, Australia. *International Studies in Sociology of Education*, 7(2): 157-180.

Lipsky, M. (1980) *Street Level Bureaucracy: Dilemmas of the individual in public services*. Beverley Hills: Sage.

Maguire, M. and Ball, S. (1994) Researching Politics and the Politics of Research: Recent qualitative studies in the UK. *International Journal of Qualitative Studies in Education*, 7(3): 269-285.

March, J. G. and Olsen, J. P. (1975) *Choice Situations in Loosely Coupled Worlds*. Unpublished manuscript, Stanford University.

McCormick and Leicester, (1999) Social Democracy in a Small Country: Political leadership or management consultancy? In A. Gamble and T. Wright (eds) *The New Social Democracy*. London: Blackwell, 131-141

McPherson, A. and Raab, C. (eds) (1988) *Governing Education: a sociology of policy since 1945*. Edinburgh: Edinburgh University Press.

Meek, V. L. and Wood, F. Q. (1997) The Market as a Steering Strategy for Australian Higher Education. *Higher Education Policy*, 10(3/4): 253-274.

Merton, R. K. (1936) The Unanticipated Consequences of Purposive Social Action. *American Sociological Review*, 1: 894-904.

Merton, R. K. (1968) *Social Theory and Social Structure*. New York: The Free Press.

Neave, G. (1997) The Stirring of the Prince and the Silence of the Lambs. In Etzkowitz, H. and Leydesdorff, L. (1997) (eds) *Universities and the Global Knowledge Economy: A triple helix of university-industry-government relations*. London: Pinter. (54-72)

Newby, H. (1999) *Higher Education in the 21st Century: Some possible futures.* Paper for Committee of Vice-Chancellors and Principals, 5 March.

Pratt, J. (1999) *Policy and policymaking in the unification of higher education..* J.Education Policy, (1999) Vol.14, no. 3, 257-269.

Prichard, C. (2000) *Making Managers in Universities and Colleges.* Buckingham: Open University Press/SRHE.

Pring, R. (2000) *Philosophy of Educational Research.* London: Continuum.

Reynolds J and Saunders M (1987) Teacher Responses to Curriculum Policy: Beyond the 'Delivery' Metaphor in Calderhead J (ed) *Exploring Teachers' Thinking.* London: Cassell.

Rhodes, R.A.W. and Marsh, D. (1992) New Directions in the Study of Policy Networks. *European Journal of Political Research,* 21, 181-205.

Richardson, J. (1997) Interest Groups, Multi-Arena Politics and Policy Change. Paper presented at Annual Meeting of the American Political Science Assocation, Washington, 28-31 August.

Rothblatt, S. (2001) Of Babies and Bathwater, *Times Higher Education Supplement,* 19 January, 9.

Ryle, G. (1949) *The Concept of Mind.* Harmondsworth: Penguin.

Scott, P. (1995) *The Meanings of Mass Higher Education.* Buckingham: Open University Press/SRHE.

Selznick, P. (ed) (1949) *TVA and the Grass Roots.* Berkeley: University of California Press.

Sporn, B. (1999) *Adaptive University Structures: An analysis of adaptation to socioeconomic environments of US and European Universities.* London: Jessica Kingsley.

Tierney, W. (1989) Symbolism and Presidential Perceptions, *The Review of Higher Education,* 12 (2): 153-166.

Trowler, P. (1998) What Managerialists Forget: higher education credit frameworks and managerialist ideology, *International Studies in Sociology of Education,* 8, 1, 91-109.

Trowler, P. (2001) Captured By The Discourse? The Socially Constitutive Power of New Higher Education Discourse in the UK. *Organization,* 8, 2, (183-201).

Wagner, L. (1995) A Thirty Year Perspective: from the sixties to the nineties, in T. Schuller (ed) *The Changing University?* Buckingham: Open University Press/SRHE.

Watson, D. and Bowden, R. (1999) *Why did they do it?: The Conservatives and mass higher education, 1979- 97.* J. Education Policy, (1999), Vol.14, no. 3, 243-256.

Weber, S. (1995) The Future Campus: virtual or reality? *The Australian,* 18 September, 28-30.

Woodrow, M. (1999) The Struggle for the Soul of Lifelong Learning, *Widening Participation and Lifelong Learning,* 1(1):9-12.

Woods, P., Bagley, C. and Glatter, R. (1996) Dynamics of Competition in C. Pole and R. Chawla-Duggan (eds) *Reshaping Education in the 1990's: perspectives on secondary schooling.* London: Falmer Press.

2 Explaining Change in Higher Education Policy

Ivar Bleiklie

Introduction

The analysis of higher education policy change in this chapter seeks to combine two perspectives. A number of theoretical approaches to the study of public policy share a common and popular assumption: policy change is the outcome of changing preferences among political actors. According to such *an actor's perspective*, policy change is the outcome of changing preferences in actors or changing power constellations between actors with different preferences (Ostrom, 1990). Sabatier and Jenkins-Smith (1993) advocate another version of an actor's perspective and emphasize that policy change is normally caused by external system events such as changes in economic and political conditions that affect actors' belief systems. An alternative to an actor's perspective is *a structural perspective* that emphasizes how underlying norms and values shapes policy change. This perspective explains policy change as an outcome of shifting values or constellations of values (Skocpol, 1992; March and Olsen, 1989). Such shifts may in turn be caused either by internal dynamics of political institutions or external events that causes internal disruptions.

Whereas it is commonplace in social science analysis to chose one of these perspective I shall consider it a likely assumption that both social action and structural sources of change may be located within the policy field in question or outside it. Accordingly, actors may change behaviour because of changing preferences resulting from experiential learning or changing positions within the field. Their behaviour may also change because their belief systems change as a result of shifting external conditions of action. Similarly, structural change may have endogenous or exogenous sources. It may be caused by internal structural tensions or result from reactions to tensions caused by changing environmental conditions such as reduced autonomy and legitimacy that may threaten the resource base of the system. In higher education systems where institutional autonomy is a central concern, much attention tends to be given to the question of to what extent change is generated by actors and events within the system or the extent to which changes are introduced and driven through by outside forces.

The following comparative analysis of higher education policy in England, Norway and Sweden in the 1980s and 1990s is based on *a dynamic regime* approach (Bleiklie 2000; Bleiklie *et al.*, 1997).[ii] I shall argue that variations in policy can be explained in terms of *policy regimes* defined as the network of actors and patterns of influence that are particular to a policy area or an entire polity. This does not mean that the content of policies *per se* can be deduced from particular regime characteristics, but it does mean that the processes that bring about change in policy can. The policy content is defined in terms of *policy design* where design is regarded as a set of characteristics that are observable by the policy instruments that are deployed (Ingram and Schneider, 1990).

The next section outlines and analyses the policy of the recent reforms by focusing on the choice of policy instruments. Then in Section 3 attention is turned to the regime characteristics of higher education policy and development of the concepts that shall be used for the analysis of regime changes. I discuss both the roles of the main actors, including central government agencies, local institutions, elites and interest groups, and the relationship between the actors. In Section 4 follows a discussion of processes of change within dynamic policy regimes and the main empirical analyses of regime changes and emerging policies under the current policy regime.

Policy Design, Reform and Change

Policy changes in higher education since 1945 may be described empirically in terms of the measures that have been introduced. The first two periods of policy change took place roughly between 1960 and 1980, and were first characterised by growth, than by democratization and to some extent by bureaucratization (Daalder and Shils 1982). The main focus here is on the third period of transition, characterised by unprecedented expansion and systemic integration that began during the latter half of the 1980s.

However, in order to define the dependent variable more precisely I shall use the concept of *policy design*. Policy design is defined as a set of characteristics that distinguish a given policy in one field, from policies in other fields, countries or periods, including policy attributes that affect the orientation and behaviour of target populations. Design in this meaning is not the outcome of any master plan, but reflects the decisions of many different people and organizational units, often acting in different contexts and places. They are not necessarily logical, or even coherent (Ingram and Schneider, 1993: 71f; Rein, 1983: xi-xii). Because Ingram and Schneider's behavioural characteristics of policy instruments correspond well with the policy dimensions that are relevant to higher education policy, their taxonomy shall be taken as a point of departure. The underlying assumption of this taxonomy is '…that public policy almost always attempts to get people to do things they might not otherwise do; or it enables people to do things they might not have done otherwise' (Ingram and Schneider, 1990: 513). They identify five different reasons why people are not taking actions needed to ameliorate social, economic or political problems:

> …they may believe the law does not direct them or authorise them to take action; they may lack incentives or capacity to take the actions needed; they may disagree with the values implicit in the means or ends; or the situation may involve such high levels of uncertainty that the nature of the problem is not known, and it is unclear what people should do or how they might be motivated (Ingram and Schneider, 1990: 514).

Then they distinguish between five broad categories of corresponding instruments or tools according to the behavioural assumptions on which they are based. Below I shall first discuss how higher education reform policy can be described in terms of policy instruments. When I refer to specific measures under one kind of policy tools, this does not mean that they belong to this specific category *per se*. This depends in the final analysis on what assumptions a measure is based. Neither does it mean that policy tools are mutually exclusive.

Changes in policy design

Over time, significant changes have taken place regarding the policy instruments that are employed, both with respect to what kind of instruments that are used and with respect to the way in which particular types of instruments are applied. The most striking development is the increasing array of instruments that are deployed. Whereas policies used to be concentrated on authority and capacity measures, they now encompass a wider array of instruments. Secondly, existing types of instruments are used in different ways. In particular, the changing management philosophies have changed the way in which authority instruments are used. Finally, in certain cases discussion may arise as to what category a particular instrument belongs because the behavioural assumptions behind its use are unclear or contested. Comparing the three countries I shall highlight similarities and differences between them rather than presenting the reform policies in detail. (Kogan *et al.*, 2000).

Authority tools are simply statements backed by the legitimate authority of government that grant permission, prohibit or require action under designated circumstances. These tools assume agents and targets are responsive to the organizational structure of leader-follower relationships (Ingram and Schneider 1990: 514). Authority tools have always been important in the state management of higher education and university affairs. However, such measures have traditionally been much more salient in the almost entirely state-owned higher education systems of Norway and Sweden than in England, where state authorities hardly tried to wield any authority at all. In the former countries, however, university legislation and other legislative measures determined such important issues as the degree structure, examinations, and the obligations of the academic faculty. Both in Norway and even more so in Sweden, Parliament made decisions on detailed matters such as the appointment of individual professors. However, from the perspective of the universities this formal control did not represent a problem as long as they felt that their autonomy and qualified judgement in academic matters were respected. In England, until 1981 'there was very little government policy for higher education.' (Kogan and Hanney 1999). Whether measured in terms of the legal status of the institutions, academic authority, mission, governance, finances, employment and academic decentralization English universities scored high in terms of autonomy. Although the relationship between the state and universities used to be close in England, it was characterised by a benevolent regime under which the universities enjoyed extensive autonomy and little authority was exercised by the state.

The reforms of the 1980s and 1990s signalled new directions in higher education policies in all three countries, but with different emphases. In England there was a clear centralization trend, although denied by central politicians and officials, whereas in Norway and Sweden the reforms came with the message that in the name of quality a new freedom was to be bestowed upon higher education by means of a move from regulation to performance control. The policy design was supposed to be radically altered by less emphasis on the traditional rule-oriented use of authority tools than previously and more emphasis on goal formulation and performance. This was portrayed as a process whereby state authority was rolled back and autonomy and decentralised decision making was put in its place. One characteristic that applied to all three countries was that higher education had become more politically salient over the years. Accordingly central government authorities, whatever their leaning, were more concerned about the cost of higher education and more interested in affecting the product of higher education institutions in terms of candidates and both basic and applied research than previously. This meant that although governments might steer in a more decentralised manner than previously, they were interested in steering a wider array of affairs and in this sense power was centralised rather than decentralised.

In England the benevolent 'private government of public money' was replaced by a new regime where the government started to formulate goals for the universities, and apply legislative and financial means in order to reach those goals with relatively little consultation with the academic community. Although new forms of *ex post* control had been introduced in Norway in the name of decentralization (e.g. activity planning and performance indicators), the new instruments did not replace, but came in addition to, the traditional detailed legislation that regulated an increasing array of university affairs. Swedish reforms were more consistent with the officially stated goals of decentralization and autonomy. The use of authority tools thus was reduced in the Swedish case. However, both economic difficulties with rising unemployment and the Social Democratic return to power in 1994 resulted in a gradual return to more centralist policies with more use of authority tools.

Incentive tools include those that rely on tangible payoffs, positive or negative, to induce compliance or encourage utilization. Incentives have traditionally been important tools in the life of academic institutions whether it is the use of student grading, competition for fellowships, research money and tenured or untenured academic positions. However, they have not been considered policy tools, but rather tools that were integral to the academic community and were used to cater to its internal concern with maintaining academic quality. Incentives were thought of as tools that were used by and within the 'republic of scholars' to motivate individuals. Conscious political use of incentive tools first commenced in the late 1980s.

In England a shift in the direction of extensive and active use of incentive tools began with the introduction from 1985/86 of the Research Assessment Exercises (RAE) whereby qualified basic units are arranged in hierarchical categories according to their research performance. Most of the research funds were dedicated to the top categories and no research funding to the bottom category. The incentives were ostensibly directed at selective research funding on a meritocratic basis, but the system also resulted in positioning departments in a hierarchy of esteem in which non-performing institutions were excluded from research funding.

In Norway the most important incentive tool, both financially and from a principle point of view, were the funds that were tied to the production of new graduates. Thus the funds for graduate candidates were supposed to be distributed as research funds to the individual teacher. Norwegian incentive tools were thus supposed to increase production of undergraduate candidates by motivating institutions to produce more graduate candidates. The idea was furthermore to produce more quality research by motivating individual teachers to be more efficient advisers.

The Swedish reforms represented yet another version of design and use of incentive tools by being exclusively directed at institutions in order to enhance competition between them. A performance-based funding system was established, partly following enrolment and performance of undergraduate students, partly on number of PhDs produced. In order not to encourage universities to focus too much on the competition for students and student processing without regard for quality, 5 per cent of their funding should be based on an evaluation of the institutions' quality development work. However, the latter measure was revoked by the incoming Social Democratic Education Minister in 1994 and never really took effect.

Capacity tools provide information, training, education and resources to enable individuals, groups, or agencies to make decisions or carry out activities. Capacity tools in connection with university policy are primarily about money. Three characteristics were common across the three countries: the formidable growth of the higher education system, the reduced per unit cost and the assumption behind government policies that higher education institutions needed to be more responsible and accountable for the resources they received. In addition it was generally believed that they ought to generate more of their own resources from other sources through competition for students and research funding. However, if we define the capacity of the higher education system in terms of qualified teachers and research funding it is clear that both the direction and use of capacity tools varied considerably.

During the early 1980s English universities faced severe cut backs and the definite end of the quinquennial budgets. From the late 1980s and during the first half of the 1990s the system expanded sharply in student as well as budgetary terms until the Age Participation Rate reached 30 per cent. By the mid-1990s the growth was halted and the government introduced measures to prevent student numbers to rise much above current levels.

The Norwegian reforms aimed both at expanding the system considerably and improving the level of funding from 1988 on, but student demand by far exceeded the plans and the planned real budget growth barely helped to keep up the level of funding. From 1993 the policy of growth was replaced by austerity and budget cuts. Furthermore, excepting the late 1980s and early 1990s, state colleges have tended to be relatively favoured at the expense of universities and scientific institutions.

The Swedish government sought to expand the higher education system in the early 1990s as part of a government strategy to fight unemployment and strengthen the economic competitiveness of the nation. However in the face of increasing budget deficits the government had to cut expenditures and limit growth. Although the Swedish system grew much less in the first five years of the last decade (from 1988) compared to both England and Norway it had an even growth curve and a stronger growth than Norway from 1993.

Symbolic and hortatory tools assume that people are motivated from within and decide whether or not to take policy-related actions on the basis of their beliefs and values. Symbolic and hortatory tools are important in university and higher education politics among other things because universities are institutions that are imbued with value, have a long history and embrace a fairly well codified although not necessarily consistent set of values and widespread norms. The most recent reforms represented a value shift and changing fundamental notions of what the university was all about. With it a new set of symbolic tools has emerged (Bleiklie 1996, 1998). As is evident from the policy documents, other written statements and our respondents, the idea of the university as a community of scholars, student or disciplines, and as a public agency to some extent yielded to the idea of the university as a corporate enterprise. In Burton Clark's recently coined concept, the idea of 'the entrepreneurial university' was on the rise (Clark 1998). The changing symbols had at one level apparently far-ranging and deep consequences because they redefined the mission of the institution as well as the content of what it was doing, the roles of the main actors and the power relationships between them. Academic institutions and individual researchers were requested to cultivate competition and entrepreneurship. The symbolic tools that come with the corporate enterprise notion of the university are closely related to other policy tools such as the authority and incentive tools discussed above. It is hard to discern clear differences between the three countries with regard to the symbolic and hortatory tools that were introduced. They may all be adequately described and analysed in terms of the corporate enterprise idea of the university and co-exist in an more or less tension-ridden relationship with more traditional academic values. However, the implications of apparent ideological innovations often are exaggerated and do not necessarily threaten traditional values. Their impact depends very much on how the new values are interpreted and what practical arrangements they sustain (Kogan *et al.*, 2000). The interesting comparative stuff lies in the fact that these apparently identical symbolic tools are used to justify different policies as should be fairly evident from our discussion of other policy tools.

Learning tools are used when the basis upon which target populations might be moved to take problem-solving action is unknown or uncertain. Learning tools are also fairly tightly related to the corporate enterprise notion of the university and New Public Management ideology with which the notion is related (Bleiklie, 1998; Pollitt, 1993). The idea that target groups can learn from experience is part and parcel of this ideology (Olsen and Peters 1996). In all three countries this led to the introduction of new policy tools, such as evaluation and changes in existing ones such as planning, reporting and accounting procedures. The underlying idea was that the organization formulates goals in mission statements, activity plans and budgets and receives feedback by means of respectively evaluation exercises, annual reporting and accounting. From this information the organization was supposed be able to enter into a learning process by which it might gradually improve its performance. By and large these were the policy tools that the actors involved seemed to have the greatest doubts about. Whereas proponents dreamed of a more efficient and goal oriented administration, opponents portrayed them as threats to academic freedom, open dialogue and reflection. With hindsight the tools were questioned on the grounds of their ritualistic character, their feeble if any effects and their symbolic, rather than substantial impact. Another unintended consequence of their introduction was the sensation that the administration of the tools and the information that had to be gathered, processed and analysed, led to bureaucratic expansion rather than improved performance.

Policy Regimes

Having observed these changes in higher education policy, it is time to consider explanations of how the changes came about. The following approach is based on the idea that a policy field such as higher education is governed by policy regimes and it is based on three considerations: 1) Policy regimes are networks of actors. The focus on the relationship between policy regimes, defined as dynamic actor networks, and policy design, is influenced by the policy network literature. The concept of a policy regime, but differs from the policy network concept in several important respects. Most policy network approaches present the networks as rather static, structural arrangements for interest representation, characterised by goal-oriented behavior (Atkinson and Coleman, 1992; John and Cole, 1997; Knoke *et al.*, 1996; Raab, 1994; Rhodes and Marsh, 1992; Richardson, 1997). Policy regimes are dynamic in the sense that the actors and the relationship between them change over time. 2) The network of actors within the policy regime is not exclusively engaged in interest politics, but may comprise any type of action that potentially bears on public policy. 3) The policy process within the dynamic regimes is not only driven by goal-oriented rational action, but may also be driven by rule-oriented institutionalised behaviour and by communicative action.

By using the dynamic network concept as a heuristic devise, we emphasize that the constellation of actors involved in policy making may vary over time as well as cross-nationally and involve a wide array of different actors that are motivated by a diversity of factors.

Dimensions of policy regimes

Theories of how policy regime characteristics affect the content of public policy abound. Initially I shall distinguish between two dimensions that have been important to theory formation in the area and can be helpful to the formulation of ideas about relevant regime characteristics. The first dimension turns on the distribution of *influence* between actors within a field of policy making. The second dimension, *cohesion,* refers to how tightly or loosely the actors are related to one another. Considering influence, I shall distinguish between two classes of theories relevant to the policy field under scrutiny. One class of theories comprises those assuming that higher education policies are made by one dominant institution or set of institutions: in our case either the central government or individual, autonomous, local institutions. In addition, we find theories assuming that higher education policies are made through some form of mediation either via elites or via organised interests.

Influence

State domination means that state agencies formulate policies that individual subordinate agencies are supposed to implement, by means of legislation and budgetary policy. Based on current knowledge in the areas of comparative public policy and administration there are ample reasons to expect considerable variation in the tightness of central control across nations, policy sectors and over time (Heidenheimer *et al.,* 1983; Lægreid and Pedersen,1999). Sources of such variations may be found in traditions of political steering, the relationship between civil service and higher educational institutions, and finally in views of the role of education and research in relation to the realization of national political goals (Becher and Kogan, 1992; Clark, 1993; Salter and Tappe,r 1994).

Institutional autonomy at its most extreme means that individual institutions, or institutions under government control, are free to make decisions independently and manage their own affairs as they see fit. The organizational arrangements for sustaining autonomy vary as is indicated by the difference between English charter institutions and the civil service status of Norwegian and Swedish universities (Kogan *et al.*, 2000). In either case autonomy may, but does not have to, imply that central government policies in a policy area amount to little more than the sum of the institutions' actions. Institutions within a certain policy sector may enjoy such a freedom, much like public research universities traditionally have in many West European countries (Ben-David and Zloczower, 1991; Rothblatt and Wittrock, 1993). Similarly, some national policy making 'styles', such as the Norwegian, tend to favour decentralised patterns of decision making that leave relatively substantial decision making authority with local agencies or institutions (Olsen, 1983).

Elitism. Elite theories assume that smaller groups of power holders can be distinguished from the powerless majority (Etzioni-Halevy, 1993). The pluralist view, emphasizes the concept of multiple and autonomous elites as an important factor in preventing the abuse of power by one ruling class or elite group. However, the idea of co-optation, ' ...the process of absorbing new elements into the leadership of policy-determining structures of an organization, as a means of averting threats to its stability or existence' (Kogan, 1984), puts in question the idea of autonomous elites. Co-opted academic elites may operate in at least three different ways: a) as part of government decision making through membership in government appointed bodies, b) by internalising, interpreting and helping implementation of government policies and c) by creating hierarchies of resource and esteem (Becher and Kogan, 1992; Kogan, 1992).

Interest Representation and interest politics can be important to many fields of public policy in a double sense. Interest organizations such as employers' associations and trade unions may regard a policy sector as a field that affects them as legitimately interested parties. At the same time, higher education itself has become an important field of work and a major employer, involving the parties on the labour market in questions relating to wages, working conditions, personnel management and workplace democracy. Similar to elite theorists, corporatists assume there are a few small groups of power holders who determine political outcomes in society (Cawson, 1983; Grant, 1985; Rokkan, 1966; Schmitter, 1974; Schmitter and Lehmbruch, 1979). The rise of liberalism and managerialism after 1980 has been taken as an indication that the role of corporatist arrangements and the influence of employee interests were weakening. However, the actual role played by corporate arrangements can safely be assumed to vary considerably both cross-nationally and cross-sectorally.

The influence dimension is here defined as a question of what type of actors constitute the network on which the policy regime is based. We do not presume that the four types of influence are mutually exclusive. Rather we shall ask what types of actors are active in higher education policy, what type of influence they represent and what the relationship between them are. It is of particular interest for us to see whether there have been any changes with respect to influence patterns in higher education during the reform period under study.

Cohesion

In the policy networks literature, network cohesion has been an important topic. My point of departure is Rhodes and Marsh's (1992) idea of a policy network as a continuum, with 'policy community' and 'issue networks' at the two opposing ends. The criteria used in this analysis are membership, integration, resources and power. A 'policy community' would thus be characterised by: its limited membership; frequent interaction with shared basic values; all participants having a resource base and the ability to deliver their members' support; and a relatively equal power distribution among the network members. On the opposite end of the continuum is the 'issue network', characterised by: a large and/or wide range of affected interests; fluctuations in contacts, access, and level of agreement; unequal resource distribution combined with varying abilities to deliver members support; and unequal powers among the group's members.

Cohesion is an important dimension of policy regimes as we have defined them. Thus corporatist arrangements of policy making can be seen as a type of policy regime, most often leaning towards the 'policy community' side of the continuum. Loosely coupled networks of elite decision-makers or autonomous institutions, however, may operate like 'issue networks' and constitute a very different type of policy regime. Considering both the variations across countries and the way in which the relationship between state and interest groups has changed over approximately the last decade and a half, an approach that allows for greater variety in the organizational expressions of such relationships seems to be called for. In the next section we shall discuss challenges to the policy regime concept and attempt to show how the dynamic regime approach can be useful for the analysis of the structuring of the English, Norwegian and Swedish higher education policy regimes.

Regime dynamics

Within a policy field the core activities of the field – such as the production and administration of rules, procedures or services – are subject to attempts by more or less cohesive networks of actors to affect and control relevant processes and events. These actors constitute a policy regime that may include local or specialised institutions, interest groups, various elites and central political-administrative authorities. State domination, institutional autonomy, elitism and interest representation represent attempts at conceptualising different ways in which a policy regime may be structured. How an actual regime is structured in this sense does not have to be theoretically predetermined, and the relationship between structuring and policy making constitutes a central part of the empirical analysis. The different types of influence represent ideal typical patterns that are not mutually exclusive. The patterns may thus appear in a variety of combinations depending on the constellation of forces that participate in policy making.

In analysing such forces we shall apply a combination of an actor focused and a structurally focused analysis of actor networks. The former kind of analysis typically assumes that rational action is the driving force of the policy process. It assumes further that policy design takes place under conditions where it is the outcome of power plays among actors who are involved in the process. The outcome depends on the positions they hold, the resources they control, the coalitions they make and the bargains they are able to strike. Policy variation across nations and over time can be explained in this perspective as the outcome of regime variation along the influence dimension, where the preferences of the members of the dominant coalition determine the outcome in each individual case. The latter kind of analysis assumes that institutionally shaped norm-oriented behaviour drives the policy process. Furthermore it assumes that policy design takes place under conditions where it is the result of a process of adaptation between existing norms and values and new arrangements. The outcome thus depends on what values and norms the actors feel obliged by, prevailing authority patterns, how actors shape reform measures to conform to current norms and how they reinterpret their values in order to accommodate the new measures (March and Olsen 1989, 1994). Policy variation can be explained as the outcome of regime variation along the normative (cohesion) dimension where the shared norms defining the community of decision-makers determine the outcome.

Thus two kinds of regime change may explain policy design: the policy preferences of those actors who make up a policy regime; and the hegemonic values and normative conceptions that are shared by all (or at least the dominant coalition of) actors in question. The two theoretical positions make up extremes of a theoretical dimension along which the array of possible explanations to policy design may be arranged. Here we find a purely rational action model at one extreme and a pure structural, norm-oriented institutional model at the other extreme. *Actor-preference* driven design processes and *value-structure* driven design processes are not mutually exclusive. We expect that actual policy designs usually do not fall clearly into one of those two categories, but are characterised by some particular mix and tensions that distinguish the process. Although we may speak of variation along a dimension delimited by two ideal typical patterns and a range of possible combinations in between, this is meant as an illustration, and as such it has its limitations. Actual policy design may be characterised by a combination of strongly preference-driven and strongly value-driven designs. Rather than arranging themselves neatly along one dimension, therefore, we are likely to find that unique combinations of characteristics measured along a number of dimensions can distinguish specific design processes.

Regime Changes

In order to understand the policy changes that were identified above we need to look closer at the actors involved, their values and the relationship between them. One implication of the higher education expansion we have witnessed since about 1965 is that the growth of the system in terms of the number of faculty, students and institutions changed significantly the qualitative content, dynamics and conditions of actions for the actors within the system. In the remainder of the chapter we shall explore the changes empirically by way of an analysis of the actors in higher education policy making and their interrelationships.

Actors and influence

In the analysis of the actors and their influence in higher education policy I shall use the typology of influence and consider to what extent there has been any development regarding the different types of influence during the period considered.

Changes in state domination

The three countries moved in different directions and from different points of departure regarding state influence. *England* moved from a situation where the state accepted financial responsibility without demanding any say in how the universities managed themselves, to one in which in the 1980s the central government was characterised by its ability to determine policies and implement them without too much deference to external groups. Ministers played a dominant role in policy formulation, but the degree of state influence is more contested regarding control over the universities once the broad policy framework has been set (Kogan and Hanney, 1999; Salter and Tapper, 1994), had a dominant role in the determination of higher education policies.

Central government higher education policies in *Norway* were until recently concerned almost wholly with issues relating to access and size and macro structure of the system. Two parallel processes seem to have developed whereby the stronger central government role in higher education also represented a move from Ministerial towards a stronger parliamentary influence, opening up for stronger influence by politically influential actors like students and state colleges, at the expense of universities and scientific colleges.

The Swedish central government and its civil servants predominantly determined higher education policy since the 1970s (Lane 1990). The Conservative coalition government of 1991–94 was successful in passing legislation that gave the institutions considerable more freedom, including the right to establish professorships. In the former period the voice of the academics seems to have been ignored, whereas academic and institutional input during the later reform process again seemed to be more significant. After the arrival of the Social Democratic government (September 1994) this change was somewhat moderated (Kogan and Marton, 2000).

Changes in institutional autonomy

Despite a presumed loss of institutional autonomy of greater state domination over *English* universities, Conservative ministers and departmental officials claimed there had been an increase in institutional autonomy where the universities became less dependent on the state for their resources. Institutional leaders undoubtedly became more powerful but their space for action was more strongly framed (Askling and Henkel, 2000). The universities have moved from a position in which they were almost uniquely trusted to run their own affairs, to a situation in which they were regarded at times with an element of suspicion, mixed with a feeling of continued respect for the quality of the top research universities.

Institutional autonomy in *Norway* has been affected by two kinds of developments in recent years. Arrangements that were traditionally regarded as safeguards for autonomy were dismantled both in connection with such arrangements as the incorporation of the universities in a national legislation and planning system and with the internal transformation of the university governing structure. The legislation meant that a functional principle replaced a disciplinary principle of representation to the governing bodies, and that external representation was mandated on the university boards. However, the meaning of the term 'autonomy' was redefined by policymakers and many institutional leaders. It no longer referred to the individual and collective autonomy of academics to make independent decisions, but came to mean decentralised decision authority of institutional leaders in relations to state authorities (Kogan and Marton, 2000).

The notion of the *Swedish* university as an 'independent' cultural institution was not really evident from the policies implemented during the 1970s and 1980s. Many reforms during the 1970s were severely opposed by academics and students. The power of the professoriate was weakened by the 1977 reform, as outside interests were granted positions on decision-making boards (Premfors and Östergren, 1978; Svensson, 1987) and further in 1983 when it was established that one-third of all representatives on the governing boards would be non-academics, representing external interests (Lane 1990). In the reform of 1993, the Conservative coalition government limited the influence of these outside groups by denying them positions on the university boards. We also observe one parallel to the Norwegian case in the sense that autonomy was redefined as a value for the institutional leadership, possibly to the extent that it weakened or infringed upon the powers of the professoriate and faculties.

Changes in elite mediation

The range of academic elites in *England* has been characterised as to some extent non-coterminous. Although the Oxbridge elites as a general class were not influential in government policy making, many of the most powerful coopted elites were at the same time members of the 'real' academic elite. Within the broad policy framework, substantive decisions affecting institutions or academic subject resources were delegated to bodies allocating teaching or research monies. These bodies consisted of 'co-opted elites', which became increasingly important in the implementation of quality assessment policies and the research selectivity exercise carried out by the UGC, and the successive funding councils. It is not clear, however, whether the co-opted elites directly affected policy making as opposed to its implementation.

The function of elites in the *Norwegian* higher education system must take into account the small scale of Norwegian society and the intimacy of a system where top civil servants in the ministries and university professors knew each other personally. Although the system had grown it was still relatively homogenous. However, in the Norwegian study we drew conclusions that were shared by the major players in Norwegian university politics: 1) There was no national higher education policy elite. 2) To the extent that there were integrated groups of powerful actors in higher education policy making, they are local or specialised. 3) The groups were often relatively loose, temporary person- or issue-based networks.

The role of academic elites and their possible co-option in the *Swedish* higher education regime are difficult to discern for primarily two reasons. 1) The Swedish university system was based on the notion of equality of institutions across the country. 2) There was a long tradition of 'expert' involvement in the policy process through the use of government commissions. Comparing the individual actors who comprised the leadership of the two major reform commissions, 'U68' and 'Högskoleutredningen 89', Bauer *et al.* (1999) have noticed quite a significant difference in background and areas of expertise. The U68 Commission members all represented central government positions. The key members of the 'Högskoleutredningen 89' were all academics. Thus, it appears that academic elite persons played a much more salient policy making role in the late 1980s and early 1990s.

Changes in corporatist mediation

Overall the role of the corporatist actors is difficult to detect in the case of *English* Higher Education, although certain actors who may be members of interest groups intersect with those admitted to decision making as co-opted elites. The interest group representing the university leaders, the Committee of Vice-Chancellors and Principals (CVCP), often encountered difficulties in representing the collective voice of institutional leaders who valued institutional autonomy above agreeing to a common line. Previously corporate interest-based networks existed in certain areas of higher education in the form of policy communities with stable, limited and consensual membership. To the extent that interest groups played a part in England they may have played their most important part in the period after elite structures started to disintegrate and before relatively stable policy communities shifted towards a larger issue network. The latter development characterised the 1980s. Thus we may say that the influence structure in England moved from implicit consensus between universities and government to governmental framing of policy without too much heed to established interest groups except where their interests were clearly aligned to current policies.

Norway has traditionally been counted among those countries where interest organizations and corporatist institutions have played an important part in national politics (Olsen, 1978; Rokkan, 1966). In higher education the situation was different. Although most university employees were unionised, their unions have not been influential. The exception was the traditional domains of labour unions such as working conditions and wage negotiations. To the extent that such issues interfered with other aspects of higher education policy, however, corporatist arrangements might make themselves felt. In general the field of work environment and the detailed regulations in that connection might in principle make the unions important and influential players, but in practice they did not seem to have exploited this potential.

The corporatist tradition in *Sweden* was evident during the late 1960s and the 1970s in the strong representation of the trade unions, industry leaders, and local government officials in the policy process. The policy network certainly leaned towards a type of policy community, with a limited number of powerful players at the negotiation table with consensus prevailing. During this time, the National Swedish Labour Market Board had a special role in the formation of higher education policy, given the goal of the welfare state to connect higher education to job purpose and job creation. During the 1990s, a shift from a 'policy community' to an 'issue network' seemed to have occurred. A wider variety of interest groups and organizations were involved in policymaking. The focus of the major reforms during the 1990s reflected the input from students as well as teachers and the business community (Bauer *et al.*, 1999). Compared to the corporatist regime before the early 1990s the 1993-reform process was characterised by a shortening of the policy process, often skipping the traditional consultation process (remiss) which may have reduced the chance of some groups, from fully expressing their policy preferences.

Actor networks and cohesion

Whereas the basic characteristics of the three higher education policy regimes seemed relatively unchanged during the first half of this century, unprecedented growth and successive waves of reform policies introduced a new dynamism from the 1960s on. These waves broke up established structures and reshaped fundamental aspects of the regimes and the relationship between the actors within them. Thus all three countries underwent broad processes of structural change that had a number of similar characteristics.

First, the size of higher education until the 1960s was by and large relatively stable; it was exposed to relatively modest demand and its political salience was low. The growth of the system made it much more politically important and the prevailing notions of what the university does and its relationship with the state changed. Until the 1960s the prevailing idea about university research still was that it was the location of a small-scale intellectual and culturally important activity, the autonomy of which it was a state responsibility to protect. With regard to education, utilitarian concerns in many cases shaped the programs and degree system. Today it has come to be conceived as a high-cost, large-scale research and educational enterprise, an economically important activity, the cost of which it is a state responsibility to control and the results of which it is a state responsibility to exploit. As higher education grew it became more interesting to the politicians. It was gradually lifted out of the purely elite, administrative sphere where top ministry officials and university professors prevailed and into the political sphere of a wider network of actors such as Parliament and interest organizations. Higher education thus became more exposed to various 'external influences' and the wider political agenda of central governments. Economic policies and in particular labour market policies thus increasingly influenced relations and decisions in higher education in all three countries.

Second, although the co-ordination of higher education institutions traditionally turned on the relationship between the state and the institutions, the institutional side changed considerably. The systems evolved from relatively few universities and national scientific institutions into much more comprehensive systems. Binary systems were developed from the 1960s in all countries but have been or are currently about to become dismantled. This meant that a large number of institutions competed for resources, academic privileges and students. They were not only concerned with absolute growth of their budgets, but also with how they fared compared to other institutions. Thus the network of actors involved increased and their interrelations have changed. As higher education became politicised, relations became formalised and affected by the attempts of central government authorities to direct, integrate and control the costs of the higher education sector.

An appropriate overall characteristic seems to be that the regimes changed from cohesive, transparent networks of few actors – mainly the leaders of a few academic institutions and top civil servants to a wider and more politicised network. Compared with present times we may say of all three countries that when the expansion started in the 1960s, the higher education systems were small, and policies were often made within what today appear as intimate, community like and informal settings were the actors knew one another personally. As the system grew it become more formal and arguably less transparent. Management based on informal knowledge and personal relationships within relatively homogenous elite groups gave way to political-administrative processes embedded in formal structures and based on formal positions. The new networks of actors were more opaque and politicised. There was a stronger focus on the competition between institutions, the needs of the students, and the labour market. The process of politicization also contributed to integrating higher education policies with welfare state and labour market policies.

Although the regimes of the three countries originally had elitist features, it is important to bear in mind the differences between them. First of all, whereas English universities were considered self-governed corporations, supported by the state, Norwegian and Swedish universities have always been part of the civil service. Whereas in England academic elites appears to have been self-governed, it is harder to distinguish between the state and the academic elite in Norway and Swedish. Furthermore, comparing the two state systems, corporate actors were more influential in Sweden than in Norway.

Both the informal cohesive community-like actor networks and the wider formal actor networks were different. In England there was a movement from an independent academic elite to a wider set of actors in which central government through ministerial influence was a particularly influential actor. The changing actor constellation in Norway went from a situation in which a state civil service elite encompassed the academic elite to a situation where central government influence manifested itself as a more politicised and parliamentary influence through which regional interests were able to influence policy making. Finally, in Sweden a state civil service elite influence first transformed into a network characterised by corporate influence and then into a wider and looser network in which 1990s academic elites, business groups and party politics played more important roles.

Conclusion

Over time, say the latter half of the last century, there has been a tendency to use a growing array of policy instruments. Traditionally public policies typically relied upon the use of authority tools and symbolic tools. An increasing diversity of public tasks and growing responsibilities during the era of public expansion until the mid-1970s made capacity and incentive tools more important. Particularly important in this connection were welfare state services and various productive tasks, in some countries also of active labour market policies and comprehensive macro economic planning. The policy shifts during the last decades, including the rise of neo-liberalism, led to changes in the directions of the use of policy instruments. The use of incentives directed at institutions as well as individuals grew, as did the use of learning tools. The latter typically manifested itself in the form of the growth of evaluation within public administration. These were all policy shifts common to the three cases. They underscore that actor strategies and their impact must be considered against a backdrop of structural change that we find in all three countries.

In addition to the focus on policy change over time, the dynamic regime approach directs our attention to cross-national and cross-sector comparison between countries and policy sectors. Let us briefly try to sum up and draw some conclusions from the observations of higher education reform in the three countries. First of all it demonstrated that reforms espousing similar ideologies varied considerably both with respect to how radical the reforms were and to how stable the policies were (Bleiklie, 2000; Bleiklie *et al.*, 1997). Although the reforms meant an increased use of incentive and learning tools in all three countries, they were used quite differently. The reform patterns had some striking differences that seem clearly related to general system characteristics of the three countries. These processes suggest that regime characteristics may be linked with policy design in different ways. The three patterns make up three types of policy styles that may be used as an aid for further studies into the relationship between institutional design and policy design.

In spite of the fact that the countries apparently moved in the same direction they did so in manners that were characterised by different national points of departure and that to some extent seemed to sustain national peculiarities. Thus the 1977 reform gave Sweden a point of departure that was different from England and Norway when the reforms of the late 1980s and early 1990s where conceived. Having introduced reforms in the 1970s that significantly reduced institutional autonomy, and tailored the educational programs to national labour market planning, the latter reforms were considered to move higher education out of the grip of the central government and closer to traditional academic values. In England and Norway the reforms were regarded as moves in the opposite direction as the state tried to gain control of higher education in order to control costs and use it in the service of general economic policy goals. In addition the politicization of higher education meant different things in the three countries. In England the influence of education ministers seems to have been particularly strong. In Sweden party politics have influenced policies and in Norway MPs have acted as representatives of regions and their local state colleges rather than as party members.

English reforms were comparatively centralised, radical and relied more on tougher measures in order to discipline non-compliant institutions. Once introduced the policy was pursued rather consistently. This pattern illustrates the confrontational style, but also the relative stability that is the aim of the Westminster style of 'winner-take-all-democracy'. This illustrates what we may call a *heroic style* of policy making. Actor preferences and their strategies were important for the initial policy change during the 1980s. Since then a new consensus seems to have emerged and the process has been more value-structure driven, characterised by a relative consensus under which the new Labour government that came to power in 1997 did not significantly alter the policies of its conservative predecessor.

The Norwegian reforms, however, were less radical. In a comparative perspective they evolved gradually in a value-structure driven process with considerable local variation as to how the reforms were implemented. The pattern illustrated the decentralised, steady and consensual political *incremental style* characterised by Olsen (1983) as 'revolution in slow motion'. Although the policies where formulated by the central government, individual institutions had considerable leeway as to how the reforms were implemented, but most importantly, incentives were used to reward those institutions and individuals who performed well.

Swedish reforms were characterised by a more confrontational style than those of Norway, but also by less political stability. Government changes led to policy changes and a varying central government control in terms of authority tools and use of incentives vis-à-vis educational institutions. The Swedish experience thus illustrates what we may call an *adversarial style* of policy making in the sense of an uneasy tug-of-war between two major political blocks with two very different visions of higher education. These policy shifts indicate that actor preferences and the tension between them have played a more important part in Sweden than in the other two countries.

References

Atkinson, M. M. and Coleman, W. D. (1992) Policy Networks, Policy Communities and the Problems of Governance, *Governance.* 5 (2): 154-180.

Bauer, M., Askling, B., Marton, S. G. and Marton, F. (eds) (1999) *Transforming Universities. Changing Patterns of Governance, Structure and Learning in Swedish Higher Education.* London and Philadelphia: Jessica Kingsley Publishers.

Becher, T. and Kogan, M. (eds) (1992) *Process and Structure in Higher Education.* Milton Keynes: Open University Press.

Ben-David, J. and Zloczower, A. (1991) Universities and Academic Systems in Modern Societies, in J. Ben-David (ed) *Scientific Growth.* Berkley, Los Angeles, London: University of California Press.

Bleiklie, I. (1996) Universitetet - fra kulturinstitusjon til kunnskapsbedrift, in I. Bleiklie (ed) *Kunnskap og makt.* Oslo: Tano Aschehoug.

Bleiklie, I. (1998) Justifying the Evaluative State. New Public Management Ideals in Higher Education, *European Journal of Education,* 33 (3): 299-316.

Bleiklie, I. (2000) Policy Regimes and Policy Making, in M. Kogan et al. *Transforming Higher Education. A Comparative Study.* London and Philadelphia: Jessica Kingsley Publishers

Bleiklie, I., Høstaker, R and Vabø, A. (eds) (2000) *Policy and Practice in Higher Education. Reforming Norwegian Universities.* London and Philadelphia: Jessica Kingsley Publishers.

Bleiklie, I., Marton, S. and Hanney, S. (eds) (1997) *Policy Regimes and Policy Design – A Dynamic Network Approach.* Bergen: LOS-senter Notat 9718.

Cawson, A. (1983) Functional Representation and Democratic Politics, in G. Duncan (ed) *Democratic Theory and Practice.* Cambridge: Cambridge University Press, 178-98.

Clark, B.R. (ed) (1993) *The Research Foundation of Graduate Education*. Berkley, Los Angeles, London: University of California Press.

Clark, B.R. (ed) (1998) *Creating Entrepreneurial Universities*. Oxford, New York, Tokyo: IAU Press/Pergamon.

Daalder, H. and Shils, E, (eds) (1982) *Universities, Politicians and Bureaucrats*. Cambridge: Cambridge University Press.

Etzioni-Halevy, E. (ed) (1993) *The Elite Connection. Problems and Potential of Western Democracy*. Cambridge: Polity Press.

Grant, W. (ed) (1985) *The Political Economy of Corporatism*. New York: St.Martin's.

Heidenheimer, A. J., Heclo, H. and Adams, C. T. (eds) (1983) *Comparative Public Policy. The Politics of Social Choice in Europe and America.*. New York: St. Martin's Press.

Henkel, M. (ed) (2000) *Academic Identities*. London and Philadelphia: Jessica Kingsley Publishers.

Ingram, H. and Schneider, A. (1990) Behavioral Assumptions of Policy Tools, *Journal of Politics*, 52 (2): 510-529.

Ingram, H. and Schneider, A. (1993) Constructing Citizenship: the subtle messages of policy design. In H. Ingram and S. R. Smith (eds) Public Policy for Democracy. Washington DC: Brookings Institution.

John, P. and Cole, A. (1997) Networks or networking? The Importance of power, position and values in local economic policy networks in Britain and France, *APSA paper*, Washington, 28-31 August.

Knoke, D., Pappi, F. U., Broadbent, J. and Tsujinaka, Y. (1996) *Comparing Policy Networks*. Cambridge Studies in Comparative Politics. Cambridge: Cambridge University Press.

Kogan, M. (1984) The Political View, in B. R. Clark (ed) *Perspectives on Higher Education*. Berkeley: University of California Press.

Kogan, M. (1992) Political Science, in B. R. Clark and G. Neave (eds) *The International Encyclopedia of Higher Education.*. London: Pergamon Press.

Kogan, M. and Hanney, S. (1999) *Reforming Higher Education*. Higher Education Policy Series 50. London and Philadelphia: Jessica Kingsley Publishers.

Kogan, M. and Marton, S. (2000) State and Higher Education, in M. Kogan et al.(ed) *Transforming Higher Education. A Comparative Study*. London and Philadelphia: Jessica Kingsley Publishers.

Kogan, M., Bauer, M., Bleiklie, I. and Henkel, M. (eds) (2000) *Transforming Higher Education. A Comparative Study.* London and Philadelphia: Jessica Kingsley Publishers.

Lægreid, P. and Pedersen, O. K. (eds) (1996) *Integration og Decentralisering. Personal og Forvaltning i Skandinavien..* Copenhagen: Jurist- og Økonomforbundets Forlag.

Lane, J-E. (ed) (1990) *Institutional Reform. A Public Policy Perspective.* Aldershot: Dartmouth.

March, J. M. and Olsen, J. P. (1994) Institutional Perspectives on Governance., in Hans Ulrich Derlien (ed) *Systemrationalität und Partialinteresse: Festschrift für Renate Mayntz.* Baden-Baden: Nomos Verlagsgesellschaft.

March, J. M. and Olsen, J. P. (eds) (1989) *Discovering Institutions.* New York: The Free Press.

Olsen, J. P. (1978) Folkestyre, byråkrati og korporativisme, in J. P. Olsen (ed) *Politisk organisering.* Oslo: Universitetsforlaget.

Olsen, J. P. (ed) (1983) *Organized Democracy.* Bergen: Universitetsforlaget.

Olsen, J. P. and Peters, B. G. (eds) (1996) *Lessons from Experience. Experiential Reforms in Eight Democracies.* Oslo-Stockholm-Copenhagen-Boston-Oxford: Scandinavian University Press.

Ostrom, E. (ed) (1990) *Governing the Commons.* Cambridge: Cambridge University Press.

Pollitt, C. (ed) (1993) *Managerialism and the Public Services. The Anglo-American Experience.* Oxford: Blackwell.

Premfors, R. and Östergren, B. (eds) (1978) *Systems of Higher Education: Sweden.* New Haven: ICED.

Raab, C. (1994) Theorising the Governance of Education, *British Journal of Educational Studies*, 42(1), 6-22 March.

Rein, M. (ed) (1983) *From Policy to Practice.* London: The Macmillan Press.

Rhodes, R.A.W. and Marsh, D, (1992) New Directions in the Study of Policy Networks, *European Journal of Political Research,* 21:181-205.

Richardson, J. (1997) Interest Groups, Multi-Arena Politics and Policy Change, *APSA-paper*, Washington, 28-31 August.

Rokkan, S. (1966) Norway: Numerical Democracy and Corporate Pluralism, in R. A. Dahl (ed) *Political Oppositions in Western Democracies.* New Haven: Yale University Press.

Rothblatt, S. (1992) *The OECD Master Plan and the Californian Dream.* Center for Studies in Higher Education. Berkley: University of California Press.

Rothblatt, S. and Wittrock, B. (eds) (1993) The European and American University Since 1800:

Historical and sociological essays, Cambridge; Cambridge University Press

Sabatier, P. A. and Jenkins-Smith, H. (eds) (1993) *Policy Change and Learning: An Advocacy Coalition Framework.* Boulder, CO: Westview Press.

Salter, B. and Tapper, T. (eds) (1994) *The State and Higher Education.* Ilford: Woburn Press.

Schmitter, P. (1974) Still the century of corporatism, in F. Pike and Th. Strich (eds) *The New Corporatism.* Notre Dame: University of Notre dame.

Schmitter, P. and Lehmbruch, G. (eds) (1979) *Trends Toward Corporatist Intermediation.* Sage: Beverly Hills.

Skocpol, T. (ed) (1992) *Protecting Soldiers and Mothers. The Political Origins of Social Policy in the United States.* Cambridge, Mass and London: The Belknap Press of Harvard University Press.

Svensson, L. (ed) (1987) *State Control and Academic Autonomy.* Stockholm: UHÄ.

3 The Role of Different Groups in Policy-Making and Implementation: Institutional politics and policy-making.

Maurice Kogan

This chapter draws on the literature concerned with two main themes: the role of different groups in policy-making and implementation; and institutional politics and policy-making. It also uses data from a three country study of higher education policy reported in Kogan *et al.* (2000), Kogan and Hanney (2000) and Henkel (2000). That research into the changing nature of the HE systems in Sweden, Norway and England in the last 25 years of the 20th century used documentary evidence and data from 90 interviews with key policy informants. There were in addition over 300 interviews carried out as part of a study of the impact of policy changes on academic identities in those countries.

In examining these two issues, we begin by articulating a set of presuppositions which are need of testing:

* in a democratic society policy changes reflect some kind of accommodation between government and the interests of various stake-holders
* the corollary is that a number of groups are involved in the generation of policy
* that changes in policy have been the result of reflection on why change was needed, and how the changes would meet discernible deficits and needs
* that changes in governmental machinery reflect the nature of the policy changes
* such drastic changes have had at least some of the impacts that policy-makers hoped to achieve.

Treated sceptically, these presumptions provide a critical framework against which to exploit the empirical material gathered in the studies referred to above and in similar one. The chapter returns to consider their robustness when subjected to this test at the end of the first part of the chapter.

Different Groups in Policy-Making and Implementation

In considering the forces at work in creating and implementing higher education policy, the basic distinction to observe is between *contextual factors* that affect policy outcomes, and the involvement of certain groups or *actors*.

Contextual factors

Contextual factors affected the policy environment. There was expansion, the spontaneous growth in demand for higher education, in the UK from more than 3% to 15% and then to over 30%, of the school leaver population. Expansion may indeed have been more a cause than a result of policy change. At any rate, without it the whole quality movement would not have been so prominent, and the relative degradation of academic power would have been less steep. The economy demanded more from higher education but was unable to sustain the funding per unit provided until the reductions of the late 1970s and the large reductions of 1981. There was an assumed growth in demand for new knowledge and its applications. Those factors had their effects, even if hardly articulated by policy in any systematic or rational way. There were also, partly acting as contextual factors and partly embodied in actors, ideologies such as those informing the emphasis on academic freedom and those advocating the claims of the market and the economy. The economic ideology, it is argued, first emerged 'as a set of state-sponsored values in the post-war years.'(Salter and Tapper, 1994) and helped drive the centralising motivation of the national bureaucrats - an interpretation they mainly reject.

Prime actors

Within the contextual factors there were the actions of the prime actors, and specifically, elite and interest groups and the ways in which they connected with each other. There is a great deal of writing about them, and I will try not to get too involved in the academic word-chopping which has surrounded their discussion.

Elites

Elite theories assume that small groups of power holders can be distinguished from the powerless majority. The classic versions distinguish elites according to their group consciousness, coherence and conspiracy. In terms of power, organization or other resources, they are able to exploit their positions to preserve their domination (Marton *et al.*, 1995). Elite analysis has typically studied top positions to find out who controls the positions where key decisions are made (Hunter, 1953).

Corporatism, too, assumes there are small groups of power holders who determine political outcomes in society (Schmitter and Lehmbruch 1979; Cawson 1986; Grant 1985). Under corporatism, political exchange is limited to a few participants who are insulated from external pressure. In the UK we had until the 1980s a 'handsome corporatist bargain' in which the universities provided knowledge and an educated elite in return for their status, resources and freedom.

The pluralist view, often called democratic elite theory, emphasizes the concept of multiple and autonomous elites. The autonomy of the elites, both from the government as well as from the other elite groups, is an important factor in preventing the abuse of power by one ruling class. But the idea of co-optation, '…the process of absorbing new elements into the leadership of policy-determining structures of an organization, as a means of averting threats to its stability or existence' (Kogan 1984), puts in question the idea of autonomous elites. Similar concerns appear in Saward's (1992) attempt to build a model of policy making in terms of co-optation.

The notion of co-optation is important in higher education policy. Co-opted academic elites may operate in three different ways: as part of decision making through membership of government appointed bodies, eg funding or research councils; by internalising, interpreting and helping implementation of government policies, for example, the CVCP in its participation in Jarratt and the QAA, and by creating hierarchies of resource and esteem (Becher and Kogan, 1992 and Kogan, 1992). In some of its actions, as in establishing the Reynolds enquiry it pre-empted government action. These forms of influence may interact to form highly varied patterns of influence within the policy sector.

Moving away from the more abstract definitions, if we take the UK scene, we can discern three groups that influence higher education policy. There are, first, the 'real' academic elites, as represented by the fellowships of the British Academy and the Royal Society. Taken collectively, the academic elite did not make much impact in recent policy changes, the British Academy less than the Royal Society, and only on a few issues. For example, much of the debate about career structures for researchers was driven by the Royal Society. No arts person has had the same influence on policy. There was not one FBA on the Dearing Committee. Individual FRSs did have influence, and, no doubt, the fact of their fellowship enhanced the assumed value of the advice they gave. But one cannot assume that individual members of the elite, working through the ABRC and the research councils, shared the same views as the two honorific societies.

> Such bodies as the Royal Society have several inner tribes pushing their own subject rather than more general policies. Connection with policy making during this period was intermittent, often personal, and episodic… many of the academic elites were remote from

the main policy concerns... They have difficulty, because of their specialisation, in communicating with politicians. The costs of the involvement are high for them. Many would not want to risk threat to their reputation.' (Interview with leading academic, 1996).

Members of the defined elite were, however, represented on the top bodies advising on scientific policy; at the time of the controversial report *A Strategy for the Science Base* (1987); of the ABRC's 23 members.12 were FRSs, 1 an FBA and there were 5 F. Engs (one of whom was also an FRS). It is claimed that, in practice, coordination of science policy in Britain tends to mean cross-membership of committees and 'the system probably only works because the people who sit on all these committees have so much in common' (Ince 1986: 28). However, one observer believed that the initiative had passed away from that elite which was effectively longing for greater selectivity. 'All those groups that operated before 1992 evaporated. What we now have is a bureaucratic system that can't cope. People can't pull the levers any more.' (Kogan and Hanney, 2000; 222).

Coopted elites are those who arrive at positions of power because Ministers have laid hands on them. They are appointed to chairs or membership of the main allocative bodies. The academic elites overlap with the coopted elites much more in the hard sciences than in the humanities. Whilst some key figures are also members of the academic elite, for the most part, however, they are not coterminous with them. They do not run the research selectivity exercises, for example, and members of the funding or research councils are rarely members of the two elite societies. Yet there is linkage. Two sets of decision-making go on. There is that of allocations through the funding bodies and research councils. But there is also a second line in which academics make judgements about who will get the top chairs and academic honours. Academic judgements are convertible into status and resources not unlike the interaction of tectonic plates: not directly connected but generating energy through the movement between them.

As for institutional leaders, some are powerful nationally, and no doubt members of the Russell Group would lay claim to that territory, but collectively as through the CVCP are not able to aggregate opinions and power well enough to change the policy flow. They are stratified: the Russell group, Oxbridge, vice-chancellors of the 'old' and newly incorporated universities. Those who have a voice need not also be members of the academic elite - as is illustrated by the way in which the quality assurance surge was handled by those from the former polytechnics. For the most part, the leadership elites in Oxford and Cambridge as represented by the heads of colleges pursue their own rather than national agendas.

What influence did these groups have? In our period, with some significant exceptions, their influence on higher education policy making was limited. We can find exceptions: for example, the influence exerted by the scientific elite on the decision to create OST and on the content of the subsequent white paper. For the most part, ministers determined the new policy thrusts, though a few members of the elites helped fashion the means and style of their implementation for example, the format of the RAE, the decision on RTX and the QAA structures.

We need to ask now how coherent they were. The literature offers (Wright, 1988; Rhodes and Marsh, 1992; Jordan, G. and Schubert, K, 1992) a continuum between a 'policy community' and 'issue networks'' at the two opposing ends of a policy network. The criteria used are membership, integration, resources and power. A 'policy community' would thus be characterised by: its limited membership; frequent interaction with shared basic values; all participants having a resource base and the ability to deliver their members' support; and a relatively equal power distribution among the network members. The 'issue network' is characterised by: a large and/or wide range of affected interests; fluctuations in contacts, access, and level of agreement; unequal resource distribution combined with varying abilities to deliver members support; and unequal powers among the group's members.

The latter seems to be the more accurate description of what we have in Britain. In that country we have a fragmented power structure and this picture differs from that of an earlier generation of elite studies that assumed that there were links between university and other elites, with an emphasis on Oxbridge, in its role in educating the wider elite (eg, Wakeford and Wakeford, 1974). It was assumed that policy making for the universities was conducted, 'by likeminded members of the elite' (Halsey, 1969, p137, Kogan, 1975) in the Treasury and the University Grants Committee (UGC) and that between them there was a high level of trust. If both government and the universities can be considered as embodying elites, conflict between them would be unlikely. But, as Salter and Tapper point out (1978: 150): 'Part of the significance of Robbins… lies in the indications it gives of the beginnings of elite fragmentation.'.

However it is doubtful that picture was true for the earlier period on the simple assumption that there was virtually no explicit policy-making before 1939, and that by the time the really big issues arose following Robbins in the mid-1960s, the power landscape was changed. It could, however, be argued that elite operation is concerned with making sure that there is no public policy-making and that any agenda for action remains with them.

In the UK coterminosity between the different influence groups has been uneven. They were not well enough connected with each other, or with government, to constitute a policy community, although there were issue networks. For example, the majority of Oxbridge heads of houses are not members of the academic elite. Of those appointed vice-chancellor since 1960, only 14% have been FRSs and 5% have been FBAs (Smith *et al.*, 1999). Individual members of the academic elite, particularly those eminent in science and technology, are part of the co-opted elite when they are appointed to research councils and allocative bodies, but the majority of co-optees are not members of the academic or institutional leadership elite.

The research problem of demonstrating strength of connection is considerable. Detailed network analyses would require access to diaries, but they would not necessarily disclose the content of the connection. Policy shifts can result from single meetings and, indeed, continuous contact may reduce the quality of the contact. Thus we have to rely on documentation and on interrogated accounts by participants that can then be compared with others.

Interest Representation and Interest Politics.

An assumption for sceptical testing, mentioned at the beginning of this paper, was that policy changes would reflect some kind of accommodation between government and the interests of the various stake-holders. For example, one might assume that general interest organizations would be interested such policy matters as higher education's role in the labour market. But, for the most part, they have not been particularly active in the UK. Overall the role of the corporatist actors is difficult to detect, although some intersect with those admitted to decision making as co-opted elites.

We could divide them between those directly concerned with higher education and others with broader spans of interest. Of the first, the Committee of Vice-Chancellors and Principals (CVCP), often encountered difficulties in representing the collective voice of institutional leaders who valued institutional autonomy above agreeing to a common line. It was able to lobby with some success in the House of Lords, where some academics sat. It was strongly opposed to the cuts of 1981 onwards, but with barely any success. It was divided on the allocation of resources. The old universities were less keen on growth. The vice chancellors were hardly consulted as a total group on introducing quality assessment or on the shift to the HEFC. When a new larger, diverse CVCP formed, it was even more difficult to get it to sing from same hymn sheet. We have noted some cooption of the CVCP to government: for example, academic audit, Jarratt and implementing performance indicators were passed to UGC/CVCP to do.

The Committee of Directors of Polytechnics were much more tightly organised. I return to them below. The AUT were never much listened to by officials or by ministers. The NUS leadership tended, even by the mid '80s, to be in the hands of people who were primarily interested in 'causes' although there was a changing acceptability. One respondent reported that at a meeting with Keith Joseph, the CVCP said 'for goodness sake overcome your prejudices and receive the NUS. Leaving the NUS out is only causing problems.' With the collapse of the binary system negotiation between central government and local government associations came to an end.

The CBI and industry were not a coherent lobby although some of the more influential industrialists were consulted often and civil servants read material produced by CBI and by CIHE and talked with them. According to a respondent though it was 'simply untrue that the concerted choir of the CBI were saying let's have a great expansion of higher education… a late conversion.'

Previously there were some policy communities with stable, limited and consensual membership. One example was those represented in The National Advisory Council for the Supply and Training of Teachers and another was the National Advisory Body (NAB) for public sector higher education funding, although this existed only for eight years in the 1980s. They tended to be constituted of virtually predictable representative groups.

In the 1980s, the predominant UK model was weak and intermittent. There was consultation rather than negotiation, and it was not as widespread or as systematic as is typical of an issue network. Earlier, there had been consensually accepted policies of expansion, and politicians did not interfere in academic matters; the buffer institutions, on which academics were represented, made active negotiation largely unnecessary. When radical reform came, UK central government deferred little to external groups in determining and implementing policies.

The influence structure moved from implicit consensus between universities and government to governmental framing of policy without too much heed to established interest groups except where their interests were clearly aligned to current policies. Some of the leading interest groups - such as CVCP - might be consulted 'incessantly' but on the whole it was consultation rather than negotiation. Former ministers and civil servants attested that relationships with main groups were episodic rather than systematic. Academics were not a group particularly close to the Government. Thatcherism regarded them as a vested interest to be controlled.

So to return to the political science categories, there are few empiricised examples of pluralistic influence in higher education (Kogan, 1992). Nor was *corporatism*, with its implications of bargaining and exchange, applicable. Nor was there much exchange (Blau, 1964); Ranson (1980); Rhodes (1981) in the sense of there being *quid pro quos*, but increasing dependence on the state and deference to its policies.

There were differences between the influence structures in UK and Norway and Sweden (Bleiklie *et al.*, 2000, Highley; Lægreid and Olsen, 1978; Peterson, 1989; Premfors, 1980). Norwegian top civil servants and university professors formed a tightly knit elite, although its characteristics changed as the system expanded. In Sweden the notion of elites is less salient; corporatism has worked through party and trade union membership in making policy change. The policy making process has occasionally broken with this tradition and from 1993 the reform process was characterised by skipping the traditional consultation process which may have reduced the ability of some groups to express their policy preferences.

The working of elites is affected by the general nature of the polity. Whereas English universities were self-governed corporations, supported by the state, Norwegian and Swedish universities have always been part of the civil service. Whereas in England academic elites appears to have been self-governed, it is harder to distinguish between the state and the academic elite in Norway and Sweden. Furthermore, comparing the two state systems, corporate actors were more influential in Sweden than in Norway.

What happened in the UK

Let me turn now from more general discussion of influences to particular cases in the UK. If the system was not strongly influenced by policy communities or interest networks, there were particular policy issues on which we can see particular groups and individuals wielding influence. On some, such as Enterprise in Higher Education, ministers created and drove the policy. The membership of Manpower Services Commission included several powerful industrialists keen on the changes, although they did not originate them. Trade unions were not mentioned in this discussion. By contrast, the establishment of TQA was a product of public sector thinking which originated in discussions between DES and PCFC heads - Stubbs and Melia. And it was soon taken over by polytechnic leaders and thrived despite opposition from the CVCP 'and from the AUT as well because they didn't like the idea of their professionalism being challenged.'

In the ending of the binary system, there was a coming together of interests between some polytechnic directors and Tory ministers. It is the one example of the successful operation of interest group pressure on government. The polytechnics succeeded in persuading government that they were trying to achieve precisely what the government wanted- for example, vocationally led education, quality measures and expansion at a relatively low unit cost. The CDP was also talking to a Government that wanted to overthrow the local authorities, with whom, by Baker's time, there was virtually no communication. The CVCP were relaxed about independence for polytechnics: 'a lot of us had polys in our cities and we saw the dead hand of local government ...' They were less happy about the ending of the binary line.

We know from several interviews that a comparatively small group of policy makers such as Swinnerton-Dyer, David Phillips, Christopher Ball, interacted with senior officials on key issues. We have accounts of dinners held by Swinnerton-Dyer at which there was discussion of concentration and selectivity. Those present included government chief scientists and industrial leaders such as Roberts, later of UCL, as well as David Phillips and Christopher Ball. Such names as Brian Flowers and Fred Dainton were also mentioned as being influential in policy discussion.

The science community probably were split down the middle on selectivity - those who thought they would benefit from research concentration were for it. In the 1984 UGC Strategy Document there was little support for research selectivity in the evidence gathered; Peter Swinnerton-Dyer, then chairman, was said to have advocated it. but in part to be responding to pressure from ministers. If the UGC had not taken the initiative the Government might have done. There was no pressure from industry. The industrial members of the UGC were not taking a lead - they tended to retain a respect for universities and the UGC that most no longer had. None of the academic elites - Royal Society, British Academy and the like- were pushing for it, but they did not oppose it (Kogan and Hanney, 2000).

On these issues the initial impetus came from ministers, through policies were rapidly picked up and elaborated by the co-opted elites. Changes of policy can be identified most with the preferences of individual Ministers. Thus Joseph would never have granted university status to polytechnics and was a believer in local government: compare him with Baker and Clark under whom such major structural changes were made. The change in style was described by one interviewee who contrasted Joseph's way of consulting the system with that of his successors:

> Baker and Clark coming in almost simultaneously in Education and Health believed that doing business in that way is what had slowed the Government down and made it impossible to make progress and that the device you had to copy was that of the blitzkrieg and they both saw themselves as sort of Panzer Generals working out policy with no

consultation - pretending after you'd propounded the policy that you were going to consult but in fact working by fait accompli, meanwhile using the propaganda machine of the Department to ensure that public opinion comes your way so that a total change took place but it's very important to see that the change was very much more a change in how you did the business than in the debate. (Kogan and Hanney, 2000: xx)

As one former minister put it: 'Government was trying to take less notice of vested interest groups.' And a former civil servant: 'Ministers consulted people who give the right answer.'(Kogan and Hanney, 2000). Policy was made largely internally with no systematic consultation with outside groups. Some interest groups were excluded, eg the local authorities. Hardly any group resisted the implementation of policies, apart from local authorities on NAB, and the CVCP on the first big cuts and on the 1988 Act. But elite groups picked up and ran with the selectivity and quality assurance policies once they were promoted politically.

Role and behaviour of civil servants.

Our interviews, and the literature (Baker, 1993; Young, 1990; Jenkins, 1996), show ministers distrusted civil servants and key changes were pushed through by them. Here our evidence conflicts with the views of Salter and Tapper of DES bureaucrats wanting to gain more control and orient HE to the needs of the economy. There were uncertain contacts between civil servants and interest groups. There were no lunches between the minister and the chairman of the CVCP, although the permanent secretary might meet him informally. The CDP had more contact, at Deputy Secretary level, than the CVCP. Such individuals as the president of the Royal Society had fairly indirect impacts in keeping the science budget up. The No. 10 Policy Unit, especially the Head, Brian Griffiths, 'played a significant part in a lot of these discussions ... there was always the transmission of a Government view, a political view, through Brian Griffiths to Kenneth Baker ... they were in continuous telephone contact on the '88 Act.'

Our evidence is weak on the changes within the central government department. But the closure on evidence and ministerial determination had effects on decision making. One former civil servant put it:

> There was no time for anybody to offer any evidence. Evidence was not wanted so perhaps better not to have it. There was no serious communication about ideas about the system. No solid block of officials communicating with a substantial body of expert opinion as in a centre for higher education studies. No serious system for getting knowledge from academics ... Little bits of evidence were brought up to support the prejudices: Keith Joseph's concerns with the [Open University] sociology of education course took many hours to investigate and to get the issue right. There were also ten years of a prime minister who deeply distrusted DES. She would turn in any direction other than

that Department - they thought too highly of themselves and were out of touch.

Parliament

Parliament does not come out as a strong force, although there was increasing interest shown by the PAC and Select Committees. More obvious was the interest shown by the House of Lords and here the briefing by the CVCP was critical, as noted above. In particular, they were active in causing changes in the 1988 Act, with its implications for academic freedom, by collaborating with peers from all parties. This was also one of the few examples where the Committee of Vice-Chancellors was able to secure consensus among its members on a substantive issue of policy.

The evidence is mixed about the influence of political advisers. Some felt that they were beginning to erode the relationship between a minister and his civil servants but other civil servants believed they were 'not, I'm happy to say, an excessive influence'. But 'The Think Tanks were influential and providing pressure - which irritated us because we were usually on the right lines anyway - on the whole they were not a malign influence. The think tanks had less influence than on schools policy. Indeed, some of the right wingers were hostile to the increased control over universities.

Conclusions

We can conclude this part of the paper by returning to the assumptions proposed at its beginning. First, we have seen that policy was not formed by any kind of accommodation between government and the interests of the various stake-holders. Secondly, certain groups were involved in the generation of policy but in no systematic way and nothing approaching a policy community was formed. Thirdly, changes in policy were not based on systematic policy analysis, on reflection on why change was needed, and how the changes would meet discernible deficits and needs. Changes in governmental machinery did reflect the nature of the policy changes - the creation of single funding councils and the brigading of science policy under the DTI are obvious examples. Finally, the drastic changes in policy certainly had some impacts but the evidence is of considerable continuity of practice and of values at the working base. Among the strongest effects were changes at the institutional level to which I now turn.

The impact of policy changes on institutional government

When we turn to the institutional level, the evidence is of a greater emphasis on management, often at the expense of professional power at the base of the system, and a strengthening of the role of the institution as a part of policy change.

Many of the government-led reforms of higher education were intended to affect the behaviour of individual academics. Such initiatives as Enterprise in Higher Education and Foresight were intended to shift the priorities and targets of academic activity. Teaching and research were now to be assessed through a public process, including student evaluation. If, however, all the reform policies must have been intended to ultimately affect academic behaviour and performance, some were mediated through institutional arrangements that ultimately, too, would affect individuals. We are concerned here, therefore, primarily with the impact of government on institutions.

The conceptual constructions of higher education institutions have almost always been based on the example of the classic research university, and particularly that which led the status hierarchy in the USA, where most of the formative writing on the subject originated. Two potentially conflicting versions might be applied to the *status quo ante*. Becher and Kogan (1980; 1992) asked whether the institution is a true level of the system. Can it generate its own values which it can pursue with the requisite authority? In an earlier edition (1980) they had concluded that it could just about establish its case as a values generator. But we were not entirely satisfied that the university was other than a holding company for the real contenders in the basic units. This picture had, however, changed by the time of our second edition (1992).

If many authorities tended to marginalise the importance of the institutional level, others, whilst sharing their view of the dominant role of the individual academic and the basic unit, gave a strong version of the place occupied by the institution. An important alternative picture is the empirically based, but also normative, ascription, produced by R. Burton Clark, of the *Distinctive College* (1970; 1992) and, more recently, the *Entrepreneurial University* (1998). In these accounts the institution is or can be a potent cultural entity capable of creating its own organizational saga, or story that it tells about itself. So we can grant status to the institution as a powerful cultural personality even before the recent reforms caused shifts of power from the working base of the system.

The Jarratt Report 1985 had long term effects on the internal management of institutions. Vice-chancellors were to adopt the role of chief executives to whom deans and heads of departments would report as line managers. The universities would create and work under a corporate plan that would be formulated by a small group drawn from the lay council and the senior academic management. The report was hostile to the power of departments. It urged the use of performance indicators, but failed to mention the functions of teachers, researchers or students - an omission not repeated in the less well publicised equivalent NAB report (NAB, 1987). Internal management is led by a resources and policy committee in virtually all institutions. The transfer of power from departments to the central institution and to a lesser extent to faculties may well have occurred anyway in part response to the pressures caused by reduced funding and increased institutional responsibilities, but was given its clearest mandate by Jarratt.

Managerialism, that is, the shift in power from senior academics and their departments to the central institution and the dominance of systems over academic values, resulted in part from institutions' need to meet new demands with fewer resources. The importance of institutional leadership was illustrated at the time of the first major cuts in 1981 (Sizer *et al.*, 1988). These shifts towards greater accountability and corporate mechanisms were now all part of the general shift in public services. In political science terms, the universities had worked to a political model in which largely equal groups competed for resources and other elements of power through negotiation. (Baldridge, 1971). Negotiative patterns hardened into processes and structures - the process known as morphogenesis. The political model remains but it is overlaid by the need of institutions to look and behave as corporate and managed entities.

Factors making for change

The key external factors making for change were expansion, cuts in the units of resource, research selectivity and quality assurance. These external policy influences strengthened the role of central managers as they sought to move their institutions towards income generation and reputation enhancement.

The intra-institutional changes included the emergence of institutional leaders as chief executives; the creation of small management groups at the centre of the institution; the centralization of power and creation of more explicit hierarchies; a stronger institutional grip on resource distribution; the institutional framing of academic work; strategic planning for stronger performance, income generation, and relationships with industry; changes in structures, procedures and institutional rules, and changes in the academic - administrative interface. I will glance briefly at each of these change factors and outcomes.

The tendency for expansion and cuts in the units of resource to reinforce central power hardly needs further explanation. The evidence is cleat that research selectivity lent more power to central institutional managers, that it made academics more visible and caused their performance to be assessed publicly. The quality assessment system changed the balance between managerial accountability and the power of the academic community. Academics began to prepare accounts of their work to be monitored by those at the institutional centre. Evaluations were in the public domain and more easily informed institutional decisions about financial and staffing allocations, salary awards and the like. It is clear that some vice-chancellors used quality assurance as an instrument of change

Institutions respond to external changes (Gumport and Sporn, 1998; Kogan 1999) and their responses become structured in terms of organizational and power structures. Many of the more important changes have been described as bureaucratization (eg Gornitzka *et al.*, 1998). This word is currently being used to mean two quite separate things. The first is the move from individual and academic power within the sometimes mythic collegium to the system or institution, and a resulting new structuration of decision making. The second is the growth of power of non-academic administrators. The first is the major phenomenon and the second a possible but not invariant consequence of it. Indeed, the opposite may happen: the shift of power from the professoriat to the university may lead to an increase in some forms of academic power (Karlsson, 1996; Dill, 1999).

Some of the established literature represents academic organization in a bureaucracy-free and romantic light : 'The community of scholars remains as a myth of considerable strength and value in the academic world.' (Harman, 1990). Middlehurst (1993) comments that, although weakened by the requirement to compete, collegial behaviour can be seen in the sharing of information, ideas and tasks, and in the professional critique of each other's work before it enters the public domain. We define it as a group of academics of equal decision-making power acting together to determine standards of entry and accreditation, to share collective resources, and to determine divisions of labour and reward systems.

The collegium has hardly ever existed except in mixed or diluted form. A group of academics within a university department may act collegially when they meet as a course committee or as a board of examiners where all voices may be equal, at least in formal terms. But universities, even when a collection of collegia, are also hierarchies in which resources are allocated, policies and promotions made. It has also been assumed (Scott,, 1995) that universities have become more bureaucratic and less collegial as they grow larger. This generalization cannot easily be applied, for example, to US universities where some of the largest are also among the most academically strong, and where the professoriat sustain a major voice in the creation of policy and in managerial decisions such as the awards of salary differentials. Bureaucratization has, however, resulted from the increased need for holistic institutional planning to meet reduced resources, the requirements of quality assurance and many other prescriptions placed upon academic work by central government policies as expressed by the funding councils.

The effects of the changing role of the institutions on internal structure can be enumerated in several ways. There has been a shift of power from senate to both council and to the vice chancellor. The nature of vice chancellors themselves has not changed in that the majority still come from senior academic ranks (Smith *et al.*, 1999) even if their role has. Our interviews give no conclusive evidence on whether there was a predisposition on the part of some vice-chancellors to encourage the onset of managerial approaches, and whether this can be related to their educational or other origins. As to their changing functions and styles, observation of systems both western and further east suggests that wherever systems either centralise or decentralise, authority at the head of institutions is strengthened. It occupies whatever space central government or the collegium yields.

There are changes in the nature of internal structures and in the relationships between academics and non-academic administrators. Within institutions, crossing cutting administrative sections concerned with external relations, market operations, quality assurance, research policy, personnel policies have taken power from the academic and specialist base and rendered decision-making subject to institutional rather than academic definitions (Kogan, 1996). At the same time, it has been noted in Scandinavian systems (Karlsson, 1996), in the USA (Dill and Helm, 1988), and in our own evidence, that the growth of central management functions has often been achieved by the placing of senior academics into administrative roles. At the same time faculties became more powerful in relationship to departments, as the needs for priority-setting and demonstration of worth became pressing (Boys *et al.*, 1988).

The thrust towards central institutional power has been reinforced by the imposed requirements to produce corporate plans and mission statements (see Mackay *et al.*, 1995). An increasing amount of information and requests come from the funding councils and these need an administrative capacity for their treatment.

Some of the more important changes in management structures have been the creation of pro-vice-chancellor roles for the development and implementation of policies cutting across the faculty and departmental lines of authority; a growth in managerial and administrative work at institutional and infra-institutional level; changes in the tasks and relative power of academics and administrators within universities; hinge or interfacial mechanisms which enable collegial decision-making to be authorised and resourced by the institution.

The earlier simple diarchical assumptions of how institutional tasks are performed no longer hold. Academics move into systems management and administrators increasingly help create the policy and procedural frames for academic work.

Academics began to feel more caught up in the corporate enterprise not only because of the power of managerialism and the impact of strategic planning but because the new conditions of resource seeking and quality grading made them more dependent on the university for support (Henkel, 2000). This had an effect on the professoriat who came under institutional influence from various directions, including: shortages of resources; the need for management within departments and for the head to carry the department with them; and the pressure from research committees established in most institutions to mimic the RAE and assess and allocate resources

The impact of changes varied according to the type of institution and the academics affected by them. Institutions were expected by the funding councils to exercise leadership in the implementation of the RAE policies. Senior academic teams in most of the universities studied (Henkel, 2000) regarded RAE as being of pivotal importance. Almost all of the 'old' universities had a pro-vice-chancellor responsible for research by the early 1990s. All universities evolved policies to improve performance. They had to consider the balance to be struck between teaching and research. At first, universities were reluctant to exercise selectivity in funding based on research performance and, indeed, many vired resources from high to low rated departments. (McNay, 1999) Only after 1996 was there substantial evidence of departmental mergers and restructuring to strengthen RAE performance (Henkel *et al.*, 2000).

In some institutions staffing policies reflected the preoccupation with RAE. These might include shifting resources to create a critical mass in the better departments and shopping for academic talent in other universities. As research performance became more important, universities shifted into what had been departmental territory. This might involve making connections with national academic policy making, and bringing new perspectives to bear on departmental research agendas.

One commentator has noted that there is a perception that universities have become more managerial but that 'most universities are still struggling to be collegial in their values but are forced in their practices to be increasingly managerial'.

Yet throughout our interviews with vice-chancellors and pro-vice-chancellors in this project and in our associated projects (Henkel, 2000 and Henkel *et al.*, 2000) many statements were made about the importance of and indeed compulsion to recognising that academic autonomy and intrinsic motivation are sustained because they are the motive power of institutions. Many believe that academic management must incorporate these assumptions. At the same time, there is more monitoring of individual behaviour and more collective action particularly in response to external assessments. The activities of the QAA will tilt the system even more in that direction.

References

Advisory Board for Research Councils (1987) *Strategy for the Science Base.* London: HMSO.

Baker, K. (ed) (1993) *The Turbulent Years. My life in politics.* London: Faber and Faber.

Baldridge, J.V. (ed) (1971) *Power and Conflict in the University.* New York: Wiley.

Becher, T, and Kogan, M. (eds) (1992) *Process and Structure in Higher Education,* 2nd edn. London: Routledge

Blau, P. M. (ed) (1964) *Exchange and Power in Social Life.* NewYork: John Wiley.

Bleiklie, I., Høstaker, R. and Vabø, A. (eds) (2000*) Policy and Practice in Higher Education.* London: Jessica Kingsley Publishers.

Boys, C.J., Brennan, J., Henkel, M., Kirkland, J., Kogan, M. and Youll, P. (eds) (1988) *Higher Education and the Preparation for Work.* London: Jessica Kingsley Publishers.

Cawson, A. (ed) (1986) *Corporatism and Political Theory*. Oxford: Basil Blackwell.

Clark, B. R. (1970) *The Distinctive College.* Chicago: Aldine.

Clark, B. R. (1986) *Corporatism and Political Theory.* Oxford: Basil Blackwell.

Clark B.R. (ed) (1983) *The Higher Education System: Academic Organization in Cross-National Perspective.* Berkeley: University of California Press.

Clark, B. R. (ed) (1998) *Creating Entrepreneurial Universities. Organizational Pathways of Transformation.* New York: Pergamon.

Committee on Higher Education, (1963) *Higher Education: Report of the Committee appointed by the Prime Minister under the Chairmanship of Lord Robbins 1961-63, (The Robbins Report).* London: HMSO.

Dill, D. D. (1999) Academic Accountability and University Adaptation: The Architecture of an Academic Learning Organization, *Higher Education,* 38(2):127-154.

Dill, D.D. and Helm, K.P. (1988) 'Faculty participation in strategic policy making.', in J.C. Smart (ed) *Higher Education: Handbook of Theory and Research,* Vol. 4. New York: Agathon.

Gornitzka, A., Kyvik, S. and Larsen, I. M. (1998) 'The bureaucratisation of universities.', *Minerva,* 36, 21-47

Grant, W. (ed) (1985) *The Political Economy of Corporatism.* New York: St.Martin's.

Gumport, P. and Sporn, B. (1998) 'Institutional adaptation: demands for management reform and university administration.', in J. Smart (ed) *Higher Education: Handbook of Theory and Research. Vol. XIV.* New York: Agathon.

Halsey, A.H. (1969) 'The Universities and the State', *Universities Quarterly,* Vol.23, no2.

Harman, K.M. (1990) 'Culture and conflict in academic organization.', *Journal of Educational Administration 27(3):* 30-54.

Henkel, M. (ed) (2000) *Academic Identities and Policy Change in Higher Education.* London: Jessica Kingsley Publishers.

Hunter, F. (ed) (1953) *Community Power Structure.* Chapel Hill: The University of North Carolina Press.

Ince, M. (ed) (1986) *The Politics of British Science.* Brighton: Wheatsheaf Books.

Jarratt Report (1985) Committee of Vice Chancellors and Principals *Report of the Steering Committee for Efficiency Studies in Universities.* London: CVCP.

Jenkins, S. (ed) (1996) *Accountable to None: The Tory Nationalisation of Britain.* London: Penguin.

Jordan, G. and Schubert, K. (1992) 'A preliminary ordering of policy network labels.', *European Journal of Political Research,* 21: 7-27.

Karlsson, C. (1996) 'The academic and administrative interface in Scandinavian universities.', *Higher Education Management,* 8(2): 29-35.

Kogan, M. (1984) The Political View, in B. R. Clark (ed) *Perspectives on Higher Education. Eight Disciplinary and Comparative Views.* Berkeley: University of California Press.

Kogan, M. (1992) Political Science, in B. R. Clark and G. Neave (eds) *The International*

Encyclopedia of Higher Education. London: Pergamon Press.

Kogan, M. (1996) *Academic and Administrative Interface.* Paper given at Institutional Management in Higher Education (IMHE) Seminar on Staffing and Institutional Infrastructures, Budapest, August.

Kogan, M. (1999) 'The academic-administrative interface.', in M. Henkel and B. Little (eds) *Changing Relationships Between Higher Education and the State.* London: Jessica Kingsley Publishers.

Kogan, M. (ed) (1975) *Educational Policy-Making. A Study of Interest Groups and Parliament.* London: Allen and Unwin.

Kogan, M. and Hanney, S. (1999) *Reforming Higher Education.* Higher Education Policy Series 50. London and Philadelphia: Jessica Kingsley.

Kogan, M., Bauer, M., Bleiklie, I. and Henkel, M. Transforming Higher Education: A Comparative Study, in I. Bleiklie, R. Høstaker and A. Vabø, *Policy and Practice in Higher Education.*

Mackay, L., Scott, P. and Smith, D. (1995) 'Restructured and differentiated? Institutional responses to the changing environment of UK higher education.', *Higher Education Management, 7(2)*: 193-205.

Manpower Services Commission (MSC) (1987) *Enterprise in Higher Eduction. Guidance for Applicants.* December 1987. London: HMSO.

Marton, S., Hanney, S. and Kogan, M. (1995) *Interest Groups and Elites in Higher Education Policy Making: The cases of England and Sweden.* Paper presented at the European Consortium of Political Research, Bordeaux, 27 April to 2 May.

McNay, I. (1999) 'The paradoxes of research assessment and funding.', in M.Henkel and B.Little (eds) *Changing Relationships Between Higher Education and the State.* London: Jessica Kingsley.

Middlehurst, R. (ed) (1993) *Leading Academics.* Buckingham: Society for Research into Higher Education and Open University Press.

National Advisory Body (NAB) (1987) *Management for a Purpose: The Report of the Good Management Practice Group.* London: NAB.

National Committee of Inquiry into Higher Education (1997) *Higher Education in the Learning Society.* London: HMSO. (The Dearing Report).

Office of Science and Technology (OST) (1993) (White Paper) *Realizing Our Potential - A*

Strategy for Science, Engineering and Technology. Command 2250, London: HMSO.

Peterson, O. (ed) (1990) *Demokrati och Makt i Sverige,* SOU, 1990:44 Huvudrapport, Allmänna Förlaget, Stockholm.

Premfors, R. (1980) The Politics of Higher Education in a Comparative Perspective: France, Sweden, United Kingdo*, Studies in Politics*, 15. University of Stockholm.

Ranson, S. (1980) 'Changing Relations Between Centre and Locality.' *Local Government Studies*, Vol.6 no.6, 13-24 Nov-Dec.

Reynolds Report (1986) *Academic Standards in Universities*. London: Committee of Vice-Chancellors and Principals.

Rhodes, R.A.W. (ed) (1981) *Control and Power in Central-Local Government Relations*. Aldershot: Gower.

Rhodes, R.A.W. and Marsh, D. (1992) 'New Directions in the Study of Policy Networks', *European Journal of Political Research,* Vol 21.

Rhodes, R.A.W. and Marsh, D. (1992) New Directions in the Study of Policy Networks *European Journal of Political Research*, Vol. 21:181-205.

Salter, B. and Tapper, T. (eds) (1994) *The State and Higher Education*. London: Woburn Press.

Saward, M. (ed) (1992) *Co-optive Politics and State Legitimacy*. Aldershot, Hants: Dartmouth Publishing.

Schmitter, P. and Lehmbruch, G. (eds) (1979) *Trends Toward Corporatist Intermediation.* Sage: Beverly Hills.

Scott, P. (1995) *The Meaning of Mass Higher Education.* Society for Research into Higher Education and Open University Press. Buckingham, UK and Philadelphia, USA.

Sizer, J. (1988) *Institutional Responses to Financial Reductions Within the University Sector*. Final Report. London: DES.

Sizer, J. (1988) *Institutional Responses to Financial Reductions within the University Sector (*Final Report). London: DES.

Smith, D., Scott, P., Bocock, J. and Bargh, C. (1999) 'Vice Chancellors and Executive Leadership in UK Universities: New Roles and Relationships?', in M. Henkel and B. Little (eds) *Changing Relationships between Higher Education and the State.* London: Jessica Kingsley

Tapper, E. and Salter, B. (1978) *Education and the Political Order: Changing patterns of class control*. London: Macmillan.

Wakeford, F. and Wakeford, J. (1974) Universities and the Study of Elites. In P. Stanworth and A. Giddens (eds) *Elites and Power in British Society.* Cambridge: Cambridge University Press.

Wright, M. (1988) 'Policy community, policy networks, and comparative industrial policies.', *Political Studies XXXVI*, 2(4): 593-612.

Young, H. (ed) (1989) *One of Us.* London: Macmillan

4 Access and Recruitment: Institutional policy in widening participation.

Brenda Morgan-Klein and Mark Murphy

Introduction: The creation of an access imperative.

The issue of widening access is now driving both national policy and a critical public debate on higher education in the UK. A key focus of debates has been the issue of fiscal policy in relation to higher education. The rapid expansion of higher education in the 1990s, particularly in the further education sector, led to an intense debate over the affordability of higher education both for the state and – following the introduction of tuition fees in 1998 – for the individual. Public disquiet over the imposition of tuition fees has in turn been fuelled by intense media interest in perceived injustices as when the seemingly well-qualified comprehensive school pupil Laura Spence was rejected by Magdalen College Oxford in 2000. The Labour Government's decision to highlight both the issues of social justice and access in policy (DfEE, 1997; SOEID, 1997; Scottish Executive, 2000) whilst simultaneously reforming student funding, has certainly been politically difficult. The fiscal controversies surrounding higher education, and student funding in particular, have been further amplified by the divergence of policy in the UK following Scottish devolution. (Cubie, 1999; Scottish Executive, 2000).[iii]

This crisis of affordability for individuals and the state has unfolded at a time when higher education in the UK has been comprehensively restructured. In Scotland the creation of new universities in 1992 from the old Central Institutions resulted in a more unified system of higher education. The emphasis on flexibility and accessibility in the former Central Institutions had the potential to stimulate change across the new university sector as these institutions participated in the same policy fora. In the same year the Further Education Colleges (FECs) in Scotland were freed from local authority management. This together with their links to the new universities allowed them to increase their higher education provision. This often involved articulation or franchising arrangements with the new universities (Osborne & Gallacher, 1995) – a process given further impetus by the University of the Highlands and Islands project. These changes helped trigger the proliferation of institutional developments traditionally associated with accessibility including credit accumulation and transfer schemes, modularization of courses, semesterization, accreditation of prior learning, the growth of open and distance learning initiatives and inter-institutional access arrangements - although not in equal measure across the university sector.

Despite these considerable changes in provision there remains well documented concern in Scotland and in the UK as a whole that the increase in participation in the 1990s has in fact done little to *widen* access giving rise to what has been called a 'crowded traditional system' (Robertson, quoted in Watson & Taylor, 1998). Sargant *et al.* (1997) report that in the UK twice as many people from social classes A and B participate than do those from D and E and similar patterns of participation are apparent elsewhere in Europe (Parjanen & Tuomi, 2000). A key characteristic of the recent expansion repeatedly emphasized in research is continued sectoral differentiation with older universities proving less accessible than the new (Schuller *et al.*, 1998; Bourgeois *et al.*, 1999; CVCP, 1998). Indeed the differential between pre and post 1992 universities in terms of non-traditional enrolments raises the possibility that increasing ghettoization in recruitment terms is now underway with low income students increasingly concentrated within newer universities (CVCP, 1998). This does not sit comfortably with a Governmental desire to create a 'learning society' (DfEE, 1998; WO, 1998; SO, 1998) and the often-repeated aim to widen access to further and higher education (Scottish Executive, 2000). Thus, increasing public awareness of the issue of access to higher education, perceived past failures, political divergence within the UK, and the fiscal crisis in relation to an expanded higher education have created a challenging set of dynamics around policy on access.

What is To Be Done? Asking questions about access

Alongside these changes, national (and global) policy on lifelong learning is increasingly contested in the academic literature. The focus on employability is criticised variously as merely 'learning to labour' (Martin, 2000) and as a form of social control (Coffield, 1999) while the model of social inclusion underlying current policies is criticised for its individualistic focus on personal deficit (Preece, 2000; Gallacher & Crossan, 2000).

Meanwhile a veritable access industry has emerged as funding councils have targeted specific resources on initiatives designed to widen access at institutional level. This has created a debate of a different kind concerned primarily with the question of efficacy or 'what works' as defined by Funding Council and institutional policy frameworks. Unfortunately these two different debates over what is to be done about access and social justice in higher education have proceeded in parallel - each failing to inform the other. Thus debates over the purpose of lifelong learning policy have largely failed to address the question of purpose and motivation in practice and in policy *implementation*. This means that the institutional policy context has often been ignored. Given the increasing sectoral differentiation in higher education and the targeting of resources designed to widen access on institutions, this is a serious omission.

Discussions of the 'what works' variety have, on the other hand, sometimes ignored questions of purpose thus offering only normative accounts of access practices which do not help us to understand motivation and purpose in practice or to construct analytical categories for understanding 'access' in action. The following discussion[iv] of institutional policy on access to higher education[v] in Scotland starts from the premise that it is not enough simply to critique policy in the abstract. Rather, any critique of current policy must also engage in and inform a debate over changes and alternatives in policy and practice and this implies firstly a critical understanding of practice and policy implementation. The purpose of this paper is to explore some of these issues in relation to institutional policy in widening access to higher education - with a particular focus on the way in which concerns over educational and social equality have become entangled with issues of market supply and demand, recruitment and institutional survival.

Mapping Access in Action

In its response to the Cubie report [vi]*Scotland a Learning Nation, (Scottish Executive*, 2000) the Scottish Executive states clearly that the *main aim* of further and higher education in Scotland is now to widen access. The consultation document makes a number of recommendations designed to target resources on the socially excluded. The Executive has already committed itself to a number of measures in response to Cubie. These include: funding for childcare support worth £8m over two years (targeted at F.E. students); means tested bursaries of up to £2000 with a further £500 available in loans for poor students (estimated at 30% of the total student population by the Executive); £10m of funding to support mature students (again estimated as helping up to 30% of the student population); and the abolition of up-front tuition fees. More recently the Scottish Executive has announced plans to provide universities with £750 per head for students from poorer backgrounds

In addition to these student support measures, a number of specific policy initiatives designed to make provision more accessible were launched beginning in 1998 with funding from the Scottish Higher Education Funding Council's Wider Access Development Grant. This is comprised four strands: development of the FE-HE interface; institutional development and co-ordination; regional fora; and selective funding. These grants have been used to fund a variety of institutional and supra-institutional developments including the establishment of four regional access fora and the Scottish Network for Access and Participation the work of which spans both the F.E. and H.E. sectors. Of particular interest in mapping access initiatives at institutional level is the historical and contemporary diversity of access routes into higher education. Seven Broad types of access initiative may be identified in the context of higher education. They are: Access Courses; Summer Schools; School-FE/HE Links; FE-HE Links; Work-based Access; Community-based Access; and Flexible Delivery. The seven types can be placed on a fairly loose continuum, initiatives at one end of which are focused on in-reach work, getting people into the institution, while at the other end the emphasis is more on the institution getting out to people, engaging in out-reach activity with schools, employers and communities.

Access as in-reach: Access programmes that can be characterised as 'in-reach' are those that place priority on recruiting potential students in to the institution. Typically a course is designed for a particular student group and, once completed satisfactorily, in most cases results in the student being guaranteed a place at the institution. Both summer schools and discrete adult access courses fit into this category. Access courses for adults are one of the more established non-traditional entry routes into higher education. They are normally of one-year duration, and successful completion usually results in securing place at university. Summer schools by comparison offer a more intensive and accelerated access route and tend to be targeted at the school-leaving cohort.

Access as flexibility: The notion of flexibility can of course be used to characterise access in general. In the present context, flexibility refers to systemic (as opposed to discrete) changes to provision associated with access including greater diversity of mode, curricula, pathways and settings. This includes, for example, the use of accreditation of prior learning (APL), credit accumulation and transfer, modularization, part-time provision, FE-HE links such as articulation and franchise agreements, use of open and distance learning and information and communication technology (ICT). These changes imply a process of de-differentiation that is presumed to benefit students by facilitating the movement between one course of study and another or by facilitating the fit between work and study

Access as out-reach: This category includes partnerships between institutions and employers, schools and communities. Out-reach activities such as these, compared to in-reach programmes, tend to be more pro-active in their efforts to widen participation. For instance, work-based access initiatives are viewed as an effective means of providing entry routes to sections of the population unable to take advantage of higher education, and involve the linking of academic credit to student/employer-negotiated projects. School-FE/HE links are becoming increasingly prominent as alternative access routes in Scotland, both formal and informal. Such links can take many forms: mentoring/student tutoring programmes, information evenings and open days, Christmas leaver arrangements, university experience weeks, and on a more formal level, the university *Compact*. The classic form of university outreach, community based access initiatives combine traditional adult education concerns with personal development and community empowerment with the development of progression into HE.

Although "traditional" access programmes – adult access and summer schools – are still quite popular and exist in most institutions, in terms of quantity of provision there has been a marked move away from these to more 'non-traditional' out-reach types of activities. This transformation in the field of access reflects a more profound shift, one connected to the shifting balance between supply of and demand for provision. Evident in current activities and the debate surrounding them is a move away from development of access provision as a response to perceived demand, to the development of access programmes designed to *create* new forms of demand. The latter approach, and this applies to 'out-reach' programmes in general, tends to be more prominent in the further education institutions and new universities. Desire to engineer change on the demand side tends not to be the concern of older universities, sticking for the time being at least with their 'in-reach' provision, combined with some more piecemeal activity in terms of flexible provision.

The Access Agenda: Equality, recruitment, marketing and institutional competition

Sectoral differentiation in the character of access initiatives adopted by institutions suggests that a range of external and internal factors underlie current practice depending on institutional type. Certainly previous research indicates a mixed set of motivations on the part of institutions involved in access initiatives. This could be said to be true for HE policy in general. As Bourgeois *et al.* put it,

> HE institutions have multiple, ambiguous and highly contested goals. The university could hardly be reduced to any single notion mission... .Because they are multiple and ambiguous, the goals of the university are also most often highly contested and conflictual (Bourgeois et al., 1999: 36).

In this regard, the CVCP report (CVCP, 1998), which characterised approaches to access as broadly elitist or broadly socially inclusive, could be viewed as overly simplistic. Elitist approaches offer only limited 'second chance' opportunities for the few deemed able to benefit, while socially inclusive approaches are committed to more radical approaches to access.

> There are those who perceive access to be a process for rescuing the (relatively few) individuals endowed by nature with the capacity to benefit from higher education, but prevented from doing so by adverse socio-economic circumstances; on the other, are those who believe that many young people from lower socio-economic groups have been excluded as a result of socio-economic disadvantage, exacerbated by an elitist higher education system. (CVCP, 1998: 112)

Other research on widening participation and institutional policy, however, suggests that that these two perspectives are more fractured than this and that institutional motivation for participating in access initiatives is often ambiguous. The report produced by the Higher Education Quality Council (HEQC, 1995) found that, while there were clear differences in institutional perspectives on widening participation, the situation was more complex than the 'usual divisions' between higher and further education or between 'old' and 'new' universities (HEQC, 1995: 17). They use the example of credit-based learning to distinguish between two main perspectives from two broad groupings.

> To the first group, credit-based learning is a useful mechanism to facilitate, for example, modularity and the transfer of students where appropriate. To the second group, the report's approach promises the emergence of a single unitary national credit framework applicable to institutions and to the world of work/employment, one which will organise all post-school education including higher education. (HEQC, 1995: 17).

This approach reflects the findings from the current research, which suggests that what Woodrow *et al.* (CVCP, 1998) term 'broadly socially inclusive' could be more accurately categorised as a 'lifelong learning' approach. Therefore it is not surprising that motivation for delivering access initiatives included a wide range of aims and concerns, such as

- A concern with social justice and/or civil society
- A commitment to vocational relevance
- Concerns about institutional competition, marketing and recruitment
- Concerns about institutional performance against performance indicators in the new lifelong learning environment.

The idea of a lifelong learning approach encompasses a variety of aims, some of which may be contradictory. The category, therefore, is left deliberately imprecise to reflect the fractured nature of institutional motivation. In particular, it is important to emphasize that professed aims such as social inclusion may mask or sit alongside more pragmatic concerns. Indeed, in the majority of our interviews, social justice concerns were often eclipsed by concerns with recruitment, marketing and institutional survival suggesting that the commitment to the rhetoric of lifelong learning is as much a reflection of dynamic marketing strategies as it is of concerns with educational disadvantage and social equality. In some instances there was little to distinguish between access initiatives and exercises in marketing and recruitment.

Institutional Survival and Recruitment

For some institutions then, widening participation, increasing access, social inclusion measures and rhetoric about lifelong learning, are closely linked with possibly more pragmatic concerns over institutional survival. In some cases, the emphasis on access in government policy is timely and fortuitous, arriving at a time when institutions are experiencing declining enrolments. A Widening Access Co-ordinator in a post-1992 university, described the recent institutional emphasis on access 'as very much a survival strategy' on the part of the university, and that 'they were lucky to have made decisions about access at the time that they did, as they can score some "brownie" points off of it'.

Issues surrounding institutional survival are particularly acute among the new universities and further education colleges. One School head in a FE College described their need to increase numbers to keep the college full, 'otherwise we have to close down courses and make staff redundant'. So the widening access agenda, for him, 'comes about at a time when it's quite useful'. The Assistant Principal of the same College viewed recent changes in delivery mechanisms in similarly functional terms, believing they were able to compete with the new university sector in terms of their 'flexibility'.

Occasionally, elements of institutional suspicion and resentment would rise to the surface when discussing issues of access. This also surfaced in the context of carrying out research into widening access. One Director of Continuing Education at a new university suggested that, because they were not a research institution, they struggled to get funding for research into widening access that could inform practice. She argued that they 'were too busy doing it' themselves. Although such concerns could not be said to be prevalent, 'research' institutions are least likely to be engaged in access initiatives, while at the same time more likely to receive research funding into widening participation. This clearly has implications for role demarcation, institutional differentiation, and more practically speaking, future attempts to incorporate elements of best practice.

In interviews with HE staff, the entanglement of recruitment concerns with the discourse of access is so pronounced in some cases that attempts to distinguish between the two led to instances of confusion over the purpose of the questions, and resulted in several blind alleys of investigation. For instance, a number of interviewees in the new universities and FE sectors when asked about their widening participation initiatives, described the *institutional* need to source untapped markets of potential students – the unemployed for instance. They discussed how large sectors of untapped academic potential remained undiscovered in areas under the remit of the social inclusion partnerships. Out-reach activities, particularly links with community groups, schools and statutory agencies, were viewed by some as a means by which more pro-active steps could be taken in recruiting students, while at the same time widening access to those who would never have considered taking courses in further or higher education.

Prevalent in both the new university sector and FE colleges is a tendency to equate access with pro-active efforts to recruit in general. One Director of Curriculum viewed their involvement with local schools as 'missionary work', with a hoped for end result that 'the message will sit there' in the schools. The institution is able to offer school pupils access to laboratories unavailable to the schools, and so this entails such pupils learning on-site. The hope is that in the future, when pupils consider their post-school options, that particular institution will sit high on their list. A school-links co-ordinator in a new university argued that the institution benefited from the publicity it received from its involvement in initiatives, helping to raise awareness of the institution as a university in the area. The university is still referred to by many locals as a college of technology, even though it has not been designated as such since the late 1980s. 'Many still see it as [specializing in] science and engineering, but they have a wider range of subjects than that. The teachers coming in from the schools are also invaluable, as they are ready to recommend [the university] to the pupils." Perhaps understandably, this notion of institutions as brand names is common among access co-ordinators, access becoming equated with access to particular institutions for some. A co-ordinator of a university Compact hoped that the 'students won't go somewhere else [after school]' and that the 'link will keep them in [the education system after school]'.

It is perhaps no surprise that this drive to recruit, often expressed in managerialist discourse, has an impact in some cases on institutional structures and practices. The impact of external change on the governance and practice of further education for instance has been well documented (Elliott, 1996; Randle & Brady, 1997). Such change proved a dilemma for one co-ordinator of a HNC in Business administration who was faced with conflicting mandates within the institution in terms of its drive towards a more university style teaching system. Staff were being encouraged to move towards one hour lectures with workshops and away from three hour courses, which were 'more like FE and access stuff'. But if they were able to 'sell three hour systems to people, then this allows more access and accessibility'. She felt that with the institution – they are 'fighting against a culture and maybe the management, in terms of them being willing to work flexibly and in the evenings'. It would be incorrect to assume that advocates of widening participation in FE colleges and new universities, because of pressure to recruit, face no further difficulties within institutions. The desire to be more flexible, for instance, can bring its own problems around staffing issues, contracts and facilities.

Widening Participation and Institutional Competition

One of the main findings of the first phase of the research is that the emphasis on institutional survival and recruitment strategy cannot be divorced from concerns with institutional competition. The differential positioning of institutions within a competitive market ensures that at least some institutions are driven to increase recruitment and identify new markets as part of a strategy for institutional survival. When it comes to survival, much depends 'upon the market strength of each institution and the "price" of different types of student' (Smith & Saunders, 1991: 11). Established universities may wish to maintain their market share of 'higher priced' types of students with little increase in the number of student places. Newer universities and some Further Education Colleges appear more likely to be concerned with the (institutional) need to increase recruitment and access. Some interviewees in the FE sector described how the new university sector was, in effect, poaching their traditional client base. Because of the increased desire to recruit students and the pressure to maintain numbers, new universities were offering degree places to students who would not have considered taking a degree previously, or who may not have been awarded a degree place, in times of higher demand.

One HNC co-ordinator in an FE college bemoaned the fact that the institution signed up with UCAS:

> This is the first time we have been involved in UCAS, and this has affected us in a major way. Applications have never previously gone through the UCAS system. Now students can make choices that were not open to them before. Universities are now offering them places, so that in a way we have shot ourselves in the foot.

An assistant principal felt that a local post-92 university and his own college were now 'fishing' out of the same pool of students, the reason being that newer universities were experiencing some difficulties in terms of both recruitment and retention. According to an open-learning programme co-ordinator, not only are the applicants being offered university places, 'they get offered places even though they have really low grades'. Another FE college member of staff offered evidence that some students who were refused places on HNCs in the College were subsequently offered places on university degree programmes.

> [That] is the reality, and there is plenty of evidence for it. Students, who we have not actually accepted for an HNC, got accepted for the degree at [university].....We have had students who have applied for advanced courses here, who we felt didn't have the appropriate background qualifications, had offered them instead a non-advanced programme, as a preparatory course, who had accepted that course, and had subsequently informed us that they weren't taking it up because they in fact had been offered a place at university. There are certain HNCs that we have closed down altogether, because effectively this happened to the whole lot of them.

One head of school at a Further Education college argued that changes in economic restructuring and labour market position in one Scottish city had a major impact on strategic positionings and shifting priorities of institutions in a Scottish City.

> I believe this [re-structuring] happened at a time when we had rising unemployment (in early 90s), and therefore there was acceptance by the government that is probably better for young people to stay in full-time education, rather than join unemployment queues, and the hope that these vocational full-time HNCs would be a positive thing. Because up until that time, HNCs had been day release courses for people in employment. That was the big movement – from part-time day attendance to get an HNC to full-time attendance. And if you like it was a way of raising the school leaving age because it kept people in full-time education.

But the situation has changed since then, resulting in another strand of shifting priorities for institutions. One FE widening access co-ordinator discusses how the changing demand from HEIs has impacted on both their own HE provision and student numbers.

> We were the first FEC to validate our own degrees, but the big issue now is, is it viable? Because the HE sector has changed. There has been a major change in that the HE sector used not to be interested in non-standard entry, they didn't want them. They were much more likely to come in through Access courses, rather than the HNC/D entry route. They would say to the FECs 'sorry we have already filled our quota for non-standard applicants'. But since a few years ago there has been a major sea change in this regard. Because now they are saying yes to such students, and again the question is survival. Funding is a big issue around pursuing CATS/credit transfer students.

From the perspective of staff and policy-makers involved, it appears that the scope for both FECs and HEIs (particularly new universities) to increase their recruitment to higher education courses is severely constrained. Returning to the context of the Scottish city above, the aggressive marketing to and recruitment of the traditional FE pool of applicants with non-standard qualifications is at least partially due to more recent changes in the labour market and the economy, which has further complicated the competitive aspect of recruitment:

> If you have high unemployment, you have numbers for everybody, so what you've also got now is that feature of very low unemployment, lowest for 20 odd years. You also have very aggressive recruitment of well-qualified people straight from school by the financial institutions. So there is big competition if you like for the school-leaving cohort. So it's not just HE pinching our students, it's that there's actually been quite a change in the demography here.

This broadening of the competitive arena is another issue that surfaced during the research. First there is the heightened competition between FECs and HEIs in addition to the already existing competition within each of these sectors. Second, the introduction of *Higher Still* has affected recruitment, so schools are also taking numbers, with students staying on to do Highers. In addition, some areas of the country are experiencing increased levels of employment which has dramatically reduced the reserve army of labour. Some institutions are now in the position of competing with the private sector for applicants/workers/students.

There are a couple of other instances of this 'fishing and poaching' phenomenon in the education sector that are worthy of note. There is some evidence to suggest that access routes themselves (at least in the way that they are defined here) are beginning to compete with each other, and are becoming involved to some degree in similar exercises of marketing and recruitment strategies. One widening access co-ordinator described how enrolments for an adult access programme, while previously buoyant, have recently lowered.

> One of the reasons for this is the fact that there are many more routes for adults now. You have a situation where [name of access programme] are trying to market their courses, add value.

There is one final dimension to competitive recruitment strategies to be considered. This relates to the relationship between the Community Education Sector, FE Colleges and HEIs. While some in the FE sector feel they are the "grousebeaters" for the HE sector, in the sense that they provide many HNC/D transfer students to HEIs, especially to the new university sub-sector, some universities are now accepting students without at least a HNC. The evidence indicates that some FE colleges are now moving away from HE provision to more community-based provision, with at least one college viewing this as their 'core business', fuelling suspicion and resentment in the community education sector. Such community-based provision would previously have been viewed as a form of pre-access for many would-be applicants because of its claimed ability to develop people's self-confidence and belief in their academic ability. Now, however, FE colleges are transforming old programmes and developing new structures so that effectively they are 'swallowing up' community-based access provision by delivering such pre-access programmes as part of their course structure.

This institutional rivalry and positioning in attempts to take advantage of different student 'markets', invites some serious questioning as to attitudes regarding the welfare of the students themselves. An assumption is made by some (although so far unsupported), that this type of institutional manoeuvring results in higher dropout rates and consequent problems with student retention as a performance indicator. One senior colleague in an FE college felt this could really only work to their advantage, as the students who withdrew from university programmes, would then 'come back on the market', and could in turn be targeted for recruitment. This has major implications for the shift in policy agendas from meeting supply to creating demand in widening participation. As a head of department in a new university put it, 'if you do set out to create demand, you will have to think about the consequences of what happens to students'. She echoes others working in the access, who stress a need for an institutional regulatory framework, and an emphasis on coherence and appropriate progression.

What is underway is a process, as one respondent put it, of 'migration' between and within sectors in which students find themselves eligible for entry onto a further rung of the educational ladder as a result of an institutional 'tidal shift'. The question that faces some institutions then is: are they doing enough to acclimatise these migrants to their new environment? On this issue too, institutional needs and student needs can become confused or at least overlap. One interviewee acknowledged that modularizing a given course of study had the simultaneous advantages of providing 'bite-sized' education for struggling students (thus improving access) and reducing official 'wastage' rates through increasing the number of official exit points (thus improving apparent institutional performance). In general there is anxiety in the FECs and new universities about the way in which working with previously excluded students may affect institutional performance against indicators and the possible funding implications that this may have for them in the future. In addition, there was a realization that these students would need enhanced learning support arrangements, or indeed that such arrangements would have to be put in place for them. As one senior FE manager put it:

> We have a situation where applicants come to us now [with] lower level qualifications than those who had previously applied to us. The challenge for us now is how do we modify our courses, to deal with people coming in with different backgrounds and different skills, not simply accepting people onto the same courses and then having very high drop-out and failure rates.

Conclusion

In our interviews with staff, and in particular institutional policy makers, social justice concerns often seemed secondary to the more general concern with recruitment and institutional survival. It does appear as though the policy initiatives that begin with the objective of *widening access* are in danger of becoming refracted at the institutional level into policies designed to *increase access*. While these differing aims are not necessarily contradictory it is not yet clear if this shift is ultimately detrimental to the aim of widening access. It could be argued that the pressure on particular institutions to increase their 'market share', not only of traditional student cohorts but also of previously 'untapped' sources, may have the effect of actually widening participation for socially excluded groups. Competition and institutional survival are forcing some institutions to be highly pro-active in their marketing strategies, particularly when it comes to the unemployed and low waged, lone parents and people with disabilities, both physical and mental. These of course are some of the categories defined as 'socially excluded' and it may be the case that survival-fuelled access initiatives succeed where more 'social-justice' approaches find it difficult to achieve their goals of reaching out to the excluded.

Regardless of whether or not this is the case, it underlines the central role of institutions in widening access and the need to examine critically institutional practices and policy *implementation*. Institutional motivation is profoundly influenced by the structure of higher education including pronounced sectoral differentiation in practice, inter-institutional competition and changes in supply and demand. This raises a number of issues. The sectoral differentiation in practice may have contributed to the bifurcation of the academic debate over access. It is unfortunate that debates over important pragmatic policy concerns and debates over questions of philosophy and purpose have failed to inform each other[vii].

Aside from the concern over whether or not purpose (social justice or institutional survival) really matters in achieving the aim of widening access, sectoral differentiation also implies qualitative differences in institutions' approaches to access. At the sharp end of inter-institutional competition, the newer universities and the FECs design ever more inventive ways of targeting potential students while older institutions provide more discrete, perhaps more limited, access routes. There is evidence of a concentration of disadvantaged students in the newer universities and the FECs. A key question for policy makers is whether or not this is compatible with social justice objectives.

Institutional goals in relation to access are diverse and often ambiguous. They are also constrained by external factors including competition and changes in demand and supply some of which will be difficult to address even at the level of national policy. Nevertheless understanding institutional motivations is a crucial first step in designing effective policy on access.

References

Bourgeois, E., Duke, C., Guyot, S. and Merrill, B. (eds) (1999) *The Adult University*. Buckingham: SRHE/OU Press.

Cloonan, M. and Turner, E. (eds) (2000) *The past, present and future of further education in Scotland: A research based guide to the literature for practitioners*. University of Stirling: Centre for Research in Lifelong learning.

Coffield, F. (1999) Breaking the consensus: Lifelong learning as social control, *British Educational Research Journal*, 25(4):479-499.

Committee of Vice Chancellors and Principals (1998) *From Elitism to Inclusion: Good Practice in Widening Access to Higher Education*. London: CVCP.

Dearing, R. (ed) (1997). *Higher Education in the Learning Society* (Dearing Report). London: National Committee of Inquiry into Higher Education.

DFEE (1998) *The learning age*. London: HMSO.

Elliot, G. (1996) Educational management and the crisis of reform in further education, *Journal of Vocational Education and Training*, 48(1): 5-23.

Gallagher, J. and Crossan, B. (2000) *What Contribution Can Lifelong Learning Make to Social Inclusion: A Review of the Research*, discussion paper. Glasgow Caledonian University: Centre for Research in Lifelong Learning.

Higher Education Quality Council (1995) *Choosing to change: Extending access, choice and mobility in higher education. Outcomes of the consultation*. London: Higher Education Quality Council.

Independent Committee of Inquiry into Student Finance (1999) *Student Finance: Fairness for the Future*. Edinburgh: HMSO.

Martin, I. (2000) Reconstituting the Agora: Towards an alternative politics of lifelong learning, in T. Sork, V. Chapman, and R. St. Clair (eds), *Proceedings of the 41st Adult Education Research Conference, Vancouver, Canada, July 2000*. University of British Columbia: Department of Educational Studies.

Osborne, M. and Gallagher, J. (1995) Scotland, in P. Davies (ed) *Adults in higher education: International perspectives in access and participation*. London: Jessica Kingsley.

Parjanen, M. and Tuomi, O. (2000) Widening access to further and higher education - An international evaluative study: A case study from Finland. Paper prepared for the Scottish Executive Widening Access to Further and Higher Education Project. University of Stirling: Centre for Research in Lifelong Learning.

Preece, J. (2000) Challenging the discourses of inclusion and exclusion with off limits curricula. Paper prepared for OU/University of East London Colloquium on Lifelong Learning.

Pritchard, J. (1999) Widening participation and the role of the Scottish Higher Education Funding Council. *Update on Inclusion: Widening Participation in Higher Education*, 2:7-8.

Randle, K. and Brady, N. (1997) Further education and the new managerialism, *Journal of Further and Higher Education*, 21(2): 229-239.

Sargant, N., Field, J., Francis, H., Schuller, T. and Tuckett, A. *A study of Participation in Adult Learning in the United Kingdom*. Leicester: NIACE.

Schuller, T., Raffe, D., Morgan-Klein, B. and Clark, I. (eds) (1998) *Part-Time Higher Education: Policy, Practice and Experience*. London: Jessica Kingsley.

Scott, P. (ed) (1995) *The Meanings Of Mass Higher Education*. Buckingham:SRHE/Open University.

Scottish Executive (2000) *Scotland, A Learning Nation*. Edinburgh: HMSO.

Scottish Office Education and Industry Department (1998) *Opportunity Scotland: A Paper on Lifelong Learning*. Edinburgh:SOEID.

Shain, F. and Glesson, D. (1999) Under new management: Changing conceptions of teacher professionalism and policy in the further education sector, *Journal of Education Policy*, 14(4): 445-462.

Smith, D. and Saunders, M. (eds) (1991). *Other Routes: Part-time Higher Education Policy*. Buckingham: SRHE/OU Press.

Watson, D. and Taylor, R. (eds) (1998) *Lifelong Learning and the University: A Post-Dearing Agenda*. London: Falmer Press.

Welsh Office (1998) *Learning is for everyone*. Cardiff: Welsh Office.

5 Resources in the Management of Change in Higher Education

Rachel Johnson

I think probably everything goes back to resources in the end in the sense that academics are asked to perform in resource terms. Research is actually now a resource input into the institution. They've got to teach students, and more students than ever before, so that's a resource issue. And they've got to do more administration than ever before by virtue of the auditing and accountability criteria which are imposed from outside. So, you could say that academics...and institutions have to do more and more for the same amount of money and the money now comes with, you know, far more strings to it than previously. And all that then creates work inside the institution.
(PVC, pre-1992 university).

Introduction

This chapter considers organizational and management responses to changes in the external environmental conditions for higher education organizations ([viii]) in the UK. It considers environmental change from the particular perspective of diminished public resources for higher education and concurrent increased regulation specifying criteria for resource allocation, purposes for expenditure, and performance measurement (Barnett 1992; Trow 1996; Williams 1989, 1991). It examines changes in the external resource environment, and varying responses to this at organizational and management levels, with reference to interviews conducted with Heads of Department (HoD) from different disciplines in 17 universities in the UK ([ix]). These are the academics who carry out the 'work' consequent on the changes cited by the above Pro vice-chancellor, and these are the academics who are responsible for getting other academics to work in new ways. Their narratives of both external funding and internal organizational and management change give contemporary accounts of the significance of resources to UK universities. They offer individual descriptions and perceptions of the imperatives for organization and management of change in the resource environment, and of the consequences of these imperatives for their own work as managers (King 1994). Each account refers to multiple contexts: the individual department; the respective discipline; and the individual organization. In sum these narratives contribute a range of perspectives to the interpretation of how higher education organizations, their management and managers are responding to changes in the external resource environment.

The analysis contained in this chapter interprets policy in terms of its consequences for the academic, academic units, and the nature of academic work. It shows how imperatives and intentions of policy, as identifiable in policy design (c.f. Bleiklie 2000, and Chapter 2, this volume), are shaped during the process of interpretation and implementation by actors within organizations. The chapter identifies common themes amongst the perceived imperatives of the changed resource environment within HoD's narratives, and yet also shows diversity of interpretation and response. HoD's share awareness of the dramatic shifts in public funding for higher education, and are alert to the consequences of this for their own organization and local unit. However, their actual responses are diverse and often contradictory, and are also contested or differently interpreted by those with whom they work.

The theoretical perspectives used in this chapter explain the diversity of response to the same policy design. Responses to policy are informed by, and formulated within the constraints of the particular social, structural and normative contexts within which the HoDs operate. Diversity is the product of the differences between organizational contexts, of the variety of ways in which policy is received and interpreted in context by different people, and of dispute between them over what would be appropriate action. Thus the aims of policy and policy design have little predictable impact on local contexts; policy is shaped through, and its outcomes contingent on the situated character of individual, social and organizational behaviour.

The significance of resources in public sector policy.

Financial resources are understood as a key lever in public sector management. Analyses of 'new managerialism' (Clarke and Newman 1997; Clarke, et al 2000) and 'new public management' (Ferlie et al 1996) emphasize the pursuit of efficiency, and the introduction of market mechanisms as major themes of policy, policy attempts to direct a particular form of management response within public sector institutions. Policy appears, therefore, to draw on the assumption that the incentives of financial resources and profits are a more valuable means to effect and control change in organizational and individual behaviour than hard managerialist command and control. Gewirtz et al (1995) identify changes in the resource environment at school level, and interpret these as attempts to establish market mechanisms and motivations in the form of a quasi-market. They highlight the following changes in the public resource environment and indicate the type of change intended in management and organization:

- Methods of public funding in which resources are allocated on the basis of contracting and competitive bidding

- A decline in public funding with the consequent imperative to access resources from new and diverse sources
- A greater emphasis on performance criteria in respect of public funds, including tight financial accountability and specification of financial responsibility at all levels.

These features are also reflected into theories of 'new public management' and 'new managerialism'. Ferlie et al (1996) identify three models of organizational behaviour, each of which is underpinned by a different and ideologically informed view of management purpose and management control technique: 'the efficiency model', 'the downsizing and decentralization model', and the 'excellence' model. The features of these are, respectively:

- Efficiency: an emphasis on greater productivity, doing more for less; target setting and monitoring; audit; a market-mindedness; and, a shift from professional to managerial control.
- Downsizing and Decentralization: the introduction of quasi-markets, in which activities are represented in financial terms using proxy measures; management by contract; delayering; market-testing; flexibility; devolved budgets; and, individual agency within tight accountability frameworks, or, 'responsibilization'.
- Excellence: either, a culture of bottom-up empowerment and organizational development, or top-down cultural engineering through leadership and corporate unity and identification.

Whilst none of the interviewees in the study offer narrative evidence that their own particular organizational context can be located within one discrete model, they do bear witness to the introduction of many of the above features into management and organization in UK universities. The complex accounts also suggest that change within universities and their management is internally contradictory. At the same time, two individuals' accounts of the same organizational context may conflict; frequently these conflicting accounts reflect the respective management levels at which the academic works: their location on the implementation staircase (Trowler, this volume). Such findings illustrate the weakness of using ideal-type models, such as those offered by Ferlie et al (1996), to represent and explain the complexities of organization and change in universities. They are, nevertheless, useful models to use for heuristic purposes during initial interpretation and conceptualization of management and organizational change.

The significance of resources to organizations

A more sophisticated means to interrogate these narratives is found in two contrasting perspectives on organizational behaviour and change. First, resource dependency theory (Pfeffer and Salancik 1978; Scott, 1992) argues that because organizations need resources for survival, they are not completely self-directed and independent. In order to obtain resources organizations must interact with external fundholders. Different external fundholders have varying quantities of funds to offer, and have various capacity to exert control over how those funds are spent within the organization. Organizations' relationships with these external fundholders depend on the importance of each external fundholder to organizational survival. For example, some fundholders may be key to survival in terms of the abundance and reliability of resources held, and that fundholder may be in a position to exert high levels of control on its allocation within the organization and to specify performance outcomes for the use of funds. Yet, if that same fundholder does not have a monopoly over resources, organizations are in a position to seek resources from fundholders who have less relative ability, or will, to exert control over allocation and performance.

Organizations exist *interdependently* with the external environment; interdependence is constituted by a pattern of dependencies to different external fundholders. The pattern of dependencies is subject to change, change which may be both externally or internally induced. Changes in the external resource environment may lead organizations to relinquish some dependencies, whilst attempting to maintain others, despite the cost of having to meet new performance criteria, because the size of potential funds outweighs the drawbacks of internal response. Organizations will attempt to manage and change dependencies in order to secure sizable, reliable or non-tied funds, or to secure funds for which there is less competition from other organizations. Yet resources that are dependable, lucrative and relatively free of constraint may not coincide in one source. Thus organizations are faced with the task of managing for stability, which means achieving a balance within and between often conflicting imperatives and constraints.

The second perspective, institutional theory, brings a cultural perspective to bear on organizational behaviour and change (DiMaggio and Powell 1983; Scott 1995). In contrast to resource dependency theory, institutional theory holds that organizational behaviour is conditioned by historical norms and traditions: all organizations within a single institutional field are subject to institution-wide ideas of what are acceptable or required structures, social relations, processes of decision making, organizational purposes or criteria of performance.

Thus the essential factors that bear on whether and how an organization may change are the norms associated with the institutional field to which the organization belongs. These norms are forces that both constrain and inform change. Thus whilst changes in the external environment suggest the possibility of, or necessity for change, internal responses are conditioned by normative beliefs that counter and resist innovation. For example, and from a rational perspective, developments in information and communications technology suggest the tutor-less classroom is both a viable and profitable means to deliver teaching. However historical norms of face-to-face contact between lecturer and student run counter to this idea, legitimate the arguments of those who resist changes to the delivery of teaching, and thus inhibit change.

Institutional theory also uses the idea of norms to explain organizational isomorphism within the institutional field. Isomorphism describes the phenomenon of similarity between organizations in the institutional field, and the mimetic, coercive and normative forces that constrain change and deviance. It is clear, however that organizations do change and develop. And, it is also fair to suggest that organizations are distinct – organizational differentiation is in part a product of local agency, strategy and context. This latter point is substantiated in the case of the higher educational field; universities are distinct, and that distinctiveness is a reflection of factors specific to the internal academic and student communities, the actions of individuals, and opportunities or constraints in respect of the immediate political, economic and geographical locality. Institutional theory is therefore subject to critique in terms of its limited potential in explaining organizational differentiation, and change in what are considered 'norms' within the institutional field (c.f. Kondra and Hinings 1998; Powell 1991). New Institutional theory (Powell and DiMaggio 1991) elaborates the cultural analysis and brings a strengthened sociological perspective to bear, extending analysis beyond the institution. Theory of organizational behaviour is connected to wider social, economic and political structures and dynamics in this more recent approach. New institutionalism thus helps address the problems associated with the previous more simplistic, isolated view of the institution.

However different universities may be, it is nevertheless fair to say that all do share some pronounced cultural, structural and social norms (Becher and Kogan 1992; Bergquist 1993; McNay 1995). Institutional and new institutional theory is thus relevant to an explanation of organizational and management change in response to a changed external resource environment. Whilst HoDs describe the imperative for organization and management in resource terms, they also describe the changes and implementation of changes in the external resource environment as a source of conflicts and tensions. Perceptions of the tensions and conflicts involved in change reflect their own personal reluctance, and resistances within the academic department, to act counter to norms and traditions in the nature and purpose of academic work. Tensions and conflicts also highlight how norms of academic work are reflected in the procedural and structural traditions of university organizations. The normative becomes an obstruction to change; narratives reveal how the normative both shapes, and provides means of resistance to changes in organization and management.

Whilst both resource dependency and institutional theories are useful to an interrogation of change in organization and higher education generally, neither is in itself sufficient. Within this chapter, the extracts show that universities are organizations highly dependent on external resource environments. Organizational change, and attempts by HoDs to implement and manage change, are attempts to both secure public funding, and also find alternative sources of funds. It is also clear that managing and implementing change is problematic, for reason of the norms which the HoDs themselves claim - or allege that others claim - are *also* legitimate imperatives. Nevertheless, HoDs' accounts suggest that what constitutes the normative 'idea' (Barnett 1990) of higher educational structures, processes and purposes is changing. One of the reasons for this change is the changed external resource environment. It is at the intersection of resource dependency and institutional theories that their respective deficiencies become clear. Yet at the same time, the intersection of these theories provides more adequate explanation of change in universities and higher education. This finding lends support to the view that a more sophisticated organizational analysis might be found in a combined, rather than contrasting theoretical perspective (Orru et al, 1991).

The remainder of the chapter draws on data from a study that involved interviews with academics at different levels of seniority: HoDs, Deans, Pro Vice Chancellors and Vice Chancellors. In the subsequent sections I use interviews with HoDs to illustrate my points. Interviews with HoDs are a valuable, and justifiable set of data because HoD are charged with both the actual implementation of senior management decisions in response to changes in the external resource environment, and also the responsibility to maintain the survival of the particular academic unit and its activities:

> you're a manager in a sense that you have the responsibility of being a buffer between the people who are actually doing all the work and running the institution from that perspective, and the people that are running the institution at the macro level. I'm a manager in the sense that, "This is the staff you've got because that's the money you've got, get on and run it". So, you've got some independence, but you've got to manage within those resources or other resources that you can conjure up from elsewhere.
> (Business Studies post-1992)

HoDs are faced with the challenges of implementing change decided by others, of initiating changes determined within the department, and managing potential contradictions between both sets of demands. At the same time, the processes and challenges of both implementing changes and managing contradictions are further complicated by complex forms and sources of resistance; resistance is exerted by the different individuals with whom the HoD deals; these may be individuals within the academic unit, or others higher up the management hierarchy. Resistance is also implicit in existing organizational structures, processes, relations and perceived purposes. It is clear therefore that HoDs operate at the point where both resources and norms form vital, explicit and contradictory contexts for action; it is at this level of organization and management that the experience and nature of conflicts and tensions is most keen and most evident. It is at this level, therefore that an intersectional analyses of resource dependency and institutional theories is both necessary for the explanation of change in universities, and useful as insight into the nature and processes of organizational change:

> HOD: Sometimes … it's OK if [members of the department] don't agree with me and they don't follow the course of action that I would like them to. But if it's important I just explain that I think [their view is] wrong, and that it's important that 'This is done', and they will do it. And I think *most* people accept that.
> Int: How would you rate importance, what kind of criteria would you use?
> HOD: Importance comes down to money.
> Int: Right, so it's very much back to resources again?
> HOD: Yes.
> (Science, post-1992)

The next section emphasizes universities' sensitivity to the changes in public funding and illustrates HoDs' perceptions of the implications of those changes for academic units and their activity. Section 4 then illustrates the 'balancing act' perceived by HODs – an act that attempts balance in terms of academic activity, social cohesion within academic units, structural coherence, managerial reasonableness or load and financial budgets. Section 5 proceeds analysis of their narratives by selecting some features identified by Gewirtz (1995), Clarke and Newman (1997) and Ferlie et al (1996) and using these as means to analyse perceptions of changed management responsibilities and accountabilities, and the use of financial incentives to induce change in the performance of individual academics.

Sustaining the organization: definitions of 'survival'

One interpretation of policy aims is that these assume institutional and organizational sensitivity to the quantities of funding available, and to the criteria laid down for its use. The character of both policy intentions, and the logic of policy design is instrumental. Funding is tied to performance (Trow, 1996); definitions and criteria for performance are elaborated at the interface between government, its agencies and higher education groupings, with the negotiated outcome reflecting the relative power of respective interest groups (Salter and Tapper, 1994). Government policy documents identify 'efficiency', 'effectiveness' and 'performance' in instrumental and economic, rather than educational terms (Johnson 2000) thus highlighting the differential distribution of power in contemporary higher education politics. However, instrumentalist accounts of social, economic and organizational behaviour assume a technical-rational relationship of change; an understanding that assumes a tightly-coupled relationship between stimulus and response tends to ignore or devalue sociological dynamics of behaviour. This chapter illustrates that, whilst the predominant discourse within HODs' narratives is that of financial resources, the imperatives of the changed public resource environment, and the implications of this for organization and management, their interpretations and intended response are governed by the social fabric and dynamics of their own contexts.

The first two sets of extracts link directly to the resource dependency perspective: they explain organizational survival in economic terms. Here the key to survival is managing change in the pattern of economic interdependencies. The subsequent discussion begins to unravel the complexities faced by the HoD in implementing changes perceived necessary as a consequence of changes in public funding conditions and the imperative to find new sources of funds. It is here that insights from the perspective of institutional theory are of use in explaining how policy intentions are shaped during the process of implementation: the process of implementation depends on the normative conditions of the institutional field, and the norms that inform and legitimate identities, structures, relations and purposes within the academic organization.

Survival strategies:

HoDs describe a range of survival strategies, many of which involve activities designed to secure, generate and deploy resources sufficient to ensure survival at the level of academic unit. The first extract describes a pressure to find new and replacement resources; the pressure for income generation is a result the lack of organizational funds and is driven by a wish to survive as viable and successful academic unit. His activities focus on forming relationships external to the organization:

> The main function is to provide the resource to enable the development of the School from

whatever source. ... It means that if we wish to remain as a School with 27 academic staff, then we need certain things. One, we need students and we can only get students by offering the courses that students want. So, we've got to make sure that we offer the courses that the market place wants. We need revenue to run. We get so much from HEFCE, but it's not enough. So, you've got to get extra – where do you get that from? It means you've got to go outside and bring in revenue. The only way we can bring in revenue is by running courses for industry or doing consultancy work based on research, so you now have an external business arm. And the whole reason for that is income generation to support the educational role. So, the Head of School is now almost a Resource Manager; Human Resources, Physical Resources, Financial Resources. And managing the financial resources drives you into the market place, whether it be regionally or anywhere in the World you now operate. Every institution's being driven down the same way.
(Engineering, pre-1992)

His interpretation of his strategy identifies a desire to seek non-public sources of funds. Maintaining the academic unit involves changing patterns of dependence and, from his perspective, this change involves economic rather than value-led solutions. His strategy is motivated less by a wish for academic autonomy than it is for *viability* as unit of activity. The strategy he considers necessary involves several compromises, and relies on changes in internal activity and norms. Curricula are defined by market demand, rather than academic impulse (Henkel and Kogan, 1999); academics have to use their research instrumentally as means to inform income generating activity, rather than just the body of academic knowledge and publication.

In a different institution, this next HOD also describes how the pressure to find new or replacement resources is conditional on change, and an acceptance of change, within the organization. The change in question involves a realignment of *internal* allegiances and collaborations. The imperative to change is signalled and supported within the institution; the strategy is to generate changes within the academic community that will lead to, and secure changed relationships with external bodies. Change is explained and justified in resource terms: innovation through inter-disciplinary co-operation increases organizational flexibility and responsiveness to the interests of external fundholders. Furthermore, because external and disciplinary co-operation is emphasized in research council objectives and funding criteria, changes in internal allegiances are also means to maintain levels of public funding:

Pressure to raise external income is another change, and there's a heavy emphasis on commercialization of research ... the message is there in all parts of the university, and the university has a long track record of good contacts with the real world. ... That's been strengthened through the creation of what's called a Research and Enterprise Office at the centre of the university, that is much more proactive in getting departments and units to do things in the way of research funding and commercial sponsorship ... I've sensed there's

more pushing, more direction from the centre of the university to alert you to opportunities and encouraging you to respond to opportunities, to do more, to make connections between departments and faculties ... trying to bring together researchers in different bits of the university where ... that might be of benefit for a particular initiative or opportunity.
(Social Science, pre-1992)

Surviving dependencies:

Resource dependency theory argues that organizational change is not independent and self-directed: organizational change both reflects, and is determined by external interdependencies. In the two examples above, HoDs explained organizational survival in terms of their work in changing patterns of dependence away from public funds towards those provided within the market place. The second extract suggested that the university strategy also incorporated a desire to maintain sources of public funding. This next extract offers one explanation of why public funding continues to be of importance to organizational survival. Here, the HoD points out that the higher education 'product' is insufficiently lucrative to finance itself in commercial terms:

The university wants not to rely on government income so much, but they always will. And having said, "Go out, multiply and be fruitful in the community and whatever", what is the internal taxation regime when we do that? And if you solely ran a unit or department on non-council income you would be very hard put to sustain its viability I suspect, unless you had a really high added value product, if you had a Stephen Hawking video selling every five minutes
(Education, post-1992)

The problem faced by universities in general, and by those without high research or industrial income potential in particular, is that higher education is expensive, and its rewards to the individual deferred, rather than immediate. Thus the cost of higher education is higher than the price the market will sustain. Whilst the intention of his own university is to reduce reliance on public funding, the HoD takes the view that the intention to eliminate dependence is illusionary. His view supports the assumptions and logic that underpin policy design: strong responses within organizations in line with government priorities will occur where there is a high level of dependence on public funds.

Thus far the narratives extracted have supported the resource dependency perspective on organizational change. Within these it is clear that the 'incentive levers' contained in policy (Bleiklie, Chapter 2 this volume) generate perceptions of the necessity to change. However, actual responses depend on relative interpretations at individual and management level, and result in different outcomes

The HoD role as survival strategy:

These first extracts tackle the question of the role and identity of the HoD. Traditionally, the HoD is an academic, and not trained or professional manager. Yet many of the HoDs interviewed defined their HoD in terms of resource and financial management. At times, they used description of their responsibilities in these areas to distinguish the academic from the non-academic aspects of their work and identity:

> Well, in the sense that I am a manager, I hold the cost centre of the Department, so I manage the budget and I manage the employment of the personnel. I oversee their pay and rations, so to speak. In the sense I'm not a manager I also have a science career and I am interested in scientific research, so I do research independently of being a manager.
> (Science, pre-1992)

He suggests that the individual HoD faces a tension: he expresses reluctance in accepting budget management as definition of his identity as an academic. Whilst many viewed teaching and research work as criteria useful in differentiating management from academic responsibilities, some saw academic work as a necessary component of both the HoD's role and capacity to function, in non-academic areas. The next HoD explains her role as both manager and academic leader; her work as an academic is crucial to her ability to develop research activity and secure the public and private income that flows from this research 'presence':

> I do all the budgeting stuff that we've got and I'm operating something like fifteen or sixteen different accounts in this department, because of the number of contracts and various things that we have. That still has to be done. But I think the big change now is ... the importance of having a presence as far as research and publication is concerned, and being able then to, to use managerial speak, 'walk the talk'. ...I am at the moment trying to lead by example, [lead] my staff who are in the learning stages of actually carrying out research themselves.
> (Business Studies, post-1992)

The former HoD is an established researcher in a traditional civic university. The latter is new to academic life, and works in an institution more typically known for its teaching. Their ideas of their roles bear relation to their respective organizational contexts.

Survival skills:

Resource and financial concerns are predominant aspects of the HoD's role. In the next extract the capacity to generate income is seen as key to the HoD's ability to enable and sustain the academic activity of his unit. The HoD experiences this remit as an onerous responsibility, and claims that it relies on skills that fall outside a traditional interpretation of academic competence:

> We have devolved budgets, so I'm responsible for the finance, salaries, everything. So I run a million-and-a-half-pound business. [Determining] whether or not you are going to employ more staff ... [is] just down to, "Can your budget afford it?". If you need more staff, you've got to generate money from outside. If you need more equipment, you've got to generate money from outside. If you want to sponsor student, you've got to generate money from outside. So, where in all your academic career were you ever trained to do that?
> (Engineering, post-1992)

Whilst he himself has experience in industry, those in his department have more experience as pedagogues, teaching large numbers of students of varying academic ability. He goes on to explain how financial and entrepreneurial skills, new competencies and attitudes are demanded of all those employed within the organization. To explain his view he cites the tensions he experiences in dealing with academics in his department and in managing the time they invest in new *and* traditional areas of work. He has to convince, support and sustain both financial and academic balances:

> There are major tensions between the academic role, as perceived, in teaching ... and external fund generation, because it's the same resource that you draw upon. You're asking the same staff who teach to also generate money from industry. There's an enormous tension there. There're cultural tensions, because they're not used to doing it, so you've got to go through a whole training and education process to give them the confidence. They've got the ability; it's just the confidence, because they're not used to going out there and working in industry. So, you're managing that, and education, of course and then just balancing the time between delivering teaching here and also having to deliver outside. So, managing that is a major tension.
> (Engineering, post-1992)

HoDs often explained how the predominant concern to provide adequate resource compromises the idea of the 'educational business'. Yet some took the view that such a compromise is a matter of fact necessity. This next HoD is from the same university as the engineer above.

> You know, the whole of the external, global situation at the moment, nobody can predict what the global finances are going to be like in the next two years. So, if we're going to go to external generation, there has to be some risk to it. Now, if you don't accept risk, then let's shut shop and say what we are is a business of pure education and we're not involving ourselves with external clients. If we are going to go for external generation,

> we have to have an element of risk strategy that goes with it … [and] I think that that culture hasn't yet happened, I don't think it's understood.
> (Applied Science, post-1992)

He argues that universities can no longer afford to think of themselves as purely educational organizations, and berates the lack of capacity within his own organization to perform in ways necessary to maintain 'educational business'. The stress is, again, on the necessity to develop new skills; and, whilst others have indicated the new palette of skills demanded of the manager and the academic, his frustration targets lack of skill at organizational level. Change imperatives require development of new skills capacity, at organizational, individual and management level. Learning is an uncomfortable experience, but is more difficult to countenance when such change devalues, and lies in tension with those skills necessary to sustain the 'core value' of higher education. This next HoD works in a large, established institution, with national profile for the quality of teaching and learning support:

> Strong management skills, perhaps at a more senior level particularly financial management skills … seem to be valued at a premium. … But I think we have to be careful that in HE our core value, our core service is still to develop and deliver knowledge and people, and I think we need to keep an eye on the balance between that endeavour, those intentions, and the skills like the new types of managerial abilities that are required to actually operate successfully.
> (Business Studies, post-1992)

Survival of the fittest:

Both resource dependence and institutional theory are coherent with a political analysis of organizations (c.f. Miller, 1995). Resource dependency argues that organizational survival is conditional on successful management of both external and internal dependencies. Internal dependence is explained in terms of competition for limited resources, and the relative power of individuals and constituencies within the organization in that competition. Resource dependency theory explains relative power in terms of the relative significance to the organization of the resources provided by different individuals or groups (Pfeffer, 1992). In contrast, institutional theory rejects an economic-rational theory as sufficient explanation of power within organizations. Instead, power is a product of the behaviour of individuals and groups within organizations, the non-economic resources they are able to monopolise and employ, and the interpretation of this behaviour by, and its impact on, others (Friedland and Alford 1991; Powell 1991).

The extracts selected so far identify that resources are a condition of survival. However, within these there are also different, non-economic and competing definitions of 'survival'. This indicates that whilst one aspect of survival involves balancing resource dependencies in order to maintain and maximise income generation, survival also depends on other factors. Many of these necessary factors appear to compromise the capacity of, or readiness within, the academic organization to direct performance on the basis of economic-rational efficiency. This is because the *effective* organization is a concept that cannot be defined purely in these narrow terms (Kondra and Hinings 1998). The survival of the academic organization depends also on its ability to maintain, develop and deliver research and teaching; survival is conditional on sustaining elements of activity and identity that are *traditional* to the notion of the academic and higher education. Whilst HoDs may struggle to survive at local level, their own actions may be viewed as threatening to others' units, or the survival of the university as an *effective* organization.

Thus whilst relative power within the university may be in part a reflection of the particular income generating capacity of the HoD's own unit, the use of such power within decisions over resource allocation is frustrated at organizational level by the existence of structures that secure cross-subsidies to units that are relatively less well off financially. When survival is not defined in terms of economic efficiency, but in ways as an intention to sustain a range of courses and disciplines within the organization, relative power within the organization lies as latent potential. According to this next HOD, in a high profile, small university in a major economic region, it is a contradiction that the university inhibits its own economic potential by restricting the capacity of the rich discipline to capitalise on its own self-generated assets, and by restricting these academics' powers to place conditions on how others use that income:

> We're the people who provide most of the money to subsidise the other groups. ... but one of the things that the senior management of the university would never let us do as the successful group is to place conditions on the unsuccessful group for allowing it to use our cash. What we wanted to do was to lay conditions down and see their business plans and ... have some say in the punishments to be metered out to them for, for not achieving. But we were never allowed to do that. So you had a situation ... where people would sit there and shrug their shoulders because they were actually the majority whenever we voted on anything, and they always won.
> (Applied Sciences, pre-1992)

Yet, a different HOD in the same university has a different view of organizational processes and priorities. He perceives that the university *constrains* academic innovation by agreeing only those courses that are viable in financial, economic terms:

> I think the increased need to demonstrate financial accountability is an aspect that fifteen years ago was not so apparent. Now whenever you put in a proposal to an academic planning committee, or plans for a new programme, there will also be a financial resource form to demonstrate that you can actually put this course on … - that when it's running it will not be a drain on the university. And that is a different approach. Clearly in business, commerce, no-one's going to do anything to make a loss.
> (Engineering, pre-1992)

Similarly, this next HoD, in a very old, large university with balance in both teaching and research, also experiences how academic plans that result in diminished income are difficult to justify or secure. He is reliant on the forces of collegial good will and the traditional norm of academic co-operation. In order to justify action that has resource implications, he seeks and requires the agreement and support of colleagues as counter-weight to the competing economic argument:

> The main thing that I had to do was to cut the student numbers and that's a really difficult thing to do because it's against the interests of the university and … the faculty because it's an income stream. It's double an income stream actually because the students are funded as science students and don't cost as much to teach as a business course. We had to go against the interests of the university and it was colossally difficult to do … It took about a year of arguing with the other Heads of Departments in the faculty and with the Dean such that they would find the problems that we were facing sufficiently great that they were prepared to suffer a bit themselves to help us relieve the problems.
> (Science, pre-1992)

Whilst the richer academic units may feel a right to greater levels of control and autonomy, their relative power, and the change desired (and desirable according to an economic rationality), is frustrated by the ability of others to mobilise structures, procedures and values as counter-balance. Their power is constrained by structures, procedures and relations that reflect, and serve to maintain an effective academic organization.

Survival of the maverick. Back door dealing:

The resource environment presents the HoD with difficult choices. The drive for economy within the organization means that expenditure totals are fixed, and each item of expenditure represents a range of opportunity costs. The HoD's choice of action often involves choosing between the individual or the collective good:

> But the problem for me of that is that I'm actually saying, "We need to spend all the money that we earn", at a time when the institution is saying, "Well of course, we should be making efficiency gains". So if I want to spend more of what I earn, somebody else has got to lose staff and that's where the tension is.
> (Applied Science, post-1992)

Nevertheless within other narratives, the exigencies of the resource environment question the viability of academic traditions. For example, this next HoD attempts to explain his own torn loyalties in a situation where depleted resources necessitate deviation from norms of collegiality or self-sacrifice in the interests of the whole. The nature of his academic subject is adaptive and inter-disciplinary, and therefore the context for his academic work must be adaptive and allow him to cross-over organizational, procedural and financial boundaries. Despite a willingness to ensure fair-play and acknowledge of others' need for survival within the faculty, he argues that resource scarcity and structural constraints indicate that his predominant concern must be to protect his own academic unit's security and future potential. It is necessary for him to engage in a degree of maverick operation:

> you can't always achieve the best for your department as well as satisfying the faculty objectives or the wishes of the eight other departments. So there are occasions when you have to fight your corner or try to step outside university procedures or have them fit your needs when sometimes they don't. ... There are a lot of occasions where you have to confront the university about the fact their systems, structures, processes are not going to get you where you want to be and you need some flexibility in there. And you have to go to whichever bit of the university you think can give you the change and the flexibility that you need.
> (Social Science, pre-1992)

This next HOD has previously held more senior posts in the university – a large metropolitan post-1992 institution with long-standing reputation for teaching across a wide range of traditional and applied disciplines. She is reluctant, but sees herself compelled, to enter into political lobbying within the university on behalf of her immediate academic colleagues. She does this in order to secure, by 'back door' action (Becher, 1988), what she understands as fair treatment in resource allocation. What is new here is the degree to which she feels compelled:

> You're balancing all the time the needs of bits against the needs of the whole and I think, I probably err towards looking after the needs of the whole and not being nasty enough about the needs of the School. ... [But] people [are] lobbying in faculties for money ... and if that gets agreed it stops spending that's needed for us. Now, that makes me angry and that's when I will start to think, "Well, OK, I'll have to go in and lobby too", because it's the only way to make sure that my staff and my provision is protected. ... You know, when people in Schools that we're subsidising are asking for more staff, I say we should get them first." I've been open about that [within the department], there's been an open discussion. But the other stuff is kind of back door, 'behind the back door' dealing.
> (Applied Sciences, post-1992).

Competition for resources may be used, explicitly, as a mechanism of management within the university. This next HoD is a highly successful and prominent academic in an innovative academic discipline, located in a university she described as recently competitive and meritocratic: extra resources were given to departments that could demonstrate high levels of academic success, and balanced finances. She describes the resource allocation procedure as a political process that involves management consideration of the potential of academic and financial plans. The decision will depend on the finite quantity available, university priorities and demands made by other constituencies in the university. The HoD shapes her plans and assesses her realistic chances in the budgeting process through sounding off the views and intentions of colleagues:

> Each Faculty has to prepare its submission and prepare their financial plans [and] the Faculty does not know what any other Faculty is bidding for and so you've got to try and listen to the soundings and balance what you're asking for relative to what's going to be available, relevant to what the thinking in the university is
> (Science, post-1992)

The rational logic of resource allocation priorities translates into social action and political manoeuvring

Agents of change. Survival and autonomy:

In the following two extracts, the HoDs' concerns shift away from structures and procedures for resource allocation or academic performance towards the restrictions on their autonomy imposed through existing hierarchical relationships and patterns of decision-making. Their respective 'arguments' with Vice Chancellors use images of outdated norms to point out the contradiction of those norms in the new resource environment. They also draw on the imperatives of the new resource environment to justify their view that it is now necessary to shift the 'rules of the game' (c.f. North, 1991). In this context the respective Vice Chancellors are cast by the HoDs as ancients who adhere to traditions of acceptable institutional and organizational activities that are anachronistic and detrimental to survival. In both cases the shift identified would enable the HoDs to implement their own respective strategies for income generation. Both HoDs take the view that a shift in existing hierarchies and organizational norms is a necessary step towards academic innovation and market sensitivity. Yet they also justify their view by describing how the income generated would *maintain* other traditional academic roles and activities:

> I mean in a range of activities, we are now encouraging staff from the HOD down to become more entrepreneurial in terms of going outside to raise money ... any sort of work that will raise money ... Whereas in the past that was almost frowned on. ... The previous vice-chancellor said, "We are not going to raise money by breaking lumps of concrete,

that's not high tech work". And my argument to the vice-chancellor was I don't care what I do to get the money, but if I can spend that money on a little post doc or research student then I'll put it to good use, but he wouldn't buy it. Now, the new Head of School said, in response to my question "If I can get 10,000 pounds for breaking up some concrete, can I use that money to run a post-doc?", "Yes, of course you can, good idea".
(Engineering, pre-1992)

Previous to changes in management structures, he was obstructed by received traditions of what counts as academic work and the power of the vice chancellor to reinforce these. The second HoD, explains how the vice-chancellor justifies current management structures by referring to norms within the institutional field. Whilst this discursive act is an attempt by the vice-chancellor to legitimate their own point of view, the HoD is unconcerned with institutional norms:

> The university sees [this] School as one of its flag-ship departments [and] wants us to be innovative, wants us to be responsive and wants us to grow. But it establishes such Delphic and labyrinthine processes and this makes my job, I think, impossible. There is that tension really which is, "Yes let's grow lets do exciting things, let's back winners" ... but the bureaucracy doesn't enable me to do it. We have a very non-devolved system. I mean the VC said to me, we had a bit of an argument actually, "Well you know in this university, unlike others, you have the most high level of autonomy as heads of department of any institution I know". To which I said, "I have autonomy to do absolutely nothing because you don't leave me with any control over staffing or budgets, so please tell me what I can do".
> (Social Science, post-1992)

Both HoDs require release from management control, and space for manoeuvre.

A balancing act: managing and surviving change

This next section illustrates the various balances the HoDs have to strike to sustain the survival of their own unit. The resource environment is uncertain and volatile. Uncertain dependencies have to be balanced against more secure sources of resource. More secure sources of funds are tied to tighter conditions, and these may conflict with the needs of alternative fundholders. Management of the local unit involves financial, academic and personnel issues, each of which present a potentially conflicting set of demands.

> I have tensions with the teaching staff about the fact that we need to produce more income on the teaching side to solve the university's supposed problem with us being in deficit. The tension there is trying to produce viable proposals for new courses ... without really having the resources ... to do proper market research on those. So, the tension is coming up with ideas and you don't know whether they're going to fly until you put them into the

marketplace. That produces the situation where staff are innovating on the curriculum side all the time, when they're very pressured and busy anyway. That's a tension.
(Social Science, pre-1992)

Processes of determining and implementing responses adequate to address resource needs involve the HoD in interpretations of the possibilities and limits of the local context, and negotiations with academic colleagues over possible ways forward. Both require the HoD to reflect on the variety of potential view points, and respective positions regarding the importance of existing norms. The HoD has more room to manoeuvre in situations where members of the department are more likely to agree to changes that involve shifts in traditions of structure, procedure, social interactions or organizational hierarchies. Narratives again illustrate the tensions that exist between resource imperatives and the mediating forces of existing organizational norms and orders. The balancing acts described by the HoDs reinforce the need for a theory of change that combines and contrasts theories of resource dependency and institutional behaviour.

Slicing the cake. Cordiality and budgets:

The balance sought by this first HOD is financial. Here the key objective is to achieve parity between academic output and resource generation. In order to avoid deficits it is necessary to plan academic work outputs in terms of financial productivity; the point of reference in planning is a balanced cash flow:

> At the end of the day no-one's going to bail us out. The days of getting hand-outs from the HEFCE if you overspend are long gone, so in effect we have to make sure that the academic side of our planning and the financial side of our planning are compatible and will ensure that the university, and at a lower level the school, will actually achieve a balanced budget
> (Humanities, pre-1992)

The same HOD considers that his own role involves arbitrating between what he perceives as unrealistic staff expectations and inflexible budgets. 'Getting the balance right' involves establishing his own financial and academic priorities, justifying them and winning agreement over the compromised expectations implicit to these priorities in a context of fixed quantities of financial 'cake'. The tasks involved in this process require explanation, patience and interpersonal skill. Within the arguably safer territory of the interview setting, the frustrations of stimulating attitudinal change in order to implement his plans are self-evident. He has to balance social cohesion with the imperatives of changes in resource, and this requires him to manage within the constraints of necessary cordiality.

> They would see me as fair. I'm always prepared to listen to the other side. I think that's important in a manager, always being prepared to see the whole picture. And I think that

staff often have an incredibly naïve awareness of the whole picture, they simply don't seem to understand that the university gets finite cake, finite amount of money and if it spends more on X it has to spend less on Y. And academic staff sometimes, amazingly, they can't understand why they can't really spend, can't have more academic staff, or more administrative staff. They ... don't seem to have the concept that there is only finite cake and its all about dividing that in the best possible way, getting the balance right.
(Humanities, post-1992)

The geese that lay the golden eggs:

The balancing act involves co-ordination of social, academic, structural and financial constraints. Each form of constraint comprises different sets of norms, interests and tensions and these impact differently on the HoD's ability to implement and stimulate change. Narratives also demonstrate that various HoDs place different emphasis on the needs and demands of each source of constraint. Most HODs identify their departmental colleagues as their key constituency. In this sense, one purpose of the balancing act is to enable those colleagues to work productively with minimal friction.

This next HOD, who had high ambitions for his small department's research income and reputation, views departmental colleagues as a resource to draw on in meeting organizational financial, academic and administrative requirements. At the same time, staff also have loyalties and responsibilities in research. The bottom line of the balance he must strike is the critical point at which the valuable staff become overloaded with the different demands made of them within the organization. The HoD needs to sustain staff in order to maintain and progress academic integrity and output:

> I have to make sure that my department is properly staffed for the tasks it wants to perform and in order to respond to signals from the university about things like the department's deficit, its teaching activities, its administrative contribution. I have to respond in a positive way to those, whilst at the same time trying to protect my staff from all those pressures so that we can continue to be a research-led, successful department. So it's a balancing act between satisfying what I think we need to satisfy within the university expectations of us ... whilst not doing too much of that that it kills the goose that laid the golden egg.
> (Social Science, pre-1992)

This next HoD found that she enjoyed juggling the budget, much to her surprise. She works in an old, established and well-resourced civic, and heads a department highly popular with students and with national reputation. She suggests that the critical point of overload has already been reached as a consequence of teaching, and suggests the need to reallocation of resources away from teaching:

We put too much resources into teaching and not enough into managing and research and everyone's too tired. So every time you ask anyone to do anything there is a horrible silence because nobody wants to do anymore because they are all doing too much.
(Arts, pre-1992)

A fair wage. Balancing income and activity:

Some Heads of Department suggest that the 'finite cake' allocated to them within the organization misrepresents the effort and activity levels of their own units. These HoD typically worked in subjects with high levels of student demand; these next 3 examples come from Business, Finance and Management related disciplines. These extracts illustrate how the economics of the new resource environment encourage a financial analysis of academic inputs and outcomes. This analysis makes the imbalance in organizational resource allocations painfully clear, and this is experienced as an unfair contradiction. The work of the first HoD involves sustaining levels of activity in a context where staff are demotivated:

> There is a perception that we have been used as a cash cow for the university and for the Faculty and as a result of that the member of staff who's faced with the final year class of 300 and the practicality of ensuring good teaching, looking after the students, dealing with things the way we should have done, has left colleagues feeling a little bit ground down, well quite substantially ground down.
> (Business Studies, pre-1992)

The imbalance causes tensions within the department; these provide an added layer of complexity to the context in which the next HoD attempts survival and change:

> We are the ones who bring in all the students and do all the teaching but the result is that other departments then have lots of leisure to do research because eventually there's cross subsidization of the funding that we bring in into the university. It is not all returned to this department. ... So that could cause tension.
> (Business Studies, post-1992)

The third HoD works in a department that merged with the faculty of business two years previously. It is a subject she felt was not recognized as creditworthy by academics in the faculty, despite levels of student demand. This forms part of her explanation for the unfair resource allocation. She struggles within her own unit, and battles with senior levels of management:

> I'm struggling at the moment, for instance, with budgetary and staffing issues. There is no relationship between the FTEs, the student numbers in the department and the budget I get. ... The discrepancy between what I have to run the department and what I should get is now over £300,000. I mean it's huge, huge. I have been battling with this for the past two years and I still don't have any more money.

(Business Studies, post-1992)

Organizational resource allocation procedures represent strategies to secure academic balance - or achieve different balances of academic activity - within a balanced university budget. Yet these procedures serve to upset the balance between academic work, income and goodwill at unit level. Work outputs, income and goodwill are some of the factors on which survival and management within the academic unit depends.

The HoD operates inside and outside the academic unit to redress the local consequences of imbalances generated at organizational level. The actions of these HoDs are less management towards changed activity than they are a battle for survival in changed circumstances; in these circumstances organizational inconsistencies are revealed and the need for changes in organizational norms, structures and processes is emphasized. The agency of the HoD is constrained by features of the existing organizational context within which they operate. The impact of policy on organizations reflects the characteristics of that organization, the relative capacity of actors to respond to and implement change, and the various strategies they devise to influence change and manage survival.

Changed responsibilities: accounting for the accounts

Many characteristics of 'new managerialism and 'new public management' outlined at the beginning of this chapter are evident in the narratives included in the discussion so far. They show, for example how elements of the quasi-market outlined by Gerwirtz et al (1995) are also now used as internal mechanisms of management incentive and control. We have seen HoDs' responses to internal contracting and competitive bidding, and the real demand at all levels of the organization to access new and maintain old sources of funds as a consequence of reduced public funds. We have also seen that these responses are various, and depend on the actual conditions of the HoD's own institution and academic unit.

One dominant feature of the narratives is worth further examination. Ferlie et al (1996) and Gewirtz et al (1995) highlight how policy concerning the financial effectiveness, efficiency, performance and accountability of public sector organizations involves the use tools of control and incentive in the form of financial accountability; specification of financial responsibility at all levels, transparency of income and expenditure flows, de-layering, devolved budgets and autonomy within tight performance and accountability frameworks.

There is evidence that senior management attempts to monopolise on the sensitivity of HoD to the quantities and conditions of funding provided within the organization.

> the aim is that … if a particular school can raise some extra money, then … the extra income you earn you will retain. … Then there's obviously an incentive to do that. And really what we're looking for is to 'incentivize' people to actually go out and raise money. In the past under the old regime … there was no incentive to go and raise extra money. … I'm afraid that that isn't viable in the current climate!
> (Engineering, post-1992)

Many of the resource-based management mechanisms characteristic of the quasi market feature within HoDs' narratives. In particular, there is a common theme of devolved responsibility and tight accountability frameworks. These accountability criteria are new means of assessing the performance of both manager and department, and result from recent devolution of budget responsibility to HoDs. This HoD appears to accept the implication of devolution: that she is budget, human resource and performance manager:

> you do need to begin to account a bit more for peoples time, for the budgets that you have. In the past you didn't because everything was centralised. In the last 3 to 4 years we've devolved budget responsibility at least down to HoD level. And that was quite a major change because … previously HoDs rarely got involved with mega sums of money. I manage a budget now of something like nearly 2 million, 1.8 million pounds that I can sign for. I suppose the department must bring in something like 3½ - 4 million possibly. So you're talking about quite large sums of money really, and I don't think you can operate that without some kind of management principles.
> (Business, post-1992)

She described this change in positive terms, she interpreted devolution as a demonstration of senior management trust and an incentive. This next HoD, who had described his previous vice chancellor as an autocrat, saw current changes in management as both opportunity, but also means of 'shifting potential blame':

> The biggest change in management has been that effectively the responsibility for managing the resource is now being put at a lower level. Whereas before it was at the vice-chancellor level, now it's at the Head of School level and, effectively, the Heads of School will be accountable if in fact their Schools don't perform.
> (Engineering, pre-1992)

Devolved budgets are tied to greater central controls and levers. This next HoD is aware that the autonomy implied by devolution of budgets is superficial because there are organization specific performance criteria to which he has to perform. Moreover, his autonomy of action extends only in so far as the strategies he devises facilitate performance in terms of an 'envelope' of acceptable performance:

I don't feel restricted in terms of the developments I would like to carry out ... or the things I would like to close down in the department. [But] I suppose I'm conscious of still having to operate within a kind of envelope whereby I will be expected to achieve a certain level of full-time equivalent students, to have my staff-student ratio at a certain level, and to be generating sufficient external income. But in *how* I do that I have a great deal, a lot of autonomy.
(Business Studies, post-1992)

In this sense, the power implicit to budget control is limited to the extent the performance of the HoD, and the ways in which resources are allocated within the department, are controlled through other mechanisms. This next HoD describes how his power is conditional on the approval of the Dean:

I mean I could be a Hitler, I could be an absolute dictator here. I have that power on administration, on research and on all of the resources, space, computing, you name it. I have all of that power. What I don't have power over is in terms of budgetary control. If I get a budget allocated to me by the Dean, then yes I have control over how the budget is allocated, but I need to negotiate and discuss that budget with the Dean
(Science, pre-1992)

However, whilst academics in management positions may be alert and sensitive to the imperatives of external and internal resource environments, it is unclear whether market-related resource imperatives are effective in stimulating and directing change at the level of the individual academic. HoDs' narratives indicate the range of tensions involved in implementing new ways of working and performing within their academic units. These tensions may in part be due to resistance to, or lack of identification with incentives in the form of financial profits. There is evidence to support the view that academics' values, interests, loyalties and motivations contrast with, and in many ways contradict, the assumption that higher or different levels of performance can be stimulated through financial incentives to the individual. One HoD suggests that 'where the system is not performing effectively, ... professional managers have a role in ensuring that we manage the achievement of our academic goals in as effective a way as possible (Engineering, post-1992). Nevertheless, he is cautious of his own idea. He adds that he would 'be concerned if a manager started to set the academic goals, because then I don't think we would be a university'.

Other HoDs describe how the lack of autonomy in budget management means that they have no means to introduce penalties and incentives on performance. This next HoD is ambivalent about this. He suggests alternative means of bringing about change, and yet identifies how his ability to manage in these terms is restricted by the finite quantity of time he can spend in negotiating new priorities and attitudes with academic colleagues:

> Yeah, there are no carrots and sticks. I'm not suggesting there should be. … Carrots and sticks are not the only way to deal with it. But the frustration is someone who is absolutely immune to anything that you try to do. To actually solve the problem you have to invest so much time that there's no way you can.
> (Education, post-1992)

The main tools available are social interaction and good relations; these are used to establish performance objectives on the basis of 'some communication, some identity of aim between and among you' (HoD Arts, pre-1992). Within the academic organization, Heads tended to express how 'management is done by the team'. In this case it became 'important that I've got all my staff on board and that they share my view … [otherwise] I'm going to have a big persuasion job on my hands'(Business Studies, post-1992). HoDs were reluctant to incorporate resource-based levers within the palette of tools available to them as managers as local units:

> If you are trying to persuade somebody to do a job for example, one of the levers one has is to say is that this will contribute to promotion, accelerate an increment or whatever, so you do have something to bargain with. But I suppose I tend to, because I operate out of a feeling of obligation to the community and to myself, I tend to hope that people will defer to that rather than to their own self interest.
> (Humanities, pre-1992)

In order to successfully negotiate and persuade academics to change, the HoD needs to identify the sets of interests, values and motivations that exist within their own unit:

> I think the key thing perhaps about being a manager of academics is that you have to find ways of harnessing that energy and that commitment and you can't do it by waving a stick, I mean, saying "You do this, and do that": it doesn't work. … I think you've got to engage people partly through the intrinsic pleasure of what they are doing. … And if you squeeze it out and they are just being mechanical deliverers of things then I think we are a bit lost really. You've got to keep some way of renewing them and energising them and this sort of thing through the subject.
> (Business Studies, post-1992)

The management of academic organizations requires forms and tools of control and incentive that *enable* academic work and work with academics' motivations:

> Management I think means motivation, it means trying to get things done, it means monitoring, it means within a university context trying to provide the minimum control to achieve that. … People can be creative, they can develop, they can follow to some extent their own interests. I think university departments … have a wide range of objectives and I think you've got to try and allow people to follow their own interests … as long as you can keep the whole thing moving forward in the right way.
> (Science, post-1992)

Many academics arrive and remain in academia because their commitments are other than high salary levels; this point applied in particular to business, applied science and engineering related disciplines. Scientific work is also better funded in commercial areas; the attraction of the academic organization is therefore one of freedom from direction and organizational performance controls. Furthermore, because much academic work, and not only that of science, relies on team and co-operative work, individual reward is a contradiction and source of potential divisiveness and ineffective work. The resource levers that are of real value to the HoD as manager are non-financial; the resources identified as effective levers of change were time, security, space, equipment and recognition. Many HoDs described these as items of expenditure available only if there was left-over in budgets, and yet their experience teaches them that they are vital to securing performance, commitment and motivation. For example, one argued that research is not stimulated by potential individual monetary rewards, but by the ability to fund it. Thus rewards for research should come in the form of a 'pot' to the department to fund the individual's future research.

> I've argued strongly that [the university should] get 10% of the research overheads back to the individuals that earned them. ... It seems to me that that's tremendous encouragement to the individual. First of all it' a bit of a reward; it's not going into your pocket but it will allow you to develop your research. Potentially it will allow you, encourage you to go out and get more money because your research has been enhanced. (Science, pre-1992)

Conclusion

The imperative for change is felt at organization, unit and individual levels, and is driven by changed conditions and quantities of funding. HoDs' ideas of the necessity of change are clear and keenly felt. Certain individual HoDs in particular institutions suggest a momentum of change in norms and traditions of academic work and organization. Changes in normative ideas of the university, and its cultural, structural, social and academic characteristics and purposes were seen as a necessary part of achieving change within their own organizations. Yet HoDs' narratives seldom suggest that any changes required have been achieved. Instead, common emphases are struggles to survive (to stand still), and to maintain balance in work, management and organization. This suggests that whilst academic organizations are clearly resource dependent, and are battling in the face of the changed resource environment, the process of responding to change in local contexts, including managing and changing dependencies, is fraught with social, structural, and value-dependent hurdles, and these mediate and reduce the speed of changes sought. Resource dependency theory appears to characterise the changes sought, but not that which has been brought about.

The HoD's ability to succeed in sustaining the academic unit, and in maintaining balance is conditional upon the management strategy adopted, and this has to pay regard to the characteristics of the local context. Resource-based incentives are not available, and ineffective in motivating the individual academics with whom the HoD has to work whilst negotiating and implementing change. Instead, the emphasis throughout the narratives is that successful management of change is achieved by working with, and within what is considered normal, acceptable and characteristic of the academic organization. Organizational survival in contemporary higher education depends on finding new markets, establishing new external and internal dependencies, and developing skills and attitudinal capacity necessary to cope with changed in priorities, imperatives and work focus. Yet it is likely that these changes in organization, management and work will become evident only incrementally, and will be contested with potentially contradictory outcome.

These conclusions highlight the deficiencies of simplistic understandings of both policy process and organizational change. Contemporary policy design and ideas of public management assume the effectiveness of financial levers, and draw on an ideologically driven, technical-rational framework of change relationships. In contrast, this chapter suggests two themes. First, that policy is crafted and has impact according to the lived practices, experiences and understandings of actors in context. Second, that policy design and management strategies should bear in mind the social nature of organizations. Contemporary policy design and management strategy are however largely devoid of such sociological implication. It is the individual HoD who has to work to render policy and management a little more human.

References

Barnett, R (1992) *Improving Higher Education: Total Quality Care*. Buckingham: Open University Press/SRHE.
Barnett, R. (1990) *The Idea of Higher Education.*. Buckingham: Open University Press/SRHE.
Becher, T. (1988) Principles and politics: an interpretative framework for university management, in A. Westoby, (ed) *Culture and power in educational organizations*. Milton Keynes: Open University Press.
Becher, T. and Kogan, M. (1992) *Process and Structure in Higher Education*. 2nd edition, London: Heinemann.
Bergquist, W. H. (1993) *The Four Cultures of the Academy*. San Francisco: Jossey Bass.
Clarke, J. and Newman, J. (eds) (1997) *The Managerial State: Power, politics and ideology in the remaking of social welfare*. London: Sage.
Clarke, J., Gewirtz, S. and McLaughlin, E. (2000) *New Managerialism, New Welfare?* London: Sage.
DiMaggio, P.J. and Powell, W.W. (1983) The Iron Cage Revisited: Institutional Isomorphism and Collective Rationality in Organisational Fields, *American Sociological Review*, (48):147-160.

Ferlie, E., and Ashburner, L. et al (1996) *The New Public Management in Action.* Oxford: Oxford University Press.

Friedland, R. and Alford, R.R. (1991) Bringing Society Back In: Symbols, Practices and Institutional Contradictions, in W. W. Powell and P. J. DiMaggio (eds) *The New Institutionalism in Organisational Analysis.* Chicago: University of Chicago Press, pp. 205-232.

Gewirtz, S., Ball, S. and Bowe, R. (eds) (1995) *Markets, Choice and Equity in Education.* Buckingham: Open University Press.

Henkel, M. and Kogan, M. (1999) Changes in Curriculum and Institutional Structures: Responses to Outside Influences in Higher Education Institutions, in C. Gellert (ed) *Innovation and Adaptation in Higher Education: The Changing Conditions of Advanced Teaching and Learning in Europe.* London: Jessica Kingsley, pp. 66-91.

Johnson, R. (2000) A Qualitative Study of Student Feedback: Lecturers' and Students' Perceptions and Experiences. Unpublished PhD thesis, University of Sheffield/Sheffield Hallam University, UK.

King, N. (1994) The Qualitative Research Interview, in C. Cassell and G. Symon (eds) *Qualitative Methods in Organisational Research: Practical Guide.* London: Sage, pp. 14-36.

Kondra, A.Z. and Hinings, C.R. (1998) Organisational Diversity and Change in Institutional Theory, *Organisation Studies,* 19(5): 743-767.

McNay, I. (1995). From Collegial Academy to Corporate Enterprise: the changing cultures of universities, in T. Schuller (ed) *The Changing University?* Buckingham: Open University Press/SRHE, 105-115.

Miller, H. D. R. (ed) (1995) *The Management of Change in Universities: Universities, State and Economy in Australia, Canada and the United Kingdom.* Buckingham: Open University Press/SRHE.

North, D.C. (1991) Towards a Theory of Institutional Change, *Quarterly Review of Economics and Business,* (31):3-11.

Oliver, C. (1991) Strategic Responses to Institutional Processes, *Academy of Management Journal* (24):183-191.

Orru, M., Woolsey Biggart, N. and Hamilton, G.G. Organisational Isomorphism in East Asia, in W. W. Powell and P. J. DiMaggio (eds) *The New Institutionalism in Organisational Analysis.* Chicago: University of Chicago Press, pp. 361-389.

Pfeffer, J. (ed) (1992) *Managing with Power: Politics and Influence within Organizations.* Boston, MA: Harvard Business School Press.

Pfeffer, J. and Salanick, G.R. (eds) (1978) *The External Control of Organisations: A Resource Dependence Perspective.* New York: Harper Row.

Powell W.W. and DiMaggio, P.J. (eds) (1991) *The New Institutionalism in Organisational Analysis.* Chicago: University of Chicago Press.

Powell, W.W. (1991) Expanding the Scope of Institutional Analysis, in W. W. Powell and P. J. DiMaggio (eds) *The New Institutionalism in Organisational Analysis.* Chicago: University of Chicago Press, pp. 183-203.

Salter, B. and Tapper, T. (1994) *The State and Higher Education*. Ilford: The Woburn Press.

Scott, W.R. (ed) (1992) *Organisations: Rational, Natural and Open Systems*, 3rd edn. Englewood Cliffs, NJ: Prentice Hall.

Scott, W.R. (ed) (1995) *Institutions and Organisations*. Thousand Oaks, Calif.: SAGE.

Trow, M. (1996) Trust, markets and accountability in higher education: a comparative perspective, *Higher Education Policy*, 9(4):309-324.

Williams, G. (1989) Prospects for Higher Education Finance, in C. Ball and H. Eggins *Higher Education into the 1990s*. Buckingham: Open University Press/SRHE, pp. 112-123.

Williams, G. (1991) Finished and Unfinished Business, in T. Schueller *The Future of Higher Education*. Buckingham: Open University Press/SRHE.

6 The Unintended Consequences of Deregulation: Australian higher education in the market place.

Di Adams

Introduction

For less than a decade, from 1988, Australia had a Unified National System of thirty six public universities, with similar working conditions, salaries and funding arrangements. From the mid 90s, the ideal of a market economy was superimposed on the sector, and enterprise bargaining gradually changed the conditions and salaries in individual institutions. The funding formulae for university operations were changed, resulting in an overall reduction in government funding to all universities. To make up the funding deficit, universities looked to entrepreneurial approaches to the selling of their 'wares', and came to regard other universities as competitors.

University co-operation evaporated under the pressure of competition, although several coalitions formed between smaller groups of universities which perceived a common interest and a marketing advantage. At the same time, international or global influences led universities into some unaccustomed behaviours, such as encouraging the adoption of expensive electronic technologies for teaching, and establishing franchise agreements for teaching materials, or sending staff off-shore to teach. Differing expectations of workloads fuelled internal tensions between various layers of the academic workforce and those charged with the management of the university, leading to disputes about academic standards, ethical practice, and administrative overload.

It is not an exclusively Australian phenomenon that universities are subject to external pressures from government and global influences and to internal dissent between academic and corporate cultures, but because of the particularly strong attachment to deregulation by the Australian government, the phenomenon has probably been experienced more intensively by Australian universities than elsewhere

This chapter analyses the intended and unintended outcomes of government and institutional policies and describes some aspects of the impact on individual academic staff and their work conditions.

Sources of data

The data for this chapter have come from primary and secondary sources. The secondary sources are reports from the Department of Education, Training and Youth Affairs (DETYA), IDP Education Australia, the Australian Bureau of Statistics (ABS); the Australian Vice-Chancellors' Committee (AV-CC); from university documents; and from newspaper articles. Primary data were collected from formal interviews and informal conversations conducted with academic and general staff within nine Australian universities (two in NSW, two in the ACT, one in Queensland, and four in Victoria). Interviews were also conducted with two research officers from the National Office of the National Tertiary Education Union (NTEU), and with four industrial officers from the branch offices of the NTEU. Data were collected from participant observation within two Australian universities, from a forum on Off-Campus Teaching with 20 participants at one of these universities and from participants at a Transnational Education Symposium held at the University of Melbourne in November 2000. Data gathered from informal conversations were validated or discarded after cross-checking with multiple respondents, or from official documents. Exit interviews were conducted with three academic staff. The universities from which data were collected included two of the old prestigious universities (commonly called 'sandstones'), two small regional universities (often called 'gumtree universities'), three of the so-called 'technological universities', one large and aggressively entrepreneurial university, and one small university with entrepreneurial aspirations.

Some of the key changes in university operations have been: diminished government funding; increased enrolment of fee-paying overseas students; a proliferation of vocationally-oriented fee-paying postgraduate courses; decreased staff student ratios; an increasing use of electronic teaching materials; and increased entrepreneurial operations, particularly off-shore.

Decreased funding

The operations of all Australian universities during the 90s have been tailored to diminishing government funding: funding provided for actual EFTSU (equivalent full-time student unit) dropped from $11,522 in 1988 to $10,463 in 1999. University revenue from Commonwealth Government grants fell from 77.1% in 1989 to 50.8% in 1998. (AV-CC, 2000). Total Commonwealth outlays on Australian universities as a percentage of GDP have ranged from 1.6% in 1975 to 0.8% in 1999 (ABS 5510.0). The proportion of public funding to Australian tertiary education is way below the OECD countries' average. The only countries with less public investment are Korea, Japan and the United States (OECD, 2000).

Fee-paying students

During the same period, the proportion of full fee paying overseas students enrolled at Australian universities increased from 4.3% in 1985 to 9.6% in 1997 (DETYA, 1998:15). A strategy used by many universities during the 90s was to offer fee-paying postgraduate coursework programs. As government funding decreased, these courses proliferated and universities searched for discipline areas that would pay for professional development with the kudos of a university award. Contracts were established with businesses and public service departments to provide specialised training, and universities competed with each other for these contracts, sometimes for very marginal profits. Some academics thought that their university had 'sold out' by training employees for a supermarket chain.

Student:staff ratios

Student to teaching staff ratios have increased by 26% in 7 years (from 14.6:1 in 1992 to 18.3:1 in 1999). Over the same period the number of Continuing Full Time Equivalent Academic staff has increased by 392 (1.3%), and EFTSU increased by 111,141 (26%).
(Data compiled from the AV-CC website and DETYA 1999).

Teaching technologies

In order to maintain a marketing advantage or market share, most of Australia's universities have embraced electronic teaching platforms, such as WebCT, BlackBoard, or First Class. This material is a useful supplement to classroom teaching. Access to on-line web-based teaching material has been useful to some students, particularly those from non-English-speaking backgrounds and students in employment. When it replaces classroom teaching completely the quality of the learning experience is the subject of dispute. The cost of establishing and maintaining the technological infrastructure and software, in addition to the staff and student training costs make this an expensive venture. Despite the lack of data to support their case, governments have maintained a belief in the cost benefits of electronic teaching. One Minister of DEETYA thought that technology would 'change the fundamental economics of higher education ... and reform the institutions' processes.' (Vanstone 1996)

Entrepreneurialism

These data show that Australian universities have been severely affected by quite sudden reductions in government funding. There was little choice but to seek alternative sources of funding when reductions of staff numbers and programs failed to meet the financial shortfalls.

The disquiet of the public (and louder discontent expressed by university staff) emanated mainly from the reduction in public funding for universities, but also from the economic rationalist ideology imposed upon university operations. Universities had been told that all new money for research must come from industry, despite the reality that industry investment in research had fallen every year since 1995. The public perception (as reported in the media and letters columns) was that a public resource was not a private business concern, and that opportunities for the youth of Australia should not be constrained by the increasing costs of a 'public' education, whether by up-front fees or as a continuing tax debt.

A growing unease of the Australian public about the stresses and strains within Australian universities during the last decade finally reached the Senate of the Australian Parliament. On October 12, 2000, the Senate established an inquiry into 'the capacity of public universities to meet Australia's higher education needs'. The terms of reference for the Senate inquiry will address *inter alia* :

> the effect of increasing reliance on private funding and market behaviour on the sector's ability to meet Australia's education, training and research needs ... and the nature and sufficiency of independent advice to government on higher education matters, particularly having regard to the abolition of the National Board of Employment Education and Training. (Parliament of Australia Senate website)

Intended Outcomes: From unity to competition

The major reform to the Australian higher education sector, which continued to reverberate throughout the 90s, was the structural change engineered by the White (Policy) Paper of 1988. This change was calculated to contribute to the Commonwealth Government's goals for the nation by producing larger numbers of skilled graduates and by ensuring a more equitable and efficient use of available resources. Nevertheless there was considerable disagreement at the time as to whether these objectives could be attained by the structural change of the new Unified National System, particularly when funding was not increased to reflect the increased student load. (Harman and Meek 1988)

Government intentions

Following the implementation of the Unified National System, most changes in the higher education sector occurred by attrition and the gradual infusion of ideology into discourse and practices rather than discrete public policies. Extensive staff cuts to the public service department whose brief was to assist the higher education sector, and the abandonment of the higher education advisory committee left the sector operating in a knowledge vacuum.

An ideological rationale for reduction in funding generated a new language of management: efficiency, effectiveness, accountability, quality assurance, responsiveness, access, self-reliance, flexibility, provider diversity, strategic planning, mission statements, productivity trade-offs. Many academics and students were unconvinced of the effectiveness of imposing managerial structures and language onto the culture of the academy and considered the definition of students as 'clients' and the learning process as 'product' to be a false representation of the university experience.

Continuing the ideological direction, accountability measures were imposed on universities in the form of annual profiles and reports, and a plan to extend the demands on documentation by the introduction of quality audits by an Australian Universities Quality Agency. It is not unusual, or undesirable for institutions to be accountable for public money, but a cynical view of these requirements is that they were designed as a demonstration to the voting public of 'value for money' rather than a procedure to make the operations genuinely transparent . A similar philosophy of 'user-pays' (on the premiss that university education is a private benefit), increased the costs of the Higher Education Contribution Scheme (HECS), particularly to law and science students, by up to 125%.

The rhetoric of the coalition government affirmed the autonomy of universities and encouraged cooperation, yet it exerted

> considerable influence in relation to their behaviour and outcomes [encouraging] an excessive stress on entrepreneurship, the naive use of arithmetical measures of performance, an over-confidence in information technology, the mechanical application of funding formulae, and the mindless pursuit of institutional growth (Osmond 1998:3)

The changes that were forced on universities by funding 'incentives' were often put into operation by university policies, but, as has been illustrated by implementation studies, the effectiveness of policies alone is minimal unless there is commitment to the policy by those who are expected to implement it. (Pressman and Wildavsky 1984) The process of steering policies of change through a university is very complex. There is a distribution of power among many semi-autonomous bodies within universities and political machinations are a frequent occurrence in the consultative or advisory bodies as well as within the faculty structure. Hence, it was possible for individuals or small groups within universities to undertake enterprises for which they had limited competence, but which nevertheless impacted on the workloads of their colleagues. Some of the unintended outcomes of these machinations will be described later in the chapter.

Some universities formed strategic alliances with other Australian universities or with overseas partners endeavouring to capture a 'market share' of potential fee-paying students. The competence of university entrepreneurs to undertake effective assessment of contracts and financial benefits, has, in many instances, proven inadequate: agents disappeared with money; costs outweighed the financial returns; fees were paid in local currency which could not be taken out of the country; and quality assurance has been compromised.

The cooperation of universities within the Unified National System was strained under the pressure of finding alternative funding sources and competing for students.

Institutional strategies

The inaugural address of the Vice-Chancellor at Royal Melbourne Institute of Technology University (RMIT) enunciated some typical strategies used by university managements to replace diminished government funding.

> As for other tertiary institutions, entrepreneurialism has been the basis of RMIT's strategies in the 1990s. We responded to a more competitive market and falling government funding with aggressive targets and plans. We achieved significant success. By 1998 our earned income was 42% of total revenue (having increased from 17% in 1992) and compared with a national average of 32%. Our student numbers have almost tripled and the diversity of students – research, Australian undergraduate, international – has also increased. In 2000, for example, international students make up some 22% of our total student body and research students account for approximately 4.5% of our higher education students. (Dunkin 2000).

The intentions of the coalition government have been few and simple: to decrease public funding to universities; to make them more accountable for the public funding they do receive; and to make them more like corporate businesses. A similar drive was expressed by Professor Chipman, one of the Vice-Chancellors close to the Minister for DETYA, and one of the team on the West Review of Higher Education (DEETYA 1997) which produced "Learning for Life - a review of higher education financing and policy" in 1997. Chipman likened education marketing to grain trading:

> ...from a purely economic point of view knowledge is now a commodity and, as with all replaceable or renewable commodities, prices have a long-term downward trend. The efficiencies and market freedoms that come with globalization can only further accelerate this downward trend (Alcorn 2000: 3).

It was not explained exactly how this price reduction would be achieved. Salaries commonly account for 50-70% of university costs, and the establishment, maintenance and training needs for infrastructure for teaching technologies are extremely high. Professor Chipman devised a strategy of expansion for his own university (Central Queensland University) through 'joint venture "no frills" convenience-focused international campuses' in Malaysia, Singapore, Hong Kong and Fiji. He did not explain what 'frills' could be omitted, nor was the concept of quality featured in the report.

One particularly aggressive strategy adopted by universities was to increase the enrolments of off-shore students. Davis *et al.* (2000:25) reported that in 1999 there were 35 universities offering programs off-shore. Data from DETYA indicated that there were 14,036 enrolled off-shore students in 1997 and by 1999 there were 26,643. The Davis *et al.* report estimated that in March 2000 the figure was 31, 850 (ibid:105). This figure may be under-estimated, since many off-shore students are enrolled via the commercial arms of universities which are not subject to the same reporting requirements of DETYA.

The espoused rationale for offering university programs off-shore was explored in the Davis *et al.* report (Davies *et al.*, 2000: 25). The strongest motivation was the generation of additional sources of income. Other reasons offered, although ranked much lower, were the chance to increase the reputation and profile of the university; to internationalise the curriculum and integrate new teaching strategies; to recruit international students to Australian campuses; staff development opportunities; and to provide opportunities for Australian students to study off-shore.

In an attempt to 'corner the market', some universities have formed consortia with strategic partners in Australia or overseas. Others, like Southern Cross University, have a policy of "proactive opportunism" (Davies, 2000: 105).The Group of Eight (Go8) comprise prestigious and older ('sandstone') universities of Australia. This group has established a Secretariat in Canberra to develop policy and lobby the government (not always in accord with the official coalition of all university Vice-Chancellors, the AV-CC). Another group comprise the technological universities of Australia, and Universitas 21 is a consortium of eighteen universities: four from North America, six from Europe, four from Asia and four from Australasia. An original partner within Universitas 21, providing business acumen and contacts, was the Murdoch company Newscorp Limited. This company withdrew from the consortium in late 2000 and was replaced by the Thompson publishing group. The aim of this consortium is to purchase academic content and on-sell it in electronic form to students with 'badging' from prestigious universities. It is unlikely that students would have any contact with the original author of the teaching material.

The University of Melbourne is an Australian member of Universitas 21, and its Vice-Chancellor is a Director of the consortium. He prioritised his twin duties to the consortium and to his university by spending six months in London as Director of Universitas 21. The University of Melbourne had already come under the public spotlight as a result of the process of privatization of Melbourne IT (a subsidiary of the University of Melbourne) which was investigated by the Victorian Auditor-General and found wanting. The Auditor-General's report raised questions about the lack of protection of the investment of the public university. Its failure:

> …to obtain an independent authoritative valuation … was a significant deficiency in the float process, in that a valuation would have provided a benchmark against which proposals from brokers and underwriters could have been better considered. (Victorian Auditor-General's Office 2000)

The Australian Securities and Investment Commission was requested to investigate the potential improprieties of share allocations being given to members of the University Council, Directors and employees of the university and its subsidiaries. Despite their vested interests, none of these members declared a conflict of interests when undertaking their duties and approving the float. This is a case of public funding from a public university underwriting the risk-taking activities of private entities with little public accountability: socialising the risks and costs, and privatising the profits. Although individuals benefited from the float and money was reinvested in further commercial enterprises associated with the university, the staff and students of the University of Melbourne did not receive any of the promised benefits.

Unintended Consequences

The intentions of government during the 90s were achieved to a great extent. By 2000, the funding from the commonwealth government was, on average, just under 50% of university income. Universities had diversified their sources of income, although still relying heavily on return from student fees. The funds from fee-paying students and the Higher Education Contribution Scheme (HECS) provided around 35% of the budget. The universities were required to assert and document their quality processes, despite the reduced funding and reduced workforce, to 'prove' to the public that they provided value for money. Nevertheless, there were unwelcome and unintended consequences of this process which received only limited acknowledgement from government bodies and university managements, if any.

'Brain drain'

An alternative view of the disinvestment in higher education is illustrated by exit interviews with academics who have left the Australian university scene. A distinguished academic exiting from the Australian National University went public with his disgust, railing at the way:

> Australia has almost disassembled its infrastructure for holding its own in research worldwide. I don't want to spend my last productive years ... watching the further deconstruction ... it's going to take at least a human generation to get back to where we were 10 years ago. (Pockley 2000:27)

The effect of the loss of experienced academic staff is not new to Australia. It has been a long tradition for younger academics to travel the world to gain experience and credibility in the old world of Europe and the new world of Northern America. It is not part of the tradition to lose so many experienced and respected academics from involuntary redundancy or from disgruntlement or disillusionment to expatriation.

Curriculum and cultural imperialism

There appears to be some disparity within data reported by Davis *et al.* (2000). On the one hand, universities report that benefits of off-shore teaching include opportunities for staff development, for designing an international focus to the curriculum and 'developments of alternate methods of delivery' (Davis *et al.*, 2000: 27). On the other hand, only 28% of respondents reported significant adaptation of the curricula for off-shore delivery, and much of this was a translation of the language of the material, or substitution of local examples in the material (ibid:39). It is not explained what aspects of that experience are considered as staff development. Certainly the experience of staff at the Off-Campus Forum at the University of Canberra did not support the view that they had experienced staff development:

> Management should respond to frontline people's needs …we need to know when future offerings will occur so that [we] can plan … I had a week's notice to teach two subjects … I had no time to prepare properly because I had to organise childcare … I worry about the quality of teaching in these environments, but I want to keep my job … There are cultural issues that have not been resolved, about learning styles and about the content, particularly for health education … our students here are not impressed when we are away [teaching off-shore]: one of them said to me: "Isn't our money good enough?" (comments from Off-Campus Forum 7 November 2000)

The quality of off-shore teaching is portrayed as excellent by the promoters of the 'product' and spokespeople for the universities. A slightly different story is told by the Davis *et al.* report in which 'impact on local courses and students' and 'stretching of resources' are listed as negative impacts of the off-shore experience and 'attention drawn to quality issues in the delivery of educational programs and their management' is a feature listed as an unexpected outcome (Davis *et al.*, 2000:27-28). All of these issues are illustrated by observations made at the Off-Campus Forum.

Academic staff interviewees who were involved in off-shore activities gave a pessimistic picture of the quality of teaching, but felt pressured to participate, despite their misgivings. Many reported that their subjects had been committed for off-shore teaching by colleagues who had financial interests in marketing the courses. Every academic interviewed felt that there was insufficient time and resources committed to adjusting their curriculum to the new circumstances. They were concerned that they were imposing culturally inappropriate teaching material onto the off-shore students, but had no useful briefings as to how they might be more culturally sensitive. Some staff were expected to immediately acquire the technical expertise to set up on-line teaching environments, with little or no technical help. Another complaint was that staff were rewarded inequitably. Different pay rates, incorporation into 'normal' workloads, consultancy arrangements and intrusion into research or semester times were features of the arrangements. Some staff were distressed that they were abandoning their home campus students and imposing additional workload on their campus-based colleagues.

Intellectual property issues

Intellectual property rights for teaching material is fraught for off-shore operations. Authors have little control of their teaching material once it has been franchised or translated into another language. Commercial entities tend to assume ownership, but it is not clear whether the selling institution has the right to sell material created by one of their employees without their consent. This situation has generated some heat and dissatisfaction among academics. One interviewee resigned from the university distressed at having her teaching material appropriated without her knowledge or consent. At one university, supposedly secure websites were raided and teaching materials downloaded for use with off-shore students. This 'appropriation' was executed by an academic colleague, with the knowledge of the Head of School. Universities have argued that they hold copyright for teaching materials created by their employees in the course of their employment, but it is recognized (by the Copyright Amendment (Moral Rights) Act of 2000) that the employee retains moral rights to the material. In the case mentioned, the moral rights of the employees to their material were violated since the works were reproduced and treated commercially with the creators not correctly attributed.

Workload and work quality

The organization of off-shore teaching has tended to disaggregate academic skills of teaching and research, and to separate out the elements of teaching, so that curriculum writing and curriculum design may be performed separately from assessment design, feedback provision and marking. The content author may have no say in the delivery of their work. They may not even be able to maintain control of the content. Sessional academics at the home campus may be engaged to plug gaps when their colleagues are called away to teach off-shore which leaves the home campus students aggrieved and the sessional staff feeling like 'academic putty' engaged only to 'plug the gaps'.

The higher stress levels of academics at entrepreneurial universities was observed by Slaughter and Leslie (1997: 225) and also emerged in interviews with academics at several Australian universities. In one case, an academic was challenged by a proposal at short notice to use her subject as an 'off the shelf' product for Malaysian students. Her personal commitment to the quality of her teaching material forced her to work throughout the night rewriting the material to make it more appropriate for these students. Other academics told how they agonised about the quality of teaching for off-shore students: how to make their material more culturally sensitive; how to condense it into a short intensive teaching period; how to assist and supervise other staff employed to teach their material when they had only one week per semester on site; how to teach effectively through an interpreter. Other personal issues which confronted them were how to organise their domestic responsibilities when sent overseas at short notice. It was evident from the interviews that academics were not given reasonable notice that they or their teaching material would be required at a particular time, and it impacted particularly on women who had responsibility for child or elder care. Yet they were expected to respond to the consequences of the poor planning of managers further up the line. Not surprisingly, "staff overload/stretching of resources" is listed as a negative impact on the faculties in the Davis *et al*. report (2000:27).

Transparency versus commercial-in-confidence

The activities of private entities within public universities are not publicly accountable in the same detail as other aspects of university operations. The cry of 'commercial-in-confidence' is heard whenever information is requested for public accountability. The amount of public money going into ventures such as Universitias 21 is not transparent, nor is the public underwriting of some commercial arms of individual universities.

The Melbourne IT company float was mentioned above as an instance of a university management operating without proper procedures. Instead of a potential profit of some $350 million, the float realised only $78.4 million. Instead of the profits going to the public university as indicated before the float, they were allocated to a further venture with a Bio-tech consortium. However, certain individuals privy to the arrangements were able to make considerable private gains. These individuals were the underwriters and their preferred clients, including members of the Council, Directors and employees of the university and its subsidiaries. (NTEU 2000)

The Australian National University (ANU) achieved notoriety with substantial losses from its commercial arm, Anutech, along with the public resignation from its Board of a Pro Vice-Chancellor of the university. Anutech was rescued at a cost of millions of dollars by the public university at the same time that academic departments were being contracted and the Butlin Archives had their budget reduced to such an extent that it would not be able to execute its charter. The threat to these archives attracted the attention of the Senate of the Parliament of Australia, in which a resolution reminded the university of its obligations to the nation and to the use of the public funds associated with the establishment and maintenance of the archives as a national resource. Another ANU venture was to enter a contract with a group of universities and a software company to develop a particular software package. The goods were not produced according to plans and ANU discovered that they had failed to ensure that any protective penalty or escape clauses were in the contract, making them liable for the breach of contract.

The University of New England (UNE) spent a considerable amount of money trying to establish a campus in Turkey and operations in Dubai and China in the early 90s. These were ultimately unsuccessful, but UNE sank perilously into debt from which it suffered for the rest of the decade.

The University of Ballarat had a franchise agreement with the Australian Business and Technology Institute (ABTI) which failed, and $800,000 disappeared from the trust funds. Ballarat University had to absorb this cost in order to salvage its reputation.

The expeditions off-shore of senior university executive and managers to sell courses, franchise teaching material, recruit students, set up twinning arrangements with foreign institutions, or set up their own off-shore campuses have been continuous and costly. It has been, however, difficult to ascertain just how costly. Certainly there were many losses during the learning experiences. At least one university experienced agents who disappeared with the institution's money; agreements with off-shore agents or institutions did not always live up to expectations; and promises of support or conditions were not always realised.

The Davis *et al.* report (2000:106) found that the majority of off-shore operations involved off-shore partners, but that responsibilities for allocating the tasks of marketing, finances, curriculum, study location and resources, student support, academic support, teaching and assessment varied according to the country of operation and its government regulations, and the contract. The Indicative Minimum Course Fees for international students recommended by DETYA for Australian universities have not been applied to off-shore courses. Off-shore courses were specifically exempted from the guidelines. Therefore this territory remained unmapped - without ethical guidelines or regulations.

There have been other education scams reported in the newspapers. Many of them involved English language classes for overseas students, and were associated with migration and visa irregularities. The many opaque and questionable dealings of commercial enterprises of universities may have provided the impetus for a Senate investigation into the activities of commercial arms of all Australian universities. This inquiry was established with a reporting date of July 2001.

There were problems with some of the fee-paying students expecting results commensurate with their fees. This issue led to considerable controversy and debate within the Australian media throughout January 2001 following the premature release of research findings from the Australia Institute (an independent think tank), which suggested that some fee-paying students had been passed against the recommendations of subject convenors. (Contractor 2001) The threat to the reputation of Australian universities did not go unnoticed or unchallenged by the National Union of Students, the National tertiary Education Union or the Australian Vice-Chancellors' Committee who issued multiple press releases of their own. This issue became a threat to the reputation of Australian universities.

Reputation

The Davis *et al.* report (2000) found that the promotion and enhancement of university reputation was a significant factor in considerations for off-shore operations, although less significant than financial return.

An aspect of reputation that emerged from interviews was that individual academic staff and committees felt constrained by fear or loyalty to camouflage or 'patch up' some of the less worthy arrangements made by their colleagues. In one case, deception (or fraud) involving the enrolment of off-shore students was 'covered' by the committee charged with quality assurance with a stern directive to the perpetrator to 'fix it up' immediately. It was felt that the university's reputation would suffer if the incident were to be made public.

Universities have traded on their reputation: their 'brand image' as it is increasingly referred to. There is a danger that the reckless chase for a dollar could result in the loss of their main tradeable entity. Nevertheless, universities and staff continue to be placed under pressure to amend assessment and accreditation procedures in order to meet marketing and client demand. Academics have told of threats to the renewal of their contracts if they do not change results for fee-paying students, and in some cases the contentious results have been changed by academics other than the subject convenor.

Threats to the moral rights of academics concerning their teaching material have been described above. Other academics have had their research thwarted after their university accepted industry funds for research groups that wanted no competition or criticism.

The competencies of managers

The training of university managers traditionally had ill-equipped them for work in a commercial environment. There was, and perhaps still is, a level of innocence, but with limited public money at stake, this naivety cannot be afforded. Many of the off-shore operations have lost money. Some managers have likened the experience to retail trading, in that they expect to have some 'loss leaders' in order to establish a market niche in the desired location. As described above, the commercial arms of some universities have also made losses, although these may be attributed to poor business decisions rather than to a deliberate marketing strategy. It is difficult to discover what costs are associated with the commercial ventures of universities, whether they are within Australia or abroad, because of the different reporting requirements for public and private entities. It is not so difficult to grasp that the costs associated with an entourage of senior academic managers travelling abroad are likely to be substantial, and given that there are many such trips undertaken from the entrepreneurial teams of all universities, there are likely to be opportunity costs as well as the financial costs.

The timely management of projects appears to be deficient. Academic staff have described the urgency with which they are advised of their proposed contributions and the impact this has on their own workload and responsibilities. In some cases the arrangements seem to have been organised overnight, and in others where contracts were signed 10-12 months previously, the academic staff members intended to be 'at the coalface' were given less than a fortnight's advance warning. An irony of the situation is that the great bulk of courses being sold off-shore are from management faculties, and yet the management of the projects most certainly did not provide the competencies of managers as described in first year management texts (eg strategic management, communication, organizational astuteness, negotiation, team leadership and empowerment, customer orientation, financial and resource management, systems perspectives, etc).

Good management would ask about the long term future of operations which had been financially successful for some institutions: would the operations continue to be financially successful if there were a change to the Australian dollar exchange rate? From the mid-90s education exports were cheap, but would they still be in demand when they were not so cheap? What would be the long-term effect of Australia signing the General Agreement on Trade and Services (GATS) which would open up national education systems to international providers and allow private access to our limited research funds? Would the educational colonisers of the developing world be colonised themselves?

The 'Learning Organisation' and its Future

There are lessons to be learned from these stories. One of these lessons is suggested in the Victorian Auditor-General's Report on the privatization of Melbourne IT:

> These considerations include risk management principles to be adopted, the need to obtain independent valuations from other parties, avoidance of any conflict of interest when persons employed in the public sector benefit from share allocations and consideration of alternative methods of sale to achieve the best outcome from the privatisation of public sector companies. (Victorian Auditor-General's Office 2000)

Lessons from the Davis *et al.* report (2000:121) are to establish processes which provide an explicit decision-making model covering strategic, educational and business dimensions; to select overseas partners in a transparent and documented process with a contract that covers the management of the relationship, measures to ensure and maintain reputation and integrity of culture; to have explicit quality assurance agreements which are resourced and reviewed; and to have a teaching and learning strategy covering entry standards, academic regulations, assessment and awards, ethical and equitable treatment of students and approval processes for courses.

The Vice-Chancellor of RMIT, appointed in 2000, made an impassioned argument for the role of the public university, expounding a theory that economic rationalism has prevented the Australian universities from performing their full community and social role. In her inaugural speech, she announced that she intended to lead her university away from entrepreneurialism and towards innovation:

> ...to continue to deepen [RMIT's] traditional expertise and broaden its integrative, collaborative capabilities [and also make a commitment to the staff, students, industry partners and communities for valuing them, helping all to reach their full potential] releasing creativity, knowledge and innovativeness (Dunkin 2000)

For a healthy higher education sector, the establishment of collegial or legislative structures could constrain those who take advantage of gaps in the system to advance their own interests at the expense of their colleagues.

The 'grey' areas between the public and private domains should be clarified and regulated. Some of the issues to be resolved include: ownership of assets; transfer of resources between domains; assumptions for the repayment of debt; and procedures for conflict resolution; and public accountability.

Some guidelines already exist. The AVCC has produced A Code of Ethical Practice in the Provision of Education to International Students by Australian Universities (1998), and the Ministerial Council on Education, Employment, Training and Youth Affairs (MCEETYA) has a Code of Practice in the Provision of International Education and Training Services (1994). Guidelines for ethical operation of other business enterprises would be a welcome addition.

The flow of fee-paying students into Australia and the flow-ons from university purchases and taxes provide windfalls to government coffers which are not acknowledged by government. A report on the returns to investment in higher education indicated that there was a net gain to government via taxes and other gains from the university sector of $2.7billion in 1997-1998 (excluding research). If these calculations are correct, it would seem that the government receives a very healthy return for its investment in universities as the estimated average rate of return is about 11%. (Borland *et al.* 2000:4)

Maintaining the essential attributes of a university education

It will be important to the future of Australia's universities to address the tension between the 'university in a suitcase' approach to education packaged for off-shore and on-shore students and the broader teaching, research and scholarship ideally practised in the Australian universities.

Accommodating cultural differences

There will be difficult and sensitive issues to address, such as the credibility and respect due to women lecturers in some countries in which women have traditionally played a subservient role. Differing perspectives of pedogogy lead to tensions when students expect lecturers to declaim, and lecturers expect to 'facilitate independent student learning'. Students who expect that fees paid will guarantee an award, will have to be made aware of the roles and responsibilities of both students and staff in the learning process.

Maintaining professional standards

There is a danger that Quality Assurance models, applied indiscriminately, will force diverse universities into a one-size-fits-all model. There is a fine line to be negotiated between quality achievement and quality measurement. Universities must resist the establishment of virtual 'call centres' staffed by an academic under-class performing academic piece-work in an electronic teaching environment. The moral rights of academics to their teaching material (in print or electronic formats) should be recognized and observed in practice, and their professional judgements of student achievement should be respected.

In some universities, university managements have used a corporate model of governance, denying a voice to academic staff. The clash of cultures (managerial and collegial) which alienates and marginalises academics has deprived these universities of a valuable source of knowledge and skills. Leadership will be required from within the academic body to use the structures and organizations available to them to claim and maintain their professional integrity.

Responsibilities

It is the responsibility of the higher education sector to educate governments and the community and to provide leadership and direction for the future of universities: to be proactive rather than reactive; and to seek innovative and cooperative ways of dealing with challenges for the sector. As one informant stated: "The whole discourse of learning at university has become public." It is up to the universities and their staff to participate in this discourse, not to remain aloof from it. For their survival, universities need to make their outcomes intentional.

Universities have a social responsibility to provide a 'real' university education, which includes the domains of affective learning and cognitive learning as well as the learning of vocational skills. Students need the attributes of critical thinking, analytical reasoning, communication and interpersonal skills, awareness of and sensitivity to cultural differences, and problem-solving skills in order to be good global citizens. It would be helpful if governments and university managers also acquired and practised these same skills.

References

ABS (no date) *Expenditure on Education: Australia.* ABS Catalogue 5510.0 various editions

Alcorn, G. (2000) "Feepaying 'shoppers' will force down prices Chipman argues", *Campus Review,* 10(46):3.

AV-CC (1998) *Code of Ethical Practice in the Provision of Education to International Students by Australian Universities.* Canberra: AV-CC.

AV-CC (2000)a *AV-CC Key Statistics.* Canberra: AV-CC.

AV-CC (2000)b *Our Universities Our Future: An AV-CC Discussion Paper.* Canberra: AV-CC.

Borland, J., Dawkins, P., Johnson, D. and Williams, R. (eds) (2000) *Returns to Investment in Higher Education.* Melbourne: The Melbourne Economics of Higher Education Research Program Report No 1.

Contractor, A. (2001) "Quest for cash: how unis cut standards", *Sydney Morning Herald,* 8 January.

Davis, D., Olsen, A. and Bohm, A. (eds) (2000) *Transnational Education.Providers, Partners and Policy. Challenges for Australian Institutions Offshore.* Brisbane: IDP Education Australia Limited.

DEETYA (1997) *Learning for Life. Review of higher education financing and policy.* Canberra: AGPS.

DETYA (1998) *Higher Education Statistics.* Canberra: AGPS.

DETYA (1999) *Selected Higher Education Finance Statistics.* Canberra: AGPS.

Dunkin, R. (2000) RMIT University: from entrepreneurial university to innovative university. Melbourne: RMIT University.

Harman, G. and Meek, V.L. (eds) (1988) *Australian Higher Education Reconstructed?: analysis of the proposals and assumptions of the Dawkins green paper.* Armidale: Department of Administrative and Higher Education Studies.

MCEETYA (1994) *Code of Practice in the Provision of International Education and Training Services.* Melbourne: RMIT University.

NTEU Media Release (2000) "Melbourne IT - How NOT to float a public asset".Melbourne: NTEU.

OECD (2000) *Education at a Glance: OECD Indicators 2000 edition.* Paris: OECD.

Osmond, W. (1998) "Karmel warns of 'seeds of decay'", *Campus Review* 8(1):3.

Parliament of Australia Senate (2000) Current Committee Inquiries – 39th Parliament.

Pockley, P. (2000) "Another team down the brain drain", *The Australian Higher Education,* 29 November.

Pressman, J. L. and Wildavsky, A. (eds) (1984) 3rd edn. *Implementation, How great expectations in Washington are dashed in Oakland*. Berkeley: University of California Press.

Slaughter, S. and Leslie, L. L. (eds) (1997) *Academic Capitalism. Politics, Policies and the Entrepreneurial University*. Baltimore: The Johns Hopkins University Press.

Vanstone the Hon, A. (1996) An address to the Business/Higher Education Round Table Annual General Meeting by the Minister for Employment, Education, Training and Youth Affairs.

Victorian Auditor-General's Office (2000). *Report on Ministerial Portfolios*. Victoria: Auditor General's Office.

7 A Comedy of Manners: Quality and power in higher education

Louise Morley

Setting the Stage

In this chapter I examine the impact of technologies for quality assurance on the affective domain. Quality assurance procedures are influencing organizational cultures, academic identities and pedagogical relations in higher education today. The central legitimating idea of higher education is changing. Higher education is being repositioned as an industry, rather than as a social institution (Gumport, 2000). Production metaphors, borrowed from industry, are now central to higher education discourse. In Britain, the academy is undergoing material and cultural transformations and is engulfed in a process of commodification. The rise of academic management, together with the rise of consumerism and political concerns with the exchange and use value of higher education have produced new professional priorities and dissonances.

This is a position paper. I would like to state that I am not opposed to accountability, nor do I embrace romantic notions of a former golden age of autonomy and collegiality in the academy. So-called university autonomy often reinforced exclusionary practices by enabling gendered, racialised networks of power to flourish, unchecked by external agencies (Morley, 1999). However, I wish to problematise the performativity that forms the basis of quality audits in higher education, in Britain, and increasingly within an international context. I would support Readings' view (1996: 18) that there is a need to separate accountability and accounting. The latter is constructing organizational realities and creating pressure and mistrust that have inter and intrapersonal consequences.

I am interested in the impact of the quality assurance movement in higher education on the micropolitics of the academy. Quality procedures require the activation and exploitation of a range of feelings such as guilt, loyalty, desire, greed, shame, anxiety and responsibilization, in the service of effectiveness and point-scoring. I wish to argue that these are having an impact on social relations in the academy.

Quality assurance is a regime of power. It also exposes the micropolitics of power in organizations in a particularly potent way. The affective dimensions of performing quality means that it is also a comedy of manners, in which all actors, like characters in a Jane Austen novel, play carefully choreographed roles.

My argument is that all the players are sceptical about the rules of the game and yet all go ahead with a ludic engagement to appease the forces of propriety, and of funding. Whereas the conceptual framework of continuous improvement can challenge routinization at work, it can also be perceived as a regulatory device. Power is relayed via the public estimation of value and worth. But, as in many systems of domination and oppression, the performativity required can create cognitive dissonance.

Post-positivist analysis has demonstrated the futility of even attempting to locate and transfer a truth of organizational life or the social world (Maynard and Purvis, 1993) . Yet, the quality machinery, with its many relay points of power in the form of external agencies, budgets, naming and shaming purports to offer some certainty and exactitude in what is perceived as an increasingly chaotic and expanding system. Quality assurance is positioned in opposition to the potential chaos of massification.

In Britain, there are currently two major accounting systems. The quality of research productivity is evaluated every four to five years via the funding council's (HEFCE) Research Assessment Exercise (RAE). This results in the grading of subject areas on a one to five point scale, with '5 star' denoting excellent world class performance. Research funding is allocated to institutions in direct proportion to the score achieved.

The second accounting system is the evaluation of teaching and learning by the Quality Assurance Agency (QAA). This process is known as Subject Review and consists of a panel of assessors from the academic community visiting subject areas in higher education institutions and grading them on 6 aspect of provision: teaching, learning and assessment; learning resources; student progress and achievement; quality management and enhancement; student support and guidance; and curriculum development and organization. The emphasis is on 'the student experience', with academics and mangers positioned as service providers. There are three primary sources of evidence: the organization's Critical Self-Assessment Document plus vast amounts of documentation about courses, procedures, regulations, practices etc. - all set out in a baseroom often the size of a modest library. Secondly, there is observation of teaching sessions, and thirdly, meetings with students (past and present), employers, academic and administrative staff. The review visit lasts four days, with the reviewed and reviewers frequently working through the night to read and produce yet further evidence to repudiate accusations of deficiency. Each of the 6 aspects is graded on a 1-4 scale, giving an overall 'best' score of twenty four, though the QAA tries to discourage institutions from simply presenting a total score. The scores are ritualistically delivered on the last day of the visit and there are no rights of appeal. As yet, there are no direct funding consequences, but the scores go into the public domain.

I contend that the two major accounting systems in higher education in Britain today are creating a pincer movement of fear and alienation. These could have detrimental long term effects on the academy. The application of quality technologies to the evaluation of research productivity and learning and teaching in the academy has been politically justified in relation to accountability, value for money, consumer empowerment, marketization, enhancing productivity, maintaining and enhancing academic standards in a rapidly enlarging sector and a globally competitive market. Recent research demonstrates (Coate *et al.*, 2000) that the increased regulation, surveillance and bureaucracy associated with quality assurance are being experienced as rituals of power and domination by UK academics.

The conceptual framework of continuous improvement can challenge routinization at work. However, it can also be perceived as a regulatory device. Numerous questions are being posed about loss of academic autonomy (Peters, 1992), the effectiveness of audits (Underwood, 1998) and the values and belief systems behind these interventions (Morley, 2000). Performance indicators and taxonomies of effectiveness are often seen as socially constructed floating signifiers (Ball, 1999; Morley and Rassool, 1999). While purporting to provide consumers with a basis for selection, performance indicators also provide powerful managerial imperatives. Hence, it is debatable whether interventions such as the QAA's Subject Review and HEFCE's RAE *measure* organizational realities, or in fact serve to *construct* them.

On the other hand, there are strong arguments in favour of holding an elite professional group and dominant organizations of knowledge production to account, particularly in relation to equity, student services, academic decision-making and access issues (Luke, 1997). In a period of changing student demographics, it is pertinent to ask whether the old elite systems and personnel can respond effectively to diversifying student needs and profiles. However, it could be argued that quality assurance processes can promote equity and social inclusion by making procedures and practices more transparent and calculable (Morley, 2000). There is a view that procedures designed to monitor and protect quality operate to reprofessionalise and modernise an elite group, rather than deprofessionalise it. The challenge by external agencies to a profession's routinized practices and claims to expertise and authority can have a salutary effect on the profession, which may emerge the stronger for the experience. Feminists have long argued that there is a pressing need to deconstruct and reconstruct the academy and to challenge patriarchal and social class privilege (Morley, 1999). However, it is debatable whether there can be an eclectic affinity between feminism, equity and quality assurance in the academy.

Higher education has largely been incorporated into the managerial state. For many, new managerialism, as a form of organizational practices, narratives and values is infused with notions of hegemonic (and somewhat dated) masculinities (Deem, 1998). Some of the discursive space opened up by feminist academics, such as process-oriented pedagogy, is at risk of closure in the stampede towards measurable outcomes and certainties. In the context of Subject Review, every taught session has to have stated learning outcomes, so negotiation, dialogue and the decentring of authority are pedagogically too risky and they could entail deviation from teacher-prescribed boundaries. Furthermore, there are fears that feminism is being co-opted into quality assurance. The process skills of feminist pedagogy are being recycled into human resource management. Deem (1998) found that feminist managers are often recruited for their interpersonal skills and that these are applied to making new managerial regimes and quality assurance procedures more acceptable. I have found that these skills are also used to repair some of the damage to colleagues caused by the unpleasantness of quality assurance techniques. For example, it is not uncommon for academics to be threatened with redundancy, or have their contracts terminated if they are considered to be research inactive. Subject Review can also an abusive and aggressive experience, with the organization and individuals structurally positioned as guilty until proven innocent. The training that Subject Reviewers receive does not sensitise them to the affective domain. Hence bullying, rudeness, sexism, unskilled, aggressive chairing of crucial meetings, are easily incorporated into the methodology to unearth organizational and pedagogical weaknesses.

What a Performance!

Current procedures for quality assurance in higher education in Britain suggest that it is possible is to capture and encode the complexities of academic life into at- a-glance league tables of excellence (Bowden, 2000). The research sophistication in the academy can easily expose how institutional averages are incomplete and statistically unstable over a prolonged period (Berry, 1999). However, academics have to operate without and within the discourse (Henkel, 2000). Gewirtz *et al.* (1995) described the process of educationalists negotiating two or more sets of values and cultures as 'bilingualism'. Different linguistic codes are invoked in appropriate contexts to represent different values and priorities. Indeed, the financial and market consequences of non-conforming are so severe that it is better to polish performances to perfection. But, as in many systems of domination and oppression, the performance can create cognitive dissonance as it is on top of considerable resentment and disaffection. The process of making tacit practices explicit requires an element of performativity and textual representation that is temporally and emotionally demanding and potentially demoralising (Jeffrey and Woods, 1996). Prescribing what must be recorded and how, is itself a system of power and governmentability. Sennett (1998) suggests that there is a mathematics of fear. Academics and managers have to decode, calculate and identify risk and reconstruct themselves textually in what is sometimes seen as creative retrospective archiving.

Professional relations are also at risk. There has been a manufacturing of consent. I described above how Subject Review is carried out by peers and co-ordinated by a government agency. Outsourcing to intermediary bodies is problematic (Neave, 1998). The use of external agents who are supposed to be temporally and spatially apart from the organization they are evaluating is divisive. Yet the auditors and assessors are drawn from the same professional group that is being assessed. There is a simultaneous loss and imposition of boundaries. There are also issues of classification, as the organization is asked to produce a reading of itself in the form of a Self-Assessment Document. This is then scrutinised by the reviewers who reclassify the organization in relation to their 'findings'. To some extent, this could be an example of capillary power and the way in which the profession has been seduced into policing itself. Neave (1998: 279) asks if the intermediary bodies are:

> ... emanations of central authority reaching out and down or are they extensions of the university world groping up and back?

Either way, critical questions about incorporation, resistance and interest representation are rasied. For example, in a market economy it is not always in an organization's interests to share information about strategies, negative experiences, anger over poor scores with competitors. Hence each organization must learn and relearn how to respond and perform in relative isolation. This minimises possibilities for resistance and lends authenticity to the grading systems.

The Aliens are Coming!

The quality movement is creating considerable fear about the public labelling of organizations and ensuing funding advantages. It is fostering competition, resentments and anxiety. Employment regimes have been reconstructed to promote the performance indicators of research productivity. For example, academics are increasingly placed on short-term contracts partly in order to eliminate time-serving complacency and generate motivation for writing and research. Scholarship is rapidly being defined as funded research with clear economic benefits to the organization. For some, the imperative to perform and produce within an alien and arbitrary signifier of worth can contribute to a corrosion of character that renders all activity meaningless (Sennett, 1998). De Groot (1997: 134) characterised academic work in the 1990s in terms of 3 themes: 'alienation, anxiety and accountability'. By alienation she means:

> ... the growing sense of separation between work and personal identity experienced by many academics and to the experience of loss of control or even influence over many aspects of teaching, learning and research (De Groot, 1997: 134).

Ball (1999: 11) argues that alienation is a result of 'inauthentic practices and relationships'. Caught between the state, employers, industry, student/consumers and the wider economic concepts of globalization, employability, international competitiveness, universities and academics in Britain are struggling with a hybrid identity that demoralises and confuses.

Suspending Disbelief

In the process of Subject Review the formerly vaunted product of the university - critical knowledge - must be suspended, while complex processes are distilled into unproblematic categories and classifications. These are then subjected to a one-way evaluative gaze that eliminates any possibility for dialogue and challenge. While one justification for the quality and standards movement is to prevent the dumbing down of higher education, it could also be argued that the quality procedures themselves represent a major form of dumbing down. It is now too dangerous to take pedagogical, epistemological or managerial risks. Everything must be knowable within the limitations of the quality taxonomies. There are dangers of organizational isomorphism and orthodoxy as vastly different institutions, without co-terminous aims, are all evaluated on the same scales.

Whether the object of inquiry is research productivity or excellence in teaching and learning, challenges exist as to how to represent one's organization textually and grammartocentrically in relation to pre-ordained, non-negotiable, socially constructed signifiers of excellence. Qualitative process are represented in material quantities. Significant rewards both for individuals and organizations follow from the effective skills of self-presentation and packaging (Broadfoot, 1998).

The university is, according to Barnett (2000: 6), 'a world open to infinite interpretability'. Yet within the quality movement, vast amounts of tacit and dynamic assumptions and practices have to be repackaged to fit the requirements of reified taxonomies and classifications. For Barnett, this raises a major contradiction in so far as the surveillance and performance involved in quality assurance represents a form of closure. This is in stark contrast to globalization, postmodernity and post-fordism which force openness of space, diversity and a reduction of boundaries.

The morality of quality can mean that any questioning of performance indicators is positioned as a resistance to public accountability, or as Readings (1996: 26) suggests 'a refusal to be questioned according to the logic of contemporary capitalism'. The higher education system in Britain is now the most audited in the world. The regulation and surveillance is on a scale that is becoming increasingly unacceptable to British academics (Coate *et al.*, 2000). Cowen (1996: 251) argues:

> In the British case..., the state has created a double market: external and internal. Double surveillance is occurring. The universities have to link with agencies outside of the university (such as industry, business and research councils) to supplement their income and the state has created, through its national evaluation system. mechanisms within which universities compete with each other, for extra financial rewards from the state for good performance.

Performance and performativity are now what are valued and evaluated. The market is the driving force for the construction of performativity. Scores have exchange and cash value in today's education market. They purport to reduce risk and provide information for consumers to make so-called informed choices. Power is relayed via the public estimation of value and worth (Neave, 1998). There is also a 'performative internationalism' (Cowen, 1996: 255). In the context of globalization, quality scores travel rapidly across national, organizational and disciplinary boundaries. A high score in the Subject Review could mean the recruitment of more high fees paying international students. A high Research Assessment Exercise grade has actual cash value and operates like a kite mark to reassure research agencies and potential research students. Hence, organizations comply and conform because the penalties and rewards are so high.

The Comfort of Commodities

Budgets for higher education institutions are dependent on compliance with policy objectives and are increasingly output-related (Middleton, 2000). Quality assurance, while being politically driven and framed, requires system-specific, common-value measures which enable products to be compared as commodities This is the ideology posing as a technology discourse (Ball, 1995). Government monitoring of micro practices is influencing the values and content of higher education. Higher education is becoming more overtly identified as a sub-system of regional and national economies (Coate, 2000). Higher education is measured against the commodity value of its outputs. In a risk society, all stakeholders seem to need endless reassurances. Funding agencies want evidence of a return on their investment and employers are calling for guarantees of 'zero defect' in their newly-employed graduates. Consequently, the employability of graduates has become a central goal for higher education.

Assessment of individuals and organizations is increasingly being seen as the central mechanism for monitoring and enhancing quality. It is questionable whether quality is being enhanced or standards measured. It is more a matter of redefining standards in terms of economic commodity values (Broadfoot, 1998). Barnett (2000: 2) argues that the modern university was based on three ideas: the Kantian concept of reason, the Humboltian idea of culture and now the techno-bureaucratic notion of excellence. Excellence itself is embedded in power relations and, despite the fact that Tony Blair stated that he wanted excellence to be the norm (DfEE, 1998), excellence is dependent on hierarchies, hegemonies and situated judgements of worth. Excellence has become a 'hoorah' word which, as Broadfoot (1998: 162) indicates has 'the capacity for almost universal legitimation'. It also 'justifies the differentiated allocation of both prestige and financial resources'.

In the context of commodification, teaching is now very much a service industry. The customer care revolution has hit the academy. As we saw above, a central element of the Quality Assurance Agency's Subject Review is the concept of the 'student experience'. Students' experiences are now more firmly located within the framework of customer care and consumer entitlements such as course handbooks, student charters and opinion surveys. A central question is whether students can fully evaluate the quality of education they are receiving. Like surgery and legal advice, it is difficult for purchasers to evaluate at the point of delivery. Evaluation is often more related to the quality of service by which it is provided (Scott, 1999). So, what is important now are features such as turnaround time for marking essays, access to tutors, transparent assessment procedures etc. As Meadmore (1998) notes, the corollary of this approach is that *what* is being taught or researched becomes less significant than that it should be done 'excellently', and that this is in fact what has happened in higher education.

Production processes and quality assurance technologies from private sector industries are being applied to education. Education in Britain is becoming Japanised in so far as production-line techniques evocative of total quality management in Nissan car factories are seen as appropriate to the public services (Morley and Rassool, 1999; 2000). Scott (1999: 194) argues that:

> Universities are no longer to be regarded primarily as institutions dedicated to research and education for the good of society as a whole so much as businesses.

It is questionable whether universities were ever entirely dedicated to the good of society, or indeed whether they represented an elite, unaccountable system. However, the elitism continues in a new form. The expansion of student numbers in Britain (from a participation rate of 15 to 32 per cent in ten years) has led to further educational stratification of students both within their universities and subsequently outside the system, by employers, and other stakeholders (Cowen, 1996). Now, it is not the title of the degree, but the institution in which it was obtained (and its place in national league tables for research productivity and quality teaching and learning) that is supposed to carry cachet.

However, there are some major contradictions. League Tables and organizational scores are supposed to influence consumer choice. Yet, in an evidence-based policy climate, with concerns about best value, there is surprisingly little evidence to suggest that quality audits are either providing information or enhancing quality and productivity. According to Segal Quince Wicksteed (1999) only 5 per cent of employers currently consult QAA reports for recruitment targeting and only 12 per cent of student applicants consider QAA reports to be the most important source of information about quality. As Yorke (1999: 18) indicates:

In the UK, only a very small proportion of the higher education provision has been found to be unsatisfactory, which raises the question of whether a rather large and heavy sledgehammer of peer-review has been used to crack a relatively small nut.

The cost of quality assurance is difficult to estimate. The official figure is 0.1 per cent of the HEFCE's teaching budget dedicated to Subject Review (Yorke, 1999). This excludes the costs incurred by institutions and the substantial opportunity costs for staff allocated to extensive preparations. When the whole organization is the unit of analysis, vast amounts of time are used ensuring ownership and information flow. So, in a policy context of best value, it is questionable what value the QAA Subject Review and RAE add. Their reliability as forms of assessment is also questionable. In Subject Review, there is an assumed causative link between teaching and learning, with an assumption that excellent teaching is followed by good learning. The whole exercise is redolent with doubtful assumptions about causative mechanisms such as that good quality student support = high student completions. Such mechanistic models socially decontextualise learning in unrealistic ways. Explanations for success and failure are frequently located in the organizational context rather than in the socio-economic terrain. For example, increasing student poverty could have detrimental effects on completion rates. However, the league table score becomes a truth and a frozen moment becomes reified for several years. Therefore a high score become the focus of desire in many organizations. This desire structures many of the priorities and activities in the academy today and permeates social and professional relationships.

At Your Service: Changing social relations in the academy

The micro-level of experience can often be where the effects of power are felt (Morley, 1999). I wish to argue that the quality assurance movement in higher education is having profound effects on the micropolitics of the academy. It has long been argued that there is a powerful affective impact of assessment in so far as it influences confidence, self-esteem and identity (Broadfoot, 1998) and Subject Review is, of course, a form of assessment. Assessment also translates dominant discourses into broad social understandings and specific practices (Bernstein, 1996). The reconstruction of students as consumers or purchasers of the educational product, alongside the policy and funding imperative for universities and academics to provide employable products and services (Dearing, 1997), has had a significant impact on social and pedagogical relations in the academy. Ostensibly, this is a form of consumer empowerment and encoding of entitlements in the face of dominant and dominating organizations of knowledge production. However, once these changing relations of service and servitude are deconstructed, it does not take long to begin to identify gendered, classed and racialised processes at play. I argue that these changing social relations represent another manifestation of abusive power relations rather than a victory for democratization.

New managerialism and the resulting dispersal of responsibility and technicization of human capacities (Barry, Osborne and Rose, 1996) have created new power relationships in the academy. The risk society has resulted in the decline of trust in professional conduct. The construct of trustworthiness is being associated with competence and reliability. Academics, traditionally constructed as producers of knowledge, have been discursively reconstructed as 'consumers of resources' (Barnett, 2000: 6). However, academics are also consumed objects who are there both to sell and mediate commodities and services.

Quality, in the public services, invariably relates to performance, standards and output, rather than to inputs such as academic employment conditions. New organizational regimes demand considerable temporal investment and emotional labour. Quality procedures require the activation and exploitation of a range of feelings such as guilt, loyalty, desire, greed, anxiety and responsibilization, in the service of effectiveness and point-scoring (Ozga and Walker, 1999). These feelings are easily activated and manipulated in today's fear-laden academic culture.

Challenging Students: Is the customer always right?

I work in an RAE rated 5* organization. This is the highest score for research excellence. This can be something of a mixed blessing where pedagogical relations are concerned. Baudrillard (1998: 61). noted how 'the sign or mark of distinction is always both a positive and a negative difference'. Working in the area of postgraduate higher education studies I frequently find myself teaching and supervising colleagues from other universities who are following master's or doctoral programmes. They have high expectations and want 'excellence' demonstrated at every opportunity. In a market relationship, students can be unforgiving if there is ever anything that is not to their liking. It is increasingly risky to invite guest speakers, to promote student presentations, to introduce anything or anyone new. Students' views are constantly sought and committed to posterity in the form of evaluation sheets which are discussed in senior level committees and made available to the QAA. Student evaluation is like a perpetual referendum, with the academy constantly on trial. In this context, quality is about gaining approval, rather than challenging certainties. This represents a major shift in the role of the intellectual and contradicts Said's (1994) view that intellectuals should fulfil an abrasive function, challenging rigidities of thought.

> Least of all should an intellectual be there to make his/her audiences feel good: the whole point is to be embarrassing, contrary, even unpleasant (1994: 9).

In the current context of quality assurance, the type of behaviour advocated by Said could result in a grievance procedure.

I explore next what I consider a critical incident, one that offers a wealth of micropolitical data and illustrates the arguments above. In one MA session, a student, who was also a colleague from professional education in a new university, gave a presentation to thirty or more students ostensibly about changing values in higher education. He produced a binaried chart to demonstrate the caring, progressive values of the organization where he worked compared with what he perceived as the negative traditionalism and disembodied knowledge of the organization where he studied. The organization where he worked was represented as student-focused and accessible to formerly marginalised students. The organization where he studied was represented as research-focused, elitist and exclusionary. This was evocative of Bernstein's observations on the marketplace in higher education (1996: 74):

> Those at the top, or near the top, of this hierarchy may maintain their position more by attracting and holding key academic stars than by changing their pedagogic discourse according to the exigencies of the market...On the other hand, those institutions which are much less fortunate in their position in the stratification...will be more concerned with the marketing possibilities of their pedagogic discourse.

The student presented no evidence, or substance for any of his truth claims. I mentioned, that, as a feminist academic, I could not relate to his assertions about a homogenised 'they'/other who all promoted and subscribed to disembodied, value-free knowledge. It transpired that he was basing his claims on one lecture by a senior male academic in the institution in which he studied. He had simply not seen or registered any of the pedagogical interactions he had had with 'less senior' teachers. He rounded off by reminding students that they should express their discontents in their evaluation sheets as in the run up to Subject Review because 'now is the year to get them!' Many of the students were embarrassed and confused, while one or two took up the invitation with a vengeance. Some of the student evaluations had the vitriol of poison-pen letters. However, in the over-audited culture of the university today, the customer is construed as always being right and their assertions, however unreconstructed and unsubstantiated have validity simply because they represent an authentic 'student voice'.

After having had the opportunity to think more clearly about the incident, I maintain that the quality culture is having a profound impact on relations between students and staff and between different academic organizations and colleagues. The quality machinery is labelling organizations and individuals by association. There are profound ontological issues at stake in the scoring of organizations. The culture of scrutiny implies deficiency and incompetence. Quality audits represent a type of organizational trauma. A low score is a badge of degradation. Within a performance culture to gain a low score is to be addressed and labelled injuriously.

Naming is a significant aspect in the constitution of identity. Butler (1997: 2) observed that: 'to be called a name is one of the first forms of injury that one learns'. The labelling of universities iterates and inscribes the discourses in a complex chain of signification. Audit and the ensuing certification and grading means that private in-house matters are now in the public domain. The results of audit provide a reified reading, which becomes a truth. For universities at the bottom of the league tables, identity is a form of negative equity. The damage to reputation becomes an attack on the competence of every organizational member. For those at the top, there is an artificial halo effect which invites the projection of a range of positive attributes on to their services. These identities have cash value in the market place.

The labelling of academic organizations frequently corresponds with the social class of the different constituencies. Elitism is reinforced and quality accolades are socially decontextualised. Some of the universities with high RAE scores have the lowest percentage of working class students. For example, between 1972 and 1993 the independent school proportion of the entry at Oxbridge increased from 38 to 57 per cent (McCrum, 1998). Major (1999) cited how the London School of Economics has more applications from the top socio-economic classes, with just under 70 per cent of UK admitted students from professional and managerial backgrounds in 1997-8. By contrast some of the new universities with lower RAE scores, such as Wolverhampton, Central Lancashire and Thames Valley have less than one third from that social group. It is worth pointing out that some of the most elite organizations also have the worst record on gender equity. For example, Cambridge did not allow women graduates full status until 1947. Even today only 6 per cent of Cambridge professors are women (compared to a national average of 9 per cent). Even at lecturer level, women only make up 15 per cent compared with 20 per cent nationally (Cole, 1998). While nationally, women students are beginning to gain more first class honours degrees than men, the reverse is true for Cambridge (Leman and Mann, 1999).

Quality assurance is producing new hierarchies and exclusions reminiscent of social class stratification. Micropolitical theory (Morley, 1999) demonstrates how it is possible to see complex macro power relations in everyday social interactions and processes. In the case of the angry students, it was the 5* label that was provoking them. The mark of distinction was being experienced as a boast, a put-down, a standard which had to be constantly attacked and mistrusted.

This critical incident exemplifies some of the damage caused to social and pedagogical relations by markets, competition and hierarchies. The student had been labelled as inferior by the positioning and status of his organization and in return he wanted to wound. As a female teacher, I provided a safe space for him to rehearse his anger. The mother/teacher elision (Shaw, 1995) meant that I had to behave rationally and coolly, offering unconditional regard and attention while he threw a series of poisoned darts in my direction. (Was this a case of marketising social relations or socialising market relations?) The Comedy of Manners is everywhere. His voice represented an example of the authentic 'student experience'. This raises questions about what forms of knowledge and values are being supported by the quality movement in higher education. James (1995: 452) argues that 'an adequate understanding of student experience is fundamentally a sociological problem'. The affective domain and equity issues do not feature in the evaluation of quality. If students are unhappy, that must be symptomatic of poor organizational inputs, rather than a consequence of what is happening for them e.g. competition, internalised oppression, anxiety, poverty.

Quality, Equity and Change

I wish to reiterate that I am not opposed to accountability. Universities should be asked some very awkward questions by funders and wider constituencies of policy-makers, employers and students about why the working classes, or socio-economic groups 4 and 5 are so under-represented in the student body. Appointment panels, senates and the state should be asked why, after several reports and research studies (Bett, 1999; Bird, 1996; Hansard Society, 1990; Modood and Acland, 1998) there are so still so few women professors or black academics at any level. Questions need to be raised about elite recruitment and retention procedures in universities at the top of the league tables. There are innumerable issues that should feature in quality audits, including: facilities for students with disabilities (Hurst, 1999; Riddell, 1999); why so many students are unable to complete their courses, despite all the organizational interventions to support them. The 1994/5 Higher Education Statistical Agency's (HESA) statistic indicated that in excess of 32,000 students withdrew from study. This is about 5.4 per cent of enrolments (Yorke, 2000). Furthermore, questions need to be raised about what universities are doing to contribute to the eradication of violence, poverty, disease, environmental disaster and social exclusion in a macro context. Quality should also be applied to employment conditions, with serious consideration of occupational stress, low morale and 'brain drain' in a micro context.

The quality agenda is attempting to deconstruct and reconstruct the academy. Other forces, such as feminist theory, have also attempted to do this (Morley, 1999). For me, a key question is whether quality assurance and the hegemonic notion of 'best practice' incorporate understanding of the affective domain and critiques of discrimination, marginalization and monoculturism. It is still unclear if there is a possibility of forging a creative alliance between feminism and quality assurance by challenging the domination of elite practices. It is uncertain whether it is possible to effect equity changes without endorsing unacceptable old ways of doing things or collude with new forms of technicism.

De Groot (1997: 139) notes that:

> More generally one should note that the resistance of much of the academic community to the new culture of scrutiny and accountability combines valid criticism of that culture with opposition to precisely the scrutiny to which feminists and others troubled by the monocultural inequities of the academy have long wished to subject it.

While quality technologies offer the promise of some reliable indicators in a complex and potentially chaotic social world, the quality discourse in higher education is riven with contradictions and discontinuities. For example, while diversity is celebrated in terms of changing the student composition, vastly differentiated organizations are evaluated on the same continuum. Within New Labour's 'beacon' approach which advocates allocating resources to excellent exemplars for others to follow, there are overt and tacit assumptions about transferable best practice. The elite universities have the highest representation of students from the top socio-economic groups. They also have the highest RAE scores. It would appear that the access agenda has an oppositional relationship to the quality agenda. Social hierarchies are reproduced via representation in quality discourses. Social classifications are translated into academic ones.

There has been a commodification of academic labour, skills and relationships (De Groot, 1997). This has been accompanied by labelling and stigmatization. The imperative to perform is creating a cognitive dissonance. The definition of universities is being left to others. Self-definitions, such as an organization's critical self-assessment document for Subject Review, are interrogated and often found wanting. Quality assurance is defining organizational subjectivity formation and producing new behaviours and relationships. New employment regimes, the omnipresent surveillance mechanisms and judgmental relationships are all contributing to a disturbing lack of safety in universities today. We have already seen in the compulsory education sector that policies involving excessive surveillance and naming and shaming have resulted in a major crisis in recruitment and retention of teachers and demoralization of that profession generally. I contend that, if the current technologies for assuring quality are not reviewed - with critical input from academic and student communities - a similar situation will soon confront the academy.

References

Ball, S. (1995) Intellectuals or Technicians? The Urgent Role of Theory in Educational Studies, *British Journal of Educational Studies*, XXXX111(3): 255-271.

Ball, S. (1999) Performativities and Fabrications in the Education Economy: Towards the Performative Society? Paper presented at the AARE: Melbourne.

Ball, S. (1999). *Performativities and Fabrications in the Education Economy: Towards the Performative Society?* Paper presented at the AARE: Melbourne. 27 November to 2 December.

Barnett, R. (ed) (2000) *Realizing the University*. Buckingham: SRHE/Open University.

Barry, A., Osborne, T. and N. Rose (eds) (1996) *Foucault and Political Reason: Liberalism, Neo-liberalism and Rationalities in Government*. London: UCL Press.

Baudrillard, J. (ed) (1998) *The Consumer Society*. London: Sage.

Bernstein, B. (ed) (1996) *Pedagogy, Symbolic Control and Identity*. London: Taylor and Francis.

Berry, C. (1999). University League Tables: artefacts and inconsistencies in individual rankings. *Higher Education Review*, 31(2), 3-10.

Bett, M. (ed) (1999) *Independent review of higher education pay and conditions : report of a committee / chaired by Sir Michael Bett*. London: Stationery Office.

Bird, J. (ed) (1996) *Black Students and Higher Education: Rhetorics and Realities*. London: SRHE/ Open University Press.

Bowden, R. (2000) Fantasy Higher Education: University and College League Tables, *Quality in Higher Education*, 6(1):41-59.

Broadfoot, P. (1998) Quality Standards and Control in Higher Education: What Price Life-Long Learning? *International Studies in Sociology of Education*, 8(2):155-180.

Butler, J. (ed) (1997) *Excitable Speech: A politics of the Performative*. London: Routledge.

Coate, K., Court, S., Gillon, E., Morley, L. and Williams, G. (eds) (2000) *Academic and academic related staff involvement in the local, regional and national economy*. Association of University Teachers Institute of Education: University of London.

Cole, M. (1998) Globalisation, Modernisation and Competitiveness: A Critique of the New Labour Project in Education, *International Studies in Sociology of Education,* 8(3):315-332.

Cole, P. (1999) To What Extent is the Culture of a University Department Supportive of Equal Opportunities for Women? *International Studies in Sociology of Education*, 8(3):271-297.

Cowen, R. (1996) Performativity, Post-modernity and the University, *Comparative Education*, 32(2):245-258.

De Groot, J. (1997) After the Ivory Tower: Gender, Commodification and the 'Academic', *Feminist Review*, 55(Spring), 130-142.

Dearing, R. (ed) (1997) *Higher Education in the Learning Society (the Dearing Report)*. London: National Committee of Inquiry into Higher Education.

Deem, R. (1998) 'New Managerialism' and Higher Education: The Management of Performance and Cultures in Universities in the United Kingdom, *International Studies in Sociology of Education*, 8(1):47-70.

Department for Education and Employment (DfEE) (1998) *Teachers Meeting the Challenge of Change* (Green Paper). London: HMSO.

Gewirtz, S., Ball, S.J. and Bowe, R. (eds) (1995) *Equity, markets and choice*. Buckingham: Open University.

Gumport, P. (2000) Academic restructuring: Organizational change and institutional imperatives, *Higher Education* 39:67-91.

Hansard Society (1990) *Women at the Top*. London: Hansard Society.

Henkel, M. (ed) (2000) *Academic Identities and Policy Changes in Higher Education*. London: JKP.

Hurst, A. (1999) The Dearing Report and Students with Disabilities and Learning Difficulties, *Disability and Society*, 14(1):65-83.

James, D. (1995) Mature Studentship in higher education: Beyond a 'species' approach, *British Journal of Sociology of Education*, 16(4):451-466.

Jeffrey, B. and Woods, P. (1996) Feeling Deprofessionalized: the Social Construction of Emotions during an Ofsted Inspection, *Cambridge Journal of Education*, 26(3):325-43.

Leman, P. and Mann, C. (1999) Gender differences in students' performances in examinations: the Cambridge University project, in P. Fogelberg, J. Hearn, L. Husu and Mankkinen (eds) *Hard work in the academy : research and interventions on gender inequalities in higher education*, 83-92. Helsinki: Helsinki University Press.

Leonard, D. (2000) Transforming Doctoral Studies: Competencies and artistry *Higher Education in Europe. Special Issue on Women and Change*, XXV(2):181-192.

Luke, C. (1997) Quality Assurance and Women in Higher Education, *Higher Education*, 33:433-451.

Major, L. (1999) A Class Apart? *The Guardian Higher Education*, 16 November, 1-3.

Maynard, M. and Purvis, J. (eds) (1993) *Researching Women's Lives from a Feminist Perspective*. London: Taylor and Francis.

McCrum, N. G. (1998) Gender and Social Inequality at Oxbridge: measures and remedies, *Oxford Review of Education*, 24(3):261-277.

McNicholl, I. and al. (eds) (1997) *The Impact of UK Universities and Colleges on the UK Economy*. London: CVCP.

Meadmore, D. (1998) Changing the Culture: The Governance of the Australian pre-millennial university, *International Studies in Sociology of Education*, 8(1): 27-45.

Middleton, C. (2000) Models of State and Market in the 'Modernization' of Higher Education, *British Journal of Sociology of Education,* 21(4):537-553.

Modood, T. and Acland, T. (eds) (1998) *Race and higher education : experiences, challenges and policy implications*. London: Policy Studies Institute.

Morley, L. (2000) Regulating the Masses: Quality and Equality in Higher Education, in K. Gokusling and C. Da Costa (eds) *A Compact for Higher Education*. London: Ashgate.

Morley, L. (ed) (1999) *Organising Feminisms: The Micropolitics of the Academy*. London: Macmillan.

Morley, L. and Rassool, N. (2000) School Effectiveness: new managerialism, quality and the Japanization of Education, *Journal of Education Policy*, 15(2):169-183.

Morley, L. and Rassool, N. (eds) (1999). *School Effectiveness: Fracturing the Discourse*. London: Falmer Press.

Neave, G. (1998) The Evaluative State Reconsidered, *European Journal of Education*, 33(3):265-284.

Ozga, J. (1998) The Entrepreneurial Researcher: Re-formations of Identity in the Research Marketplace, *International Studies in Sociology of Education*, 8(2).

Ozga, J. and Walker, L. (1999) In the Company of Men, in S. Whitehead and R. Moodley (eds) *Transforming managers*. 107-119. London: UCL Press.

Peters, M. (1992) Performance and accountability in post-industrial societies: The crisis in British universities, *Studies in Higher Education*, 17(2):123-139.

Readings, B. (1996). *TheUuniversity in Ruins*. Cambridge, Mass.; London: Harvard UP.

Readings, B.(ed) (1996) *The University in Ruins*. Cambridge, Mass.London: Harvard UP.

Riddell, S. (1999) Chipping Away at the Mountain, *International Studies in Sociology of Education*, 8(2):203-222.

Said, E. (ed) (1994) *Representations of the Intellectual: The 1993 Reith Lectures*. London: Vintage.

Scott, S. (1999) The Academic as Service Provider: is the Customer 'Always Right'? *Journal of Higher Education Policy and Management*, 21(2):193-202.

Segal Quince and Wicksteed (1999). *Providing public information on the quality and standards of higher education courses*: Report to DENI, HEFCE, HEFCW, QAA, SHEFCE. Cambridge: Segal Quince and Wicksteed.

Sennett, R. (ed) (1998) *The Corrosion of character : the personal consequences of work in the new capitalism*. New York: Norton.

Shaw, J. (ed) (1995) *Education, Gender and Anxiety*. London: Taylor and Francis.

Slee, R. (1998) Higher Education Work in the Reductionist Age, *International Studies in Sociology of Education*, 8(3):255-270.

Underwood, S. (1998) Quality assessment: some observations, *Perspectives*, 2(2):50-55.

Yorke, M. (1999) Assuring Quality and Standards in Globalised Higher Education *Quality Assurance in Higher Education*, 7(1):14-24.

Yorke, M. (2000) The Quality of the Student Experience, *Quality in Higher Education*, 6(1):61-75.

8 Exploring the Implementation Gap: Theory and practices in change interventions

Paul R. Trowler and Peter T. Knight

Introduction

This chapter combines elements of a theory of how higher education is with attention to implications for practice. It is based on reflection on data and insights which came out of our work, together and separately, on professional practices of teachers, on organizational socialization of academics entering new higher education contexts, on the ethnographic study of one English university and on the experiences of Deaf academics in a hearing environment.

At the heart of what follows is the position that the unreflective espousal of theories that are based on Enlightenment epistemologies and mechanistic depictions of management and organizations misleads practice. Our counter-position derives from different philosophies (especially phenomenological and pragmatic ones), and from psychologies that attend to the role of context and contingency. More immediately, our position is influenced by developments in Sociology (For example, Luhman, 1995), Organizational and Management Studies (Flood, 1999; Brown and Duguid, 2000; Wenger, 2000), Education (Fullan, 1999), and complexity theories (van Geert, 1994; Bryne, 1998; Cilliers, 1998). We say that a theoretically-alert view allows better thinking about what might be and ways of working towards it.

With Clegg *et al.* (1999: 5) we note that for many years those studying organizations divided the field of study into two categories: the micro, which focussed on the individual, and the macro, which focussed on the organization. Similarly, academic approaches to educational change have also, in the past, tended to concentrate on these two levels. Fullan's well known books (1991, 1993) focus on them, moving between the school as a learning organization and the individual as a change agent, the latter exemplified in this paragraph:

> I define change agency as being self-conscious about the nature of change and the change process...The individual educator is a critical starting point because the leverage for change can be greater through the efforts of individuals, and each educator has some control...over what he or she does, because it is one's own motives and skills that are at question...I am not talking about leaders as change agents...but of a more basic message: each and every educator must strive to be an effective change agent. (Fullan, 1993: 12-13).

However in his more recent work (e.g. 1999), partly deriving from reflection on chaos theory, Fullan has pointed to the significance of systemic approaches to change: recognising the organic character of social groups and the significance of the chemistry of people within organizations.

We argue here that an examination of the meso level of social processes operating in workgroups has much to offer an understanding of both organizations and change.

Conceptualizing Institutional Change

Too often institutional change is conceived either tacitly or explicitly in over-simple terms. There are a number of dimensions to this and some sophisticated reasons for it.

First organizations are characterized as culturally rather simple. Most depictions of cultures in universities see them as slotting into one of a small number of pigeonholes: usually four (Cameron and Ettington, 1988; Becher, 1988; Bergquist, 1993). Thus, for example, Bergquist sees universities as being either 'collegial', 'managerial', 'negotiating' or 'developmental', or a mix of two of them. This perspective is often replicated in common-sense depictions of institutions by members of them and by external evaluators:

> The report noted the significance which the University attached to the introduction of ISO 9001 as a means of ensuring consistency of systems and a disciplined **culture of compliance** at a time of rapid growth and organi*zatio*nal change. (QAA Audit Report University of Wolverhampton, Nov 1999, emphasis ours).

> The audit team considered initially that these procedures [of academic validation and review] appeared to be cumbersome, but was interested to learn from academic staff and senior management about the extent to which these procedures were the foundation of the **University's culture and working practices**. (QAA Audit Report, Coventry, June 2000, emphasis ours).

> [There is a] culture of self-questioning and reflection. ….Heads of school who met the team confirmed this strategy, and spoke of a **culture of access** …. (QAA Audit Report,Greenwich, May 2000, emphasis ours).

The first characteristic of dominant discourses about institutional change in higher education to which we draw critical attention is that they involve considerable *contextual simplification*.

Second is the technical-rational approach to change usually adopted by those given formal responsibility for it. Doers resolutely adopt 'common-sense' views of organizational change that scholars know are faulty, often involving "sweeping expressions of leadership and mission, reengineering and empowerment, strategy and stakeholding: the bromides and platitudes of the dominant management literature of the 1980s and 1990s" (Clark, 1998: 128). This perspective emphasizes efficient, goal- or vision- directed processes in organizations. Control is directed from the top and may operate through tight-coupling, where strong lines of command are intended to ensure that what happens is a faithful replica of what had been planned. This 'hard managerialism', with its taste for the apparatus of measurement and control, has considerable emotive appeal in some circles and equally limited efficacy when complex human operations are in question. In these circumstances, the 'soft managerialism' is often used with its deployment of loosely-coupled approaches in which responsibility may be devolved to local units which are thus subject to 'steering at a distance' (Kickert, 1991), particularly by discursive capture which limits the scope of discussion and thought through the language developed and used to 'capture' reality. Even so, roles and responsibilities within organizations are still seen as clearly and easily delineated in line with precisely defined and expressed tasks, the stages of accomplishment of which are regularly monitored. The organization as a whole is assumed to act as a co-ordinated unit with an unproblematic conception of the objectives of policy and change initiatives. The assumption is that the outcomes of properly-led change processes are predictable. Ideas that the world simply is not like this, or that it is only like this in stable systems doing determinate tasks in established ways - in calcifying systems - are unheard, ignored, or treated as excuses for a lack of commitment, a lack of competence, or both.

This top-down technical-rational understanding of change assumes that if sufficient energy can be elicited from those involved by enthusiastic leaders with a clear vision of change then large scale transformations can be accomplished relatively quickly and economically. Good planning, clarity of goals, clear direction of energies and careful monitoring of outcomes can lead to the realization of intended outcomes (Cerych and Sabatier, 1986). Failures are attributed to ill-will, indolence, ineptitude or indiscipline. We argue below that this too is an inaccurate depiction, at least in universities. The problem with this analysis of institutional change is, at best, *causal simplification*. As Fullan (1999: 3) says "the jury surely must be in by now that rationally constructed reform strategies do not work..."

Next there is the problem that the connotative and affective luggage which innovations usually carry largely go unrecognized by those with formal responsibility for bringing change about. Both leaders and change theorists have devoted considerable attention to the personal attachment people have to the status quo, seeing this as lying at the root of resistance to change. They are right to see that those on the ground have an emotional investment in present practices and affective responses to the fact of change - any change - and to the innovation itself. Here it is important to appreciate that practitioners' attachment to the way things are is entwined with the nature of skill and expertise itself. An influential account of expertise holds that skilled practice is intuitive, flowing and *a*rational so that 'An expert's skill has become so much a part of him that he need be no more aware of it than he is of his own body' (Dreyfus and Dreyfus, 1986: 30). Professional identity and, by referral, that part of self-identity associated with work, is bound up in practice and this emotional attachment to practice is not an aberration that should yield to rational argument or superior force. It is the way being an expert is. These affective charges guarantee that apparently-similar changes will get different meanings attached to them and be laden with emotion and connotative codes. The precise form they take will vary from context to context. Hence the notion of a singular innovation being put into practice in different locales is deceptive. Innovations get meanings in practices (Fullan, 1991; Brown and Duguid, 1991). This is the problem of the *obliteration of meaning and affect*.

Finally there is a problem associated with the fact that policy-making, curriculum-planning, strategy-devising and other long-term planning activities for change occur within a micro-social context which is distinct from the practices to which these planning activities relate. Even when the planners are, in other contexts, practitioners themselves, the different social context of planning means that the complexities of practice, familiar and obvious to practitioners, become occluded for the planning group. Also obscured are the issues raised by a particular innovation in relation to the context of practice: the unique set of problems and opportunities that are innovation-specific. This is the problem of *contextual occlusion*. The micro-social planning context obscures what are sometimes otherwise well-known characteristics of the context of practice.

Throughout this section we have argued that there is a complexity about social practice that differs sharply from the generalising and reductionist assumptions of Enlightenment positivism. Where 'rational' managers see this complexity as a corruption of pure essences and take their task to be one of cleansing, the view we have developed says that complexity *is*. There are no Platonic essences and attempts to separate signals from noise, figure from ground, the individual and the social are not just wrong, they seriously impede well-being, and being well.

An Alternative Perspective

By constrast we offer a rather different perspective on change in organizations. We suggest that institutional cultures are protean and dynamic, not singular and static. Any university possesses a unique and dynamic multiple cultural configuration which renders depiction difficult and simple depictions wildly erroneous. So, values, attitudes, assumptions and taken-for-granted recurrent practices may be as different from department to department, building to building in one HEI as they are between one university and the next. As one university leader has said:

> I've come to see that - just as 'all politics is local' - on most campuses there are in fact dozens of microenvironments with sharply divergent cultures: good-spirited, productive departments coexist along-side dysfunctional ones. As a faculty member once explained to me: 'When we go to work in the morning, we go to our department'....(Marchese, 1999: vii)

The apparent significance of this diversity may appear slight to those gazing at higher education though the wrong end of an analytical telescope instead of through a microscope. Ignoring it significantly reduces the illuminative power of any depiction.

The multiplicities that are apparent when looking at the meso-level, at departments and workgroups, are produced by (and produce) social processes operating within task-based workgroups within the universities. In order to understand how such groups generate these multiple cultures we commend social practice theory, or what Gherardi (2000) calls 'practice-based theory'. This thinking is located within a long tradition that holds that individuals' (professional) engagement with the world is largely social. Extended joint engagement on a project involves the development of recurrent practices and sets of meaning which are localized, endogenous in character. This involves the development of rules, including rules of appropriateness, conventions, taken-for-granted understandings, connotative codes and so on. At the same time particular ways of interacting with the technologies employed to achieve tasks also evolve and become taken for granted. In their teaching practices, for example, university departments develop ways of thinking about their students, approaches to course design and implementation, assessment practices and uses of technologies which become invisible to members of those departments but which can seem odd, novel, exciting or just plain wrong to others. Underpinning these practices are values, attitudes and ideologies that are partly developed and communicated locally.

Meanwhile, as well as developing *shared* characteristics the process of identity construction and development is going on at the individual level through interaction processes which occur as individual participants engage with each other and their work projects. At one and the same time communities of practice *and* the public identities of the participants involved are developing. Eraut (1993; 2000) believes that most human learning does not occur in formal contexts and points to the importance of 'non-formal learning'. He observes that a great deal of information in education is acquired piecemeal: images and impressions are built up on the basis of comments, overheard remarks and fleeting incidents rather than only from more systematic and formalized sources. So, learning, identity construction, affect and meaning *necessarily* come with the social practices of committee meetings, staff meetings, informal interactions in corridors or over coffee, as well as through email messages and memos.

Members of the group draw on and enact behaviours, meanings and values from the wider environment in somewhat different ways, partly depending on their age, gender, ethnicity, professional experience and so on. For example men and women bring their particular experience of sex-role socialization with them and meet expectations associated with gender roles from others in their daily practice. This 'sex-role spillover' (Nieva and Gutek, 1981) can have important implications for the experience and effectiveness of practice (Trowler, 1998). So too with age, 'race' and other social structural characteristics.

Of course workgroup members operate within a common organizational environment which has its own sets of rules (professional codes or course validation procedures, for example), taken-for-granted attitudes and conventions. Professional identities are constructed within a 'given' (or structural) framework of, for example, formal roles such as Head of Department or course co-ordinator which themselves often have exogenously-derived connotative codes associated with them. These will be different for different institutions: the role of the Head of Department and Dean are quite different, for example, in British 'new' (unchartered) universities compared to 'old' (pre-1992) ones and in most countries these roles have distinctive institutional features.

So, given that HEI are complex institutions, characterised by a multiple cultural configuration, that change initiatives are received and understood in different ways in different contexts and that innovation is socially constituted through social practice in locally contingent ways, then conceptualizations of change needs to be modified accordingly - and to become more sophisticated than those depicted above. In contrast to technical-rational and positivist approaches we see organizations as networks of networks (Blackler, Crump and McDonald, 2000) or, to put it another way, as constellations of communities of practice (Wenger, 1998). An implication is that it can be hard to be certain about what is to be selected from the environment and identified as the system that is to be taken as the organization (Checkland, 1981; Luhman, 1995; Wenger, 2000). We identify the following characteristics of this connectionist position (Strauss and Quinn, 1997):

- Activity (or practice): Following Vygotsky, we take action to involve social engagement with the world, either directly, or through the use of social tools, including signs and rituals. This is elaborated by Wertsch (1998: 13) who sees almost all human action as 'mediated action' which means simultaneously attending to 'Act, Scene, Agent, Agency, Purpose'. An important corollary is that the nature of the activity is not objectively discernible but is defined by the participants. Engagement on a research project is an example. The character of what the project means may appear to be objectively 'given' but is actually socially constructed in the process of doing it. 'Activity systems' consist of groups of individuals in distinct roles engaged in a common activity using mediating artefacts and operating on the basis of largely shared rules and conventions. There are clear parallels in this with the pragmatist thinking of Dewey and G. H. Mead in the USA. One of our papers (Trowler and Knight, 2000) extends this exploration of activity systems and higher education.

- Community of practice: a closely interacting group of practitioners within which contextualised, situated learning is always happening and is legitimized (Lave and Wenger, 1991). The research project team or teaching team may form a community of practice within a research centre or department. A single community of practice may incorporate a number of activity systems, depending on the number of distinct projects or activities they are engaged in, and a person may belong to a number of communities of practice.

- Identity: is not a fixed entity but a relational process and for this reason is sometimes referred to in terms of 'subjectivity' (Prichard, 1999) or the self (Mead, 1913), although these terms carry subtle but important differences. Wenger (1998: 153) makes the point that we know who we are by what is familiar, understandable, usable and negotiable while we know who we are *not* by what is foreign, opaque, unwieldy and unproductive, that is by *otherness*. Notice, though, that this differentiation is not intended to signify separation but to use Merleau-Ponty's insight (1973; 135, 134) that, 'The experience of the other is always that of a replica of myself, of a response to myself...The mystery of the other is nothing but the mystery of myself', the source of '...an unexpected response I get from elsewhere'. So, self and other are connected and personal and social identity is thus relational in character, involving simultaneously both a positive and negative positioning. Partly because of this, identity (or, better, identities) is not singular and fixed but situationally contingent upon the multiple, dynamic connections or social practices.

- Meaning and affect: as distinguished from information (Baumard, 1999) is a product of being. Meaning implies the way we understand the world and our place in it. It involves knowing about things, sometimes tacitly: the way they interconnect and the way we relate to them, including connotative codes, associations and feelings, that they carry. Thus, for example, higher education regulatory agencies such as the QAA and its procedures carry meaning for HE professionals over and above the information they have about such agencies. This meaning will vary from location to location to a greater or lesser extent. As we noted above, interesting questions arise about the extent to which meaning is the product of intentional learning (Eraut, 2000) as distinct from the learning that derives from simply being. Although answers to these question have enormous implications for attempts to change practice (Knight, 2002), it is not necessary to provide them here, where it is sufficient to say that even an on-message organization has many meanings.

- Discourse: language too is a form of social practice, one which is both conditioned by and conditions the social structures which give regularity and a certain degree of predictability to behaviour. Examples of such structures include educational ideologies, class structures and so on. While discursive repertoires are partly exogenous to a community of practice and imported into it, the social construction of reality within a community of practice also involves discursive creation, negotiation and contest as well as simple articulation. We see language practices and other social practices as instantiating each other.

- Technology: the role of technology within social practice is not limited to the simple use of tools. The tools and techniques used for achieving ends are themselves bound up in constructivist social processes. The fact that photocopying machines and desktop computers were initially predicted to be irrelevant to office practice (Brown and Duguid, 1991) demonstrates the important interactions between technology and social practice. Within the existing (situated) practices at the time of their invention it was true that they were and would be redundant: it was difficult to envisage any alternative. However the introduction of technologies changes practice and so the nature of the constructed social world, as brief reflection on the use and effects of email communication in universities will illustrate. At the same time social practice shapes the way technologies are defined and used within the large range of possibilities that they frequently present.

Social practice theory, then, takes this mix of features, concepts and characteristics of social groups and ponders upon how they interact in various social settings under different relations of power between actors, discourses, tools and rules. We have set out a theoretical approach to how this occurs elsewhere (Trowler and Knight, 2000). In our book on leadership in university departments (Knight and Trowler, 2000) we have also posted some warning signs about problems associated with some versions of social practice theory. The more significant of these are associated with the concept of 'community' and with the need to retain sight of the operation of power and of wider structural features while focussing on micro-social processes. We lack the space to reprise those warnings here so we will merely signal them as we move now to illustrate social practice theory with an example.

An Illustration: The 'new route' to the PhD.

The vignette that follows is based on real events at the English chartered university, 'Hilltop'. It is designed to illustrate some of the ideas discussed above. The narrative moves from the national policy-formulation context down to the institutional and then workgroup context. It demonstrates the consequences of contextual and causal simplification, the obliteration of meaning and affect and contextual occlusion. It shows how the six important themes in social practice theory introduced above were played in this case.

Policy Formulation at National Level

This vignette concerns a proposal to develop a new, American-style, route to a professional PhD via taught doctoral programmes in the UK. The Vice-Chancellor of Hilltop university was on good personal terms with a nationally known and respected non-party political figure in HE policy development, Professor Proselytiser. Informally they discussed the latter's enthusiasm for a 'new route' to the PhD in the UK: Proselytiser's vision of an 'enhanced' PhD.

Proselytiser's argument was that the traditional British PhD digs intellectual wells which are too deep, too narrow and too divorced from economic and commercial needs, including career needs of PhD students. As a result the overseas PhD market was increasingly being lost to North America where, it was argued, taught doctorates provided the breadth and requisite skills for the needs of both the economy and the individual.

Later Prof. Proselytiser put a bid to the funding council, HEFCE, designed to implement proposals to rectify this situation and - perhaps unsurprisingly - it was accepted. A consortium of universities was assembled. The 'new route' would be designed to offer 'what the sponsors want', an American-style PhD, yet one which is better than those available in the USA:

> The consequences for British interests and for the UK's share of the overseas student market [of a drain of PhD students to the USA] should not be under estimated…. As already mentioned, some [of the provision which underpins British PhDs at the moment are] spatchcock taught elements into PhD programmes on an ad hoc basis for individual students. Sponsors are scornful of this amateur approach…. The developmental elements will be in pulling this all together within the participating universities and overcoming the considerable conservatism that exists in some subject areas….[so that provision is of the same order as] in the USA, which is the competition we are seeking to excel. (Proselytizer, 2000: 2).

The new taught programme would enable the students to develop a range of skills drawn from a menu…

> which might include
> - Group work, problem solving, communications
> - Advanced/specialist IT
> - Languages
> - Media related skills
> - Business methods/enterprise skills
> - Intellectual property rights
> - Technology transfer
> - Formation of spin-out, high technology companies
> - Experience of sophisticated equipment and advanced techniques not necessarily encountered in the main research project

- Teaching skills (Proselytizer, 2000: 4)

At Hilltop University there was little or no consultation or even awareness of this agreement until the new Dean responsible for postgraduate studies, Professor Postgrad, was given details of the scheme. He was invited to a meeting in London about it and required to encourage existing doctoral programmes at Hilltop to join the pilot phase. After that meeting Prof. Postgrad also became enthused about the 'new route' and set to work attempting to recruit pilot programmes.

At Hilltop….

By now any university programme agreeing to be involved in the pilot scheme had less than a year to re-design their syllabuses, achieve re-validation of their schemes and appropriately staff and resource the new programme. Resourcing for all this was left vague, though it was clear that HEFCE funding would mainly go to market research and evaluative activity rather than the development and provision of the programmes. Substantial resources would have come from the universities involved.

At Hilltop the issue was first raised publicly at the Graduate School Committee of the university, chaired by Prof. Postgrad, and individuals were tasked to sound out and secure commitment to change in the proposed direction from existing doctoral provision. A paper from Prof. Proselytiser was circulated and postgraduate programme and research directors were invited to sign up to the first phase. The paper articulated in detail the arguments about the proposal set out above and a set of deadlines was outlined:

* now - 5 months' time - development of programmes in 'new route' model
* in 10 months' time - recruitment to 're-badged' versions of current programme
* between 1 month's time to 13 months: formal approval for new 'new route' models
* between 1 month's time to 13 months: marketing new model
* between 1 month's time and 23 months: continuation of marketing and recruitment
* in 23 months' time - new schemes started

The proposal was put to a small number of these directors in an individual process of 'tell and sell' and below we detail the response from one programme, the Doctoral Programme in Implementation Studies in the Department of Policy Sciences at Hilltop University.

An Analytical Pause in the Narrative

Here we pause to comment on the four key problems: contextual and causal simplificaion, the obliteration of meaning and affect and contextual occlusion. The planning group - separate from professional practitioners although drawn from them - had not involved them in the planning stage, but had handed to them an already constructed and discursively constituted 'vision' as set out in Prof. Proselytiser's paper. There was no attempt to consider how this might be received in different universities, or what particular implementation issues would need to be addressed. The assumption appeared to be that, given sufficient resources from HEFCE and the prospect of increased recruitment and more successful progression to work, programme leaders would be enthusiastic and would themselves 'tell and sell' to their colleagues. This misses the fact that even with one of the universities involved, Hilltop, the doctoral provision in different departments were highly diverse and could not simply be pigeonholed into one, rather derogatory, category. This is one element the contextual simplification here. Second, implicit in the approach to change adopted here was a resource-based management model of institutional change (Johnson, this volume). As Johnson points out, underlying this perspective are sets of assumptions, derived from new managerialist ideology, about the power of resource dependency to influence units or individuals. The resource-dependency model of causation, then, was the significant simplification of causality here, together with the 'tell and sell' methodology associated with it. In addition there appeared to be no reflection on the likely response from those on the ground to either the language or the substance of the proposals, or to the critique of an activity to which, in many cases, they had spent years of their professional lives. Here we see the obliteration of meaning and affect. Finally, the plan for implementation and the timescales involved revealed a lack of reflection on the complexities associated with such a radical proposal: the occlusion of the context of practice as far as the planners were concerned.

None of this is, or should be, much of a surprise to many of those involved, yet they they remain unconsidered in the formulation of this policy and in the implementation plan. The reasons for this apparent paradox relate back to the problem of contextual occlusion. Reynolds and Saunders (1987) suggest that planning and imagining practice are difficult to reconcile. Involving those at the 'delivery' level in the planning of change does not necessarily enable planning groups to integrate local knowledgeability into the policy-making process, as these authors demonstrate with their research on curriculum planning for schools:

> While working with a group of teachers who had been asked to prepare curriculum guidelines for colleagues, we had noticed how frequently but fleetingly individual teachers voiced doubts about the ways in which particular curriculum statements were likely to be regarded or disregarded by their fellows. Generally these interpolations were rapidly overridden and superseded by sustained argument amongst the whole group which shifted attention back to the form and wording of the guidelines themselves. The flow of discussion consistently moved away from the rehearsal of teachers' likely thinking to rehearsal of justifications of the curriculum text itself. (Reynolds and Saunders, 1987: 195)

One explanation for this dissociation between curriculum planning and professional thinking about everyday work practices lies in the situated character of professional practice. This is exemplified in this case by the different social and intellectual processes involved in (curriculum) planning in the context of a particular planning group which are significantly different from those involved in actually 'delivering' a lesson. Thus the supposed benefits of collegial planning or leadership are not, in practice, realized. This helps explain:

> how the conventions that underlie curriculum writing and debate can be well adapted to public justification and course administration but segregated from the tacit norms that teachers draw upon in evolving working practices between themselves, administrators, their pupils and the situations that they recurrently experience. (Reynolds and Saunders, 1987: 213)

Narrative and Analysis at the Workgroup Level

The Director of the Doctoral Programme in Implementation Studies circulated details of the 'New Route' proposal, including Prof. Proselytiser's paper to colleagues centrally involved: the 'doctoral workgroup'. Their responses ranged from the cautious to the negative through to hostile. They raised what are, from a practitioner's perspective, perfectly obvious questions. These concerned the impossibly tight timescale for planning and validation, the resource implications for the Department and workgroup, the fact that the university's accommodation and catering standards were not high enough for even current provision or sufficiently oriented to the needs and expectations of mature postgraduates. Staffing issues, particularly the multiple demands on staff and the intensification of academic work generally were important elements of the response. Underlying questions concerned the flow of resources in the scheme and the profitability question: what was the payoff for the resources immediately needed to mount this scheme? In this sense the ground-level response was coherent with a resource-dependency model but was not in the predicted direction: resource issues evinced resistance rather than compliance.

More important, though, were the meanings of this proposal for this established workgroup and their affective responses to it. First, because of their disciplinary specialisms, this particular group was highly politically literate and fully aware of policy developments in the UK over several decades. They located this proposal in that context, seeing it as an instance of marketization occurring in other professions, in schools and within HE over some time. For them this was an instance of what Barnett (2000) has called the 'slide to performativity' in British HE. This was a push for more vocational relevance in the HE curriculum, a critique of what had gone before and, associated with them, a shift in power in terms of who defines knowledge appropriate to be taught in universities. Significantly, this proposal was associated with the Teacher Training Agency, and members of the workgroup had personal as well as academic and analytical experience and knowledge about that organization's history and methods, which seemed to owe a debt to Sun Tzu:

> Reduce the hostile chiefs by inflicting damage on them, and make trouble for them, and keep them constantly engaged, hold out specious allurements, and make them rush to any given point (Sun Tzu, 1963: VIII: 10).

The discursive repertoires utilized in Proselytizer's proposal and exemplified in the extended quote above elicited a negative reaction also. One of the individuals in the workgroup reacted strongly to this: "I find some of the language in the document offensive".

Social Practice Theory: the significance of this vignette

We turn now to briefly apply social practice theory to this vignette in order to highlight how it illuminates the events and how the narrative illustrates that theoretical approach. This Doctoral Programme workgroup had been in existence for seven years, and individuals within it had been interacting for much longer than that. During that time they had developed a set of working relationships, recurrent practices, values and attitudes which formed the basis of their operation. There was internal conflict and power was manifested in different ways. This operated in such a way as to establish hegemony for alternatives preferred by some and to marginalize others. A fairly stable and well-formed community of practice was in existence.

The nature of *this* Doctoral Programme, what it aimed to do and how it approached that task, had been developed over this period as members of the community of practice had engaged with providing it. Thus sets of meanings were developed *in situ* and meanings derived from other contexts were re-shaped in this specific situation. New course members were also inducted into this community through their engagement with the activity. For them identities were importantly affected as they came to define themselves as researchers, albeit emergent researchers at first, and the public identities of the staff were also in the process of being shaped in the process of engagement in this activity. The community of practice had, in short, developed social structural characteristics: both its own rules, involving normative elements and codes of signification, and sets of resources which were both allocative and authoritative in character (Giddens, 1984, xxxi and p. 17). These related in particular to what counts as good research, appropriate ways of disseminating it and the purposes of research in general.

Tools, both discursive and technological, were simultaneously shaped in the context of this workgroup and themselves shaped the development of recurrent practices in the group. Underpinning these practices was a mix of traditionalist and progressivist educational ideology (Trowler, 1998) which stressed the importance of dialogue in the educational experience, of close inter-personal interaction. The medium-to-high technology tools used - the telephone and fax, web sites, email lists, and photocopier - while important, remained secondary to interpersonal dialogue based on a Socratic model which was implicit for much of the time but also explicitly expressed and grounded in empirical pedagogical research on which members of the group had been engaged. Thus the Programme website stated that:

> The programme's design depends heavily upon building a mutually supportive spirit among a group of people with overlapping professional and academic interests. Our current participants tell us that this is one of the most successful and valuable elements of the programme. (Doctoral Programme website).

All of this was some distance away from the enterprise ideology and its associated discursive repertoires and assumptions about the use of technology as articulated in Professor Proselytizer's paper. His proposal, then, landed in an alien territory and evoked a set of responses which, from an insider's position, are rather predictable but which, viewed from a macro perspective, would be difficult to understand and appreciate. The microscope, not the telescope, is the appropriate instrument to examine the ways in which specific proposals for innovation are likely to be received and 'implemented' in specific locales.

The enacted organization

This example shows that the organization is not quite as those who are accustomed to reify human achievements might imagine. It has a legal existence that continues beyond the involvement of any particular people, it is co-ordinated and, rather as a planet can be treated in Newtonian physics as a point with mass, so there are lots of senses in which the organization can be unproblematically treated as an super-human entity. But its boundaries, centres of action, rules and decisions are enacted as well as encoded. Wenger (1998) shows this well with study of the apparently routine processing of insurance claims where practice seeped out of the interplay of policy, the need to get work done, uncertainties, time pressures, technology and norms. The organization that people making insurance claims encountered was the insurance company *as enacted by* the claims-processing staff.

If there is an enacted aspect to organizations as manifested in their routine business, this is all the more so, as the example above suggested, in novel situations. Hilltop University's form, structures, rules and history certainly contributed to the decision-making net but there is also a sense in which it was specifically enacted in the interactions that led to *localized* policy on new doctoral programmes being created. Boundary issues - what counts as in the system and what is treated as outside it; membership issues - who participates in the decision-making and how; meaning issues - the rules that get used and their interpretations; and power issues – the processes by which decisions are found to have happened all arise when activity systems, such as departments or workgroups, face novel problems. Yet the ways in which such issues connect in dynamic systems largely constitute the organization experiencing the problem.

Furthermore, this enacted quality is more apparent when we look at sub-units, such as departments, in the loosely-coupled systems that universities usually are. Our vignette shows that the workgroup had a distinct profile, constituted out of power-pervaded interactions, which is likely to be quite different from the profile enacted on a different issue. Sometimes the department is tantamount to its leader, sometimes it is senior academic staff, sometimes students are part of it and sometimes support staff are regarded as members. This enacted quality should not be exaggerated but nor should the organizational morphing be ignored. Doing so makes the mistake of acting as if the organization were as it appears rather than what it does. Reification may be analytically convenient but it is a form of simplification. Reliance on reification lies behind many innovation attempts that sagged: they mistook appearance for reality. Appearance is a part of the network of what is.

Implications for Practices

Implications for practice are many and negotiable according to site, context and time. The argument presented here that change is situationally contingent unfortunately applies equally to any advice on how to improve policy-making and implementation. However, fifteen general observations are:

1. The argument that change forces need to be directed to workgroups at least as much as to institutions and individuals does not imply that success is to be had by scaling down and applying the determinate rationality of linear systems thinking that has characterized so many approaches to change management. Workgroups may be small systems but our claim is that, whatever their similarities to each other, they are (i) also distinctly different from one another (ii) complex, in the sense that their workings are not to be predicted and understood according to the model of Newtonian physics.

2. This is an endorsement of philosophies that emphasize the facticity and historicity of being. They do not treat contingency as impediments to understanding transcendental essences but as fundamental aspects of existence. It is also an endorsement of psychologies that emphasize the situatedness of cognition, arguing that the specific and the general are interwoven and need to be conjointly understood. It is strengthened by research into schools that draws attention to contingencies as important factors affecting what departments do, resist and are unable to do (Sammons *et al.*, 1997; Turner and Bolam, 1998; Gray *et al.*, 1999). Similar ideas are to be found in studies of organizations in general that highlight context (Blackler, 1995) and the subjective, fluid quality of sensemaking (Weick, 1995).

3. This position also takes from the same sources the view that affect, or mood, as Heidegger put it, is as fundamental as cognition. Work in management and organizational studies is increasingly treating affect as something of significance (Weick and Westley, 1996; Goleman, 1998). Hargreaves' (1998) analysis of reform efforts in schools leads to the claim that schoolteachers' feelings in the face of

change have important ramifications for the success of the intended changes. At the minimum, this position says that change interventions need to be emotionally literate.

4. This perspective on change echoes Gould's (1996) account of evolution as 'punctuated equilibrium'. It derives from complexity theories, with their paradoxical story that significant change is not common (see Farrell, 2000, for an analysis of resilience of the grammars of schooling) and that small changes can have unexpected and disproportionate effects (van Geert, 1994; Bryne, 1998). Van Geert's account of complexity also said that fundamental changes are rare and he used the mathematical concept of the power law to show that they are the product of many small changes. He added that change is not one-directional and that oscillations are the norm. In reality, '…the shortest line between two points,' he suggests, 'is the wiggle' (1994: 153), arguing that large changes are typically preceded by large drops in performance. Fullan (1999) has begun to explore some of the implications for changing schools, emphasising that the metaphor of complexity is not compatible with outcomes-driven, micro-managed change interventions. Complexity implies assembling the ingredients that make for good outcomes and supporting good working practices in the belief that good change is more likely to emerge than if other strategies were used.

5. Complexity metaphors indicate that the same effect can come from different causes and that similar causes can have different effects (van Geert, 1994). Research has shown that that this is true of 'improving' high schools (Gray et al., 1999), which tend to have got on to improvement trajectories from one of five 'portals' (improvement strategies). Conversely, schools adopting the same improvement strategy can have different outcomes. Engagement with innovation and the experience of success seem to be necessary conditions for sustained improvement, although the evidence is that they are not sufficient. An

implication for HEIs is that it would be unfortunate were departments to be marched to a single beat since the experience of successful innovation is what matters, not the exact innovation itself. So, a university hoping to make a fundamental difference to teaching and learning quality by requiring all departments to introduce new learning environments should anticipate that there will be a considerable range of outcomes and recognize that learning quality might better be improved by encouraging a diversity of innovations.

6. A further implication of complexity theories is that regress and progress go together. This is consistent with Fullan's position in his 1991 *The New Meaning of Educational Change*, namely that changes emerge in the process of implementation, which implies that the quality of support for implementation processes has a marked effect on the fate of change interventions. The complexity metaphor arguably re-inforces that view by stressing the importance of the ingredients over the plan, and the priority of the processes over intended outcomes.

7. The case for outcomes-based approaches to curriculum planning is weakened by this analysis of change forces. A process model of curriculum planning may be more authentic (Knight, 2001b).

8. This analysis has implications for the work of staff and educational development professionals, suggesting that they might contribute most to interventions by working as consultants with departments, engaging with them in processes that are likely to interact with the specifics of the workgroup's situation in ways likely to lead to some outcomes that are reckoned to be valuable. There are recent reports of staff development professionals deliberately adopting a department-focused strategy (Boud, 2000; Hicks, 2000) but they are presented as exploratory work associated with specific projects. A more radical position, implied by our analysis, is for staff development professionals to work as consultants on a long-

term basis with departments. Not only would this enhance departmental capacities but it would also help staff developers to work with a sensitive appreciation of workgroup contingencies. For many this would be a substantial role move, from trainers to consultants (Knight, 1998) who would operate within a dynamic process model of change.

9. It may be inferred that the practice of inviting departments to bid for funds to achieve changes that they contractually promise to deliver is misconceived.

10. Staff development professionals might also consider the claim that the widely-approved notion of reflection as a means to learning sits uneasily with the view we have been sketching. The substantial interest that has been shown in reflection *for*, *in* and *on* action is beginning to be challenged by (i) questions about the distinction between reflection and any old thinking (Parker 1997) (ii) the competing claims of 'metacognition' (Hacker *et al.*, 1998); (iii) unease with the metaphysical assumptions behind both metacognition and reflection. With reference to (iii): it is disputed that cognition can capture the causes of practices. One line of enquiry holds that affective factors that largely escape cognitive capture play a great part in actions and practices while another line argues that the situations into which we are cast influence what we do in ways that elude awareness (Donnelly, 1999). Consider, for example, Heidegger's account of the woodworker's craft;

> A cabinetmaker's apprentice, someone who is learning to build cabinets and the like, will serve as an example. His learning is not mere practice, to gain facility in the use of tools. Nor does he merely gain knowledge about the forms of things he is to build. If he is to become a true cabinetmaker, he makes himself answer and respond to the different kinds of wood and to the shapes slumbering within the wood - to wood as it enters into man's dwelling with all the hidden riches of its nature. In fact, this relatedness to wood is what maintains the whole craft. Without that relatedness, the craft will never be anything but empty busywork, any occupation with it will be determined exclusively by business concerns. Every handicraft, all human dealings are constantly in that danger. The writing of poetry is no more exempt from this than is the business of thinking. (Heidegger, 1968: 14-15).

Here, knowing is in the situation, which is understood to include purpose and materials. It is not just in the actor and, as such, it eludes all but the rare times of authenticity. More simply, this is a view that reflection may help people to capture something of their thinking *and* that it is relatively insensitive to the ways in which settings and practices shape thought, feeling and action.

11. If we learn by being and doing as well as by cognitive means, the idea that reflection is a high road to improving professional practice has limited reach. An alternative is that learning follows doing (Weick, 1995). A consequence of that position is that it may be more powerful to promote professional learning through direct attention to the quality of daily workgroup practices and discourses than it is to take the rational step of invoking reflection to alter espoused theories. Nor is this the same as bringing reflection and practice together in the form of praxis because the concern here is with the workgroup's practices and discourses rather than with the sense that any individual makes of the relationship between her or his espoused theories and logic-in-use. The reflective gaze is a limited one, too easily falling on the individual's cognitions. Even where it extends to praxis, it may be too attracted to the exceptional and be insufficiently aware of what is unexceptional because it is normal. This is not to say that the concept of the reflective practitioner is a sham but rather to add to it

an awareness that embedded discourses and practices also teach. Attempts to improve what is done are therefore acts of professional development. In a sense this endorses sophisticated work on learning by apprenticeship (Guile and Young, 1998) but, rather than restricting apprenticeship to novices, extends it to all members of the workgroup on a continuing basis.

12. This view of the importance of workgroups means that the induction of new staff is something that can scarcely be done through central provision because most learning takes place through being in the workgroup. This position has been developed in our accounts of the experiences of people in their first, full-time academic job (Knight and Trowler, 1999; Trowler and Knight, 1999). That aligns induction with continued professional learning.

13. This approach creates a paradox about learning to lead. If so much learning happens through engagement with the discourses and practices of a workgroup, how are outsiders to learn to lead?

14. Departments will continue, no doubt, to be audited with the aid of performance indicators, including deeply dubious summative assessment data (Knight, 2001a). This is not very compatible with the account we have given of social practices. There is a stronger case for expert appreciation of workgroups' normal discourses and practices with a view to treating accountability as a means of enhancing capacity for change. The notion of appreciation is the same as Eisner's concept of educational connoisseurship (1985), which holds that education is too complex a process to be fairly appraised by any means except something akin to the processes of aesthetic appreciation.

15. A pro-vice-chancellor was complaining that he did not have power in his university and wondering who did. Heads of department and team leaders may have more power than anyone else but this view of higher education institutions

says that really no-one has it: power is distributed, a feature of the network of interactions that comprises the HEI. Individuals have some power but the net has the power. We argue that change strategies that put the department at the centre provide a better account of the way things are than those that privilege institutional management or that treat individual academics as free and powerful agents. Better still, approaches to change that are based on the view that although some have more power than others, it is sufficiently distributed throughout the system that systemic approaches to change processes are needed in preference to targeted interventions to produce determinate changes.

References

Barnett, R. (ed) (2000) *Realizing the University in an Age of Supercomplexity*. Buckingham: Open University Press/SRHE.

Baumard, P. (ed) (1999) *Tacit Knowledge in Organizations*. London: Sage Publications.

Becher, T. (1988) Principles and Politics: an interpretative framework for university management, in A. Westoby (ed) *Culture and Power in Educational Organizations* (317-328). Buckingham: Open University Press/SRHE.

Bergquist, W. H. (ed) (1993) *The Four Cultures of the Academy*. San Francisco: Jossey Bass.

Blackler, F. (1995) Knowledge, Knowledge Work and Organizations: An Overview and Analysis, *Organization Studies*, 16,6:1021-1046.

Blackler, F., Crump, N. and McDonald, S. (2000) Organizing Processes in Compex Activity Networks, *Organization*, 7, 2:277-300.

Boud, D. (2000) Situating academic development in professional work, *Journal of Academic development*, 4(1): 3-10.

Brown, J. S. and Duguid, P. (1991) Organizational Learning and Communities of Practice: toward a unified view of working, learning and innovating, *Organization Science*, 2(1): 40-57.

Brown, J. S. and Duguid, P. (eds) (2000) *The Social Life of Information*. Cambridge MA: Harvard University Press.

Bryne, B. (ed) (1998) *Complexity Theory and Social Science*. London: Routledge.

Cameron, K. S. and Ettington, D. R. (1988) The Conceptual Foundations of Organisational Culture, in J. C. Smart (ed) *Higher Education: handbook of theory and research*. Vol 4:356-396. New York: Agathon.

Cerych, L. and Sabatier, P. (eds) (1986) *Great Expectations and Mixed Performance*. London: Trentham.

Checkland, P. (1981) *Systems Thinking, Systems Practice*. Chichester: John Wiley.

Cilliers, P. (ed) (1998) *Complexity and Postmodernism*. London: Routledge.

Clark, B. (ed) (1998) *Creating Entrepreneurial Universities: organizational pathways of transformation*. London: Pergamon.

Clegg, S., Hardy, C. and Nord, W. (1999) Introduction: Organizational Issues, in S. Clegg, C. Hardy, and W. Nord (eds) *Managing Organizations: current Issues*. London: Sage, 1-10.

Donnelly, J. F. (1999) Schooling Heidegger: on being in teaching, *Teaching and Teacher Education*, 15:933-49.

Dreyfus, H. and Dreyfus, S.(eds) (1986) *Mind Over machine*. Oxford: Blackwell.

Dyer, C. (1999) Researching the Implementation of Educational Policy: a backward mapping approach, *Comparative Education*, 35(1): 45-61.

Eisner, E. (ed) (1985) *The Educational Imagination,* 2nd edition. New York: Macmillan.

Eraut, M. (1993) The Characterisation and Development of Professional Expertise, *Educational Management and Administration*, 21(4): 224-232.

Eraut, M. (2000) Non-formal learning and tacit knowledge in professional work, *British Journal of Educational Psychology*, 70, 113-136.

Farrell, J. P. (2000) Why is educational reform so difficult? *Curriculum Inquiry*, 30(1): 83-103.

Flood, R. L. (ed) (1999) Rethinking <u>The Fifth Discipline</u>. Routledge: London.

Fullan, M. (ed) (1991) *The New Meaning of Educational Change*. London: Cassell.

Fullan, M. (ed) (1993) *Change Forces*. Brighton: Falmer Press.

Fullan, M. (ed) (1999) *Change Forces: The sequel*. London: Falmer.

Gherardi, S. (2000) Practice-based Theorizing on Learning and Knowing in Organizations, *Organization*, 7(2): 211-223.

Giddens, A. (ed) (1984) *The Constitution of Society*. Cambridge: Polity Press.

Goleman, D. (ed) (1998) *Working with Emotional Intelligence*. New York: Bantam Books.

Gould, S. J. (ed) (1996) *Dinosaur in a Haystack*. London: Jonathan Cape.

Gray, J., Hopkins, D., Reynolds, D., Wilcox, B., Farrell, S. and Jesson, D. (eds) (1999) *Improving Schools: Performance and potential*. Buckingham: Open University Press

Guile, D. and Young, M. (1998) Apprenticeship as a conceptual basis for a social theory of learning, *Journal of Vocational Education and Training* 50(2):173-192.

Hacker, D., Dunlosky, J. and Graesser, A. (eds) (1998) *Metacognition in Education Theory and Practice*. Mahwah NJ: Lawrence Erlbaum Associates.

Hargreaves, A. (1998) The emotional practice of teaching, *Teaching and Teacher Education*, 14(8):835-854.

Heidegger, M. (1968) *What is Called Thinking?*, trans. J. Glenn Gray. New York: Harper Row.

Hicks, O. (2000) Intergration of central and departmental development - reflections from Australian universities, *Journal of Academic Development*, 4(1):43-51.

Kickert, W. (1991) *Steering at a distance: a new paradigm in public governance in Dutch higher education*. Paper presented to the European consortium for Political Research, Colchester, University of Essex, March.

Knight, P. and Trowler, P. (2000) Department-level cultures and the improvement of learning and teaching, *Studies in Higher Education*, 25(1):69-83.

Knight, P. and Trowler, P. (eds) (2001) *Departmental Leadership in Higher Education: new directions for communities of practice*. Buckingham: Open University Press.

Knight, P. T. (1998) Professional obsolescence and continuing professional development in higher education, *Innovation in Education and Training International*, 35(3):241-248.

Knight, P. T. (2001a) The Achilles' heel of quality -- the assessment of student learning. Paper presented to the CRQ End of Quality Conference, Birmingham, 25-27 May.

Knight, P. T. (2001b) Complexity and curriculum: a process approach to curriculum making, *Teaching in Higher Education*, 6, 3, 69-83.

Knight, P. T. (ed) (2002) *Being a Teacher in Higher Education*. Buckingham: Society for Research into Higher Education & Open University Press.

Knight, P. T. and Trowler, P. R. (1999) It takes a village to raise a child, *Mentoring and*

Tutoring, 7(1):23-34.

Lave, J. and Wenger, E. (eds) (1991) *Situated Learning: Legitimate Peripheral Participation.* Cambridge: Cambridge University Press.

Luhman, N. (1995) *Social Systems*, trans. J. Bednarz and D. Baecker Stanford CA: Stanford University Press.

Marchese, T. (1999) Foreword, in I. Hecht, M. Higgerson, W. Gmelch and A. Tucker (eds) *The Department Chair as Academic Leader*. Phoenix: American Council on Education and Oryx Press, vii-x.

McNay, I. (1995) From Collegial Academy to Corporate Enterprise: the changing cultures of universities, in T.Schuller (ed) *The Changing University?* 105-115. Buckingham: The Society for Research into Higher Education and Open University Press.

Mead, G. H. (1913) The Social Self, *Journal of Philosophy, Psychology and Scientific Methods*, 10: 374-380.

Merleau-Ponty, M. (1973) The Prose of the World, in C. Lefort (ed) *Trans. J O'Neill*. Evanstown IL: Northwestern University Press.

Merleau-Ponty, M. (1973) *The Prose of the World*. Ed. C. Lefort. Trans. J O'Neill. Evanstown IL: Northwestern University Press.

Nieva, V. F and Gutek, B. A. (eds) (1981) *Women and Work: a psychological perspective*. New York: Praeger.

Parker, S. (ed) (1997) *Reflective Thinking in the Postmodern World*. Buckingham: Open University Press.

Prichard, C. (1999) *Identity Work - moving the 'theory of the subject' from 'division' to 'depth' in critical organizational analysis*. Paper for the Critical Management Studies Conference, Manchester School of Management, UMIT, July.

Prozelytiser, P. (2000) *A New Route to the PhD: A collaborative project funded by the HEFCE*. Mimeo.

Quality Assurance Agency (1999) *Audit Report on University of Wolverhampton*, November. Gloucester: QAA.

Quality Assurance Agency (2000) *Audit Report on Coventry University*, June. Gloucester: QAA.

Quality Assurance Agency (2000) *Audit Report on University of Greenwich*, May.

Gloucester: QAA.

Reynolds, J. and Saunders, M. (1987) Teacher Responses to Curriculum Policy: Beyond the 'Delivery' Metaphor, in J. Calderhead (ed) *Exploring Teachers' Thinking.* London: Cassell.

Sammons, P., Thomas, S. and Mortimore, P. (eds) (1997) *Forging Links: Effective schools and effective departments.* London: Paul Chapman.

Strauss, C. and Quinn, N. (eds) (1997) *A Cognitive Theory of Cultural Meaning.* Cambridge: Cambridge University Press.

Sun Tzu (Trans Griffith, S. B.) (1963) *The Art of War.* Oxford: Clarendon Press.

Trowler, P. (1998) *Academics Responding to Change: new higher education frameworks and academic cultures.* Buckingham: Open University Press/SRHE.

Trowler, P. and Knight, P. (1999) Organizational Socialization and Induction in Universities: Reconceptualizing theory and practice, *Higher Education,* 37:177-195.

Trowler, P. and Knight, P. (2000) Coming to Know in Higher Education: Theorising faculty entry to new work contexts, *Higher Education Research and Development.* 19(1): 27-42.

Trowler, P., Corker, M. and Turner, G. *Exploring the Hermeneutic Foundations of University Life: Deaf academics in a hybrid community of practice.* Paper delivered to the SRHE annual conference, 14-16 December, 1999

Turner, C. and Bolam, R. (1998) Analysing the role of the subject head of department in secondary schools in England and Wales, *School Leadership and Management,* 18(3): 373-88.

van Geert, P. (ed) (1994) *Dynamic Systems of Development: change between complexity and chaos.* Hemel Hempstead: Harvester Wheatsheaf.

Weick, K. (ed) (1995) *Sensemaking in Organizations.* Thousand Oaks CA: Sage.

Weick, K. E. and Westley, F. (1996) Organizational learning: affirming an oxymoron, in S. Clegg, C. Hardy and W. R. Nord (eds) *Handbook of Organizational Studies,* 440-458. London: Sage Publications.

Wenger, E. (2000) Communities of practice and social learning systems, *Organization,* 7(2):225-246.

Wenger, E. (ed) (1998) *Communities of Practice: learning, meaning and identity.*

Cambridge: Cambridge University Press.

Wertsch, J. V. (ed) (1998) *Mind as Action*. Oxford: Oxford University Press.

****

All Rights Reserved © 2014 Paul Trowler

---

i   A station is defined as 'both a physical place where the social order is imposed upon the individual and the social positioning of that individual in the system of social relations' (Fiske, 1993: 12).

ii   The empirical analysis is based on data from two main sets of sources, written documents and personal interviews with politicians, ministry officials and university leaders and a conceptual approach developed in connection with the International Study of Higher Education Reforms (Kogan et al. 2000) by Bleiklie, Hanney and Marton (1997). For detailed presentation of the three countries see Bauer et al.(1999), Bleiklie et al. (2000), Henkel (2000), and Kogan and Hanney (1999).

iii   In Scotland the newly imposed tuition fees were quickly replaced by a graduate endowment abolishing 'up front' fees creating a situation where English students at Scottish universities were liable for fees in the first instance which their Scottish counterparts were not

iv   This paper draws primarily on work undertaken for a current research project Widening Access to Higher Education in Scotland, a one-year project funded by the Scottish Executive. Co-researchers are Professor Mike Osborne and Professor Jim Gallacher. The views expressed in this paper are of course the authors' own.

The research aims to answer a series of research questions by sampling policy and practice in eight case study institutions across Scotland (Further Education Colleges and Higher Education Institutions) and in Finland, Australia, France, England and Canada; and by interviewing relevant staff and participating students. Key research questions include:

1.   What forms of intervention have been put in place to break down barriers, and increase representation among under-represented groups within Scotland, elsewhere within the UK, and selected other comparable countries?

2.   What policy levers can be developed to encourage higher participation rates within HE?

3.   What patterns of participation are emerging and how are these changing?

The research was designed to include a focus on four different layers in the debate over policy and practice in access: International, national, institutional and initiative. The current paper draws on the institutional and initiative strands of the research, and includes information gathered from 40 interviews with personnel in FE colleges and universities. These included both key policy makers in each institution and also personnel involved in the operational part of access policy, namely widening access co-ordinators and a number of project workers and organisers. Interviews were carried out in eight case study institutions, five HEIs and three FECs. This split provided an opportunity to compare and contrast policy and provision in the two different sectors, while also allowing a closer look at articulation and other forms of linkages between the two sectors. Both sets of institutions were chosen to reflect the range of institutional types (local, HE-focus, rural, distance provision for the FE sector; Ancient, old and new for the university sector).

v   By higher education we mean higher national and degree level provision that may be offered either in further education colleges or in higher education institutions.

vi   The Cubie Inquiry into student finance was set up following the Scottish elections. The Labour /Liberal Democrat coalition created considerable pressure for reform of student finance since the Liberal Democrats had promised to abolish tuition fees.

vii   Also of relevance here is the restructuring of adult and continuing education within the pre-1992 universities in the late 1990s which has sometimes had the effect of divorcing theory and practice in the area of access to higher education.

viii   For the purposes of this chapter 'organisation' refers to the individual university; 'institution' refers to the field of higher education in which universities are located.

ix   Data are drawn from a two year Economic and Social Research Council funded study (grant no ROO237761) conducted by a team of researchers based at Lancaster University. The study was a qualitative examination of manager-academics' and academics' perceptions of the management of UK universities during the period October 1998 – November 2000. The project team consisted of the author and Oliver Fulton, plus Rosemary Deem (now Graduate School of Education, University of Bristol) Sam Hillyard (now School of Social Relations, Keele University), Mike Reed (Dept of Behaviour in Organisations, Lancaster University) and Stephen Watson (now Henley Management College). Heidi Edmundson was the project administrator. The methodology progressed in three phases. First, focus groups were conducted with senior academics from 10 different cognate discipline areas. These explored the meaning of management and change in higher education. Second, 10-12 semi-structured individual interviews were conducted at 17 institutions, with Heads of Departments, Deans, Pro vice-chancellors and the Vice Chancellor. These examined manager-academics' own management practices, values and tasks, their career trajectories, preparation and learning needs. Third, four of these 17 institutions were chosen as sites for case studies. Here a range of interview and observational methods were used to interrogate the perceptions of management practices and organisational cultures held within the wider academic, trades union, administrative, manual staff and student communities. Further details are available from the author

Printed in Great Britain
by Amazon